THE
GLOBAL
EDUCATION
GUIDEBOOK

Humanizing K–12 Classrooms Worldwide
Through Equitable Partnerships

Jennifer D. Klein

Solution Tree | Press
a division of
Solution Tree

555 North Morton Street
Bloomington, IN 47404
800.733.6786 (toll free) / 812.336.7700
FAX: 812.336.7790

email: info@SolutionTree.com
SolutionTree.com

Visit **go.SolutionTree.com/21stcenturyskills** to download the free reproducibles in this book.

Printed in the United States of America

21 20 19 18 17   1 2 3 4 5

Library of Congress Cataloging-in-Publication Data

Names: Klein, Jennifer D., author.
Title: The global education guidebook : humanizing K-12 classrooms worldwide
    through equitable partnerships / author: Jennifer D. Klein.
Description: Bloomington, Indiana : Solution Tree Press, [2017] | Includes
    bibliographical references and index.
Identifiers: LCCN 2017006040 | ISBN 9781943874637 (perfect bound)
Subjects: LCSH: Education and globalization. | Education--International
    cooperation. | Community and school--Cross-cultural studies.
Classification: LCC LC191 .K55795 2017 | DDC 379--dc23 LC record available at https://lccn.
loc.gov/2017006040

Solution Tree
Jeffrey C. Jones, CEO
Edmund M. Ackerman, President

Solution Tree Press
President and Publisher: Douglas M. Rife
Editorial Director: Sarah Payne-Mills
Managing Production Editor: Caroline Cascio
Senior Production Editor: Tonya Maddox Cupp
Senior Editor: Amy Rubenstein
Copy Editor: Evie Madsen
Proofreader: Ashante K. Thomas
Text and Cover Designer: Laura Cox
Editorial Assistants: Jessi Finn and Kendra Slayton

For Ella and Alex.

And in memory of Mauricio, my first global graduate.

I would hurl words into this darkness and wait for an echo, and if an echo sounded, no matter how faintly, I would send other words to tell, to march, to fight, to create a sense of the hunger for life that gnaws in us all, to keep alive in our hearts a sense of the inexpressibly human.

—Richard Wright,
Black Boy (American Hunger)

Acknowledgments

i was raised to know every open wound on this earth
is a wound of mine

—Andrea Gibson

I can't start this book without expressing deep gratitude to my parents, Edward A. Klein and Sally V. Klein, for swimming against the tides and making educational choices that allowed my sister, Heather F. Zubieni, and me to flourish as creative thinkers. My experiences at the School in Rose Valley in Pennsylvania and the Jefferson County Open School in Colorado allowed me to think for myself and engage with the world in meaningful ways throughout my childhood, and for that I am eternally grateful. I also want to recognize a few of the educators who have had a direct influence on my educational worldview, including educational thought leaders Judith Baenen, Arnie Langberg, Rick Posner, and Grace Rotzel, whose ideas live at the heart of my practice.

I ended up quoting most of my thought partners in this book; thank you all for your insights and honesty, and for contributing to this important conversation. If your interview or correspondence didn't make the cut, please know that I still value your voice and perspectives—they are still reflected here, if only indirectly. I am grateful to be able to include so many amazing people in this book, particularly my most important thought partner, Mark Thomas, with whom I learned more about global education than we could ever have predicted. This book contains many global education thought leaders and project creators, including Suzie Boss, Jen Corriero, Holly Emert, Willy Fluharty, Michael Furdyk, Terry Godwaldt, Lucy Gray, Michael Graffin, Ed Gragert, Travis Hardy, Steve Hargadon, Kate Ireland, Tim Kubik, Susan Lambert, Arnie Langberg, Julie Lindsay, Dan Lutz, Adam McKim, Dana Mortenson, Lisa Petro, Dave Potter, Rekha Puri, Linda Sills, Homa Sabet Tavangar, Ross Wehner, and Jesse Weisz. I am particularly grateful for the insights and support of my international partners over the years, including Saed Abu-Hijleh, Yasser Alaa Mobarak, Angie Balata, Benjamin Barney, Federico Cartín Arteaga, Falastine Dwikat, Doris Köhn, Hindogbae Kposowa, Beesan Ramadan, and Samuel Ochieng Phabian. Each of you has taught me a great deal about how to do this work better over the years, and I am grateful for your friendship.

I'm grateful to the teachers and administrators whose stories I've referenced, quoted, or mentioned through example without naming you, including Holly Arida, Graham Altham-Lewis, Maile Black, Jeanne Boland, Betsey Coleman, Maria Conte, Jackie Cvar, Rachel Dionne, Jason Dorn, Brett Elebash, Frank Garrett, Christopher Gauthier, Kristen Goggin, Heidi Hutchison, Kathleen Kirkpatrick, Arnetta Koger, Rich Lehrer, Hilary McArthur, Rob McGuiness, Ashley Miller, Misty Moore, Flora Mugambi-Mutunga, Jonathan Reveal, Jodie Ricci, Hillary Rubenstein, Dave Suchanek, Susan Turner, and Meg Zimmerman. I'm also grateful to the young leaders who offered their stories and perspectives, including Katie Horvath, Kennedy Leavens, and Sophia Fuller.

I am fortunate to be part of multiple networks of educational change makers whose ripples cross and intersect constantly. I am eternally grateful for the opportunities I've had to support educator and school transformation with my family at World Leadership School (Colorado), and I am grateful to Ross Wehner, Erin Hawk, Maria Selde, and Sarah Binger for your continual support and inspiration, even when I'm at my worst. Other communities I've been fortunate to work closely with include TakingITGlobal (Toronto), the Centre for Global Education (Edmonton), the Center for Global Education at Asia Society (New York), Sierra Leone Rising (formerly the Kposowa Foundation), the Institute of International Education (Washington, DC), the Buck Institute for Education (California), and the Research Journalism Initiative (Palestine).

A very special thank you to my friend and thought partner Jill Ackers-Clayton for your wisdom, friendship, and ability to talk me off every ledge. Thank you to Amy Rubenstein and Tonya Maddox Cupp for knowing how to support me as an anxiety-prone writer, to Carrie Watterson for helping make it look like I know APA style, to Morgan Schoenrock and Chris Mizell for transcribing interviews, and to Natalie Bograd for helping to increase my public presence. It clearly takes a village to write a book.

I'm grateful to every creative influence I've had, starting with my grandmother, Esther Michaelman Klein, a concert pianist and the first adult to call me a writer. I am grateful to the performers I watched from the depths of Broadway orchestra pits, to the voice of the cello that permeates every memory from my childhood, to my writing school peers and teaching colleagues, to the slam poets and activist artists who share their truth unapologetically—particularly those who have partnered with classrooms, including Andrea Gibson, Sonya Renee Taylor, and Franny Choi. Thank you for every note and for every beautiful word.

Finally, I am most grateful to every student who passed through my classroom, for the words you found to describe your experiences and for the laughter and learning I always enjoyed in your presence. Thank you for using your gifts to make the world a better place.

Solution Tree Press would like to thank the following reviewers:

Christy Barham
Director of Digital Learning,
  Professional Development, and Media
Rockingham County Public Schools
Eden, North Carolina

Nicolle Boujaber-Diederichs
Social Studies Teacher
Lake Nona High School
Orlando, Florida

Laurie Clement
Technology-Enabled Learning and
  Teaching Contact
Windsor-Essex Catholic District
School Board
Windsor, Ontario, Canada

Kyle Dunbar
Technology Integration Specialist
Alexandria City Public Schools
Alexandria, Virginia

Rebecca Gurley
Global Studies and World Languages
  Academy Coordinator
Tallwood High School
Virginia Beach, Virginia

Craig Perrier
High School Social Studies Specialist
Fairfax County Public Schools
Fairfax, Virginia

Wendi Pillars
ESL Teacher
Jordan-Matthews High School
Siler City, North Carolina

Tina Schmidt
Third-Grade Teacher
St. Ignatius of Antioch Catholic School
Yardley, Pennsylvania

Dyane Smokorowski
Instructional Technology Coach
Andover Public Schools
Andover, Kansas

Karen Stadler
IT Coordinator
Elkanah House Senior Primary
Cape Town, South Africa

Maryann Woods-Murphy
Gifted and Talented Specialist
New Jersey Teacher of the Year, 2010
Nutley Public Schools
Nutley, New Jersey

Visit **go.SolutionTree.com/21stcenturyskills** to download the free reproducibles in this book.

Table of Contents

About the Author

 **Jennifer D. Klein**, a product of experiential project-based education herself, taught college and high school English and Spanish for nineteen years, including five years in Central America and eleven years in all-girls education. In 2010, Jennifer left teaching to begin PRINCIPLED Learning Strategies, which provides professional development to support authentic student-driven global learning experiences in schools. She has a broad background in global educational program planning and evaluation, student-driven curricular strategies, single-sex education, student service travel, cultural inclusivity, and experiential, inquiry-driven learning.

From 2010–2017, Jennifer worked as a consultant and teacher coach for a variety of educational organizations, including World Leadership School (Colorado), TakingITGlobal (Toronto), the Centre for Global Education (Edmonton), the Buck Institute for Education (California), the Institute of International Education (Washington, DC), and the International Studies Schools Network of the Center for Global Education at Asia Society (New York). In 2017, Jennifer was hired as head of school at Gimnasio Los Caobos, a preK–12 project-based school outside of Bogotá, Colombia. As a school leader, writer, speaker, and bilingual workshop facilitator, Jennifer strives to inspire educators to shift their practices in schools worldwide.

Jennifer's articles have been published in *Independent School*, *The NSSSA Leader*, and *The Educational Forum*. She has blogged for a variety of forums, including *EdWeek*, The Partnership for 21st Century Learning, *World Leadership School*, the Buck Institute for Education, and her own *Shared World* blog. She has facilitated workshops in English and Spanish in Brazil, Canada, Colombia, Costa Rica, Honduras, Mexico, Palestine, Sierra Leone, and the United States. Jennifer holds a bachelor of arts from Bard College and a master of arts from the University of Colorado at Boulder, both in literature and creative writing.

To learn more about Jennifer's work, visit PRINCIPLED Learning Strategies (http://principledlearning.org) and follow her at @jdeborahklein on Twitter.

To book Jennifer D. Klein for professional development, contact pd@SolutionTree .com.

FOSTERING GLOBAL CITIZENSHIP BY MEETING IN THE MIDDLE

There could be no creativity without the curiosity that moves us and sets us patiently impatient before a world that we did not make, to add to it something of our own making.

—Paulo Freire

I like to use the phrase *meeting in the middle* when talking about building equitable, reciprocal global partnerships. What does it look like to meet in the middle? The middle is not a destination, particularly when it comes to classroom-to-classroom partnerships that occur predominantly or entirely online. Teachers or students from two or more countries might travel physically to meet during a partnership, creating a more personal, face-to-face opportunity as a component of a long-term online experience. But meeting in the middle doesn't rely on physical travel; it's about students and the educators who guide them seeing others as the people they are, without judging or trying to change them. It's about meeting others *where* they are, figuratively speaking, and of crafting rich experiences that benefit all involved. It's about seeing other humans in all their wholeness, for their strengths, weaknesses, and goals, not just their circumstances. It's about seeing the essential humanity in others by acknowledging that every person has his or her own complex set of gifts, needs, and hopes. It's about celebrating all we have in common and learning from what we see differently. It's about learning *from* and *with* one another as real partners, not being observers who simply learn *about* each other. It's about trust, building relationships over time, and helping students see the world and their lives through someone else's eyes. And it's about equipping students to become the kinds of "patiently impatient" change makers Freire (1998) describes (p. 38).

Global education has experienced a boom since the mid-1990s, when it quickly became popular in schools worldwide. Connected educators around the globe are using new technologies to engage with communities and individuals, but many of those connections are not as equitable as they could be, by which I mean that they are founded on a deeply ingrained deficit mindset most teachers don't realize they have, which usually includes inaccurate assumptions about intelligence and capacity. Those inaccuracies don't do justice to what every child in every context has to offer the conversation. In fact, many connections are based on exploitative foundations by well-intentioned teachers who use global education simply to observe or *solve for*, rather than immersing students in what they can *learn from* others. In my experience, this approach can unintentionally dehumanize partners. For example, I've seen many young people come away from global learning experiences with the impression that they've "saved" a community, instead of seeing that community as perfectly capable of saving itself. Giving students the opportunity to engage directly with the world can be life changing, often providing a sense of purpose that motivates and grounds young people well into adulthood. But if that sense of purpose is based on the belief that one country or cultural group can save or fix others, these experiences may be causing more harm than good. We need a global educational revolution that puts equity at its core—one in which partners on all sides know they have something to learn *and* to teach, and one in which all partners have a voice and collaborate on equal footing.

> *Giving students the opportunity to engage directly with the world can be life changing, often providing a sense of purpose that motivates and grounds young people well into adulthood.*

Why I'm Here

As an elementary student at the School in Rose Valley in Pennsylvania (an early progressive model developed by Grace Rotzel) and a graduate of the Jefferson County Open School in Colorado (the United States' second public alternative school focusing on experiential education, founded by thought leader Arnie Langberg), I was lucky to be in globally connected, student-driven educational systems that fostered my passion and purpose. At these schools, thinking differently was a merit, and being willing to oppose authority for the sake of what Vladimir Nabokov (1980) calls "a too early moonbeam of some too early truth" was practically a graduation requirement (p. 372).

My educational experiences in the 1970s and 1980s included a great deal of outdoor and expeditionary learning, meaning that I learned by doing beyond the classroom walls. I experienced global learning and partnerships long before there were technologies to simplify those connections. My first global learning expeditions were two work trips with Open School to Sonora, Mexico, in ninth and tenth grades, during which my peers and I helped rebuild rural schools in small mountain communities through a partnership between the United States and Mexico. We provided the labor force, and the Sonoran government identified the school most in need of repair and provided paid foremen and materials.

I was on desk duty both years, which meant stripping, repairing, and then re-painting all the students' wooden desks. I remember working in the shade in a beautiful courtyard and seeing my first scorpion. I remember sitting in the local church during breaks, feeling a connection between Catholicism and Judaism that I'd never recognized before, a sort of universal spirituality I still connect with today. I remember that the local women cooked a huge traditional meal midweek for our celebration, and we played in the river with children and adults from the community. I remember my friend Shankaron, a refugee from Ethiopia, riding a horse for the first time—and her bellowing laugh as the horse forded the river with Shankaron up high. I remember tastes and smells, trying my very poor Spanish, and laughing with the children when I failed to communicate well. I remember a lot of laughter and feeling oddly connected to that place, which I can't even name or find on a map, and to the people who lived there. And I remember that I had a deep urge for more—more learning, more travel, more connecting across the differences that usually separate us.

I was able to get more; at the end of my junior year, in May of 1985, I left Colorado to spend six months living and working in Israel/Palestine and two months traveling through Europe to complete three of my passages for high school graduation. While the experience created a great deal of political and spiritual discord I still struggle with today, it was a real, raw, and hugely formative experience that still motivates everything I do. It took me many years to figure out how to turn a difficult experience into constructive action, but in the fall of 1995 I started teaching tenth-grade English in Costa Rica to the children of presidents, ministry officials, and the most powerful business leaders in the country. From that moment forward, my classroom became my platform and my platform was, in a nutshell, *global citizenship*—not just an understanding of the world but an urge to respond constructively and collaboratively to our shared challenges.

Early in my teaching career, in the late 1990s, the global education landscape changed significantly. In 1997, the Lincoln School where I taught in San José, Costa Rica, established one of the very first videoconferencing suites in a Central American school, marking the beginning of a new era in technology-enabled global education. Suddenly, students didn't need to go anywhere to make connections and have authentic conversations with people around the world. They could engage with the world from *inside* the classroom, and even though physical travel remained a priority, teachers could create transformative experiences without spending money, fuel, or time in transit. Technology meant we didn't have to wait until students were old enough to travel, either; even our youngest students could make connections with real people anywhere on the planet, as long as their teachers had access. It has taken several decades for mobile technology to narrow the digital divide more significantly, but online connections are increasingly accessible to students from more diverse socioeconomic backgrounds.

Since the late 1990s, technology-enabled global education has blossomed into a powerful movement, particularly as technology access has become increasingly equitable—though we still have improvements to make. Nearly every teacher I know is anxious to find a global partner—a classroom his or her students can work with to foster intercultural skills and see the world through a different lens. The tragedies of September 11, 2001, created new urgency around building better relationships between the United States and key regions of the world, and several public policy groups issued reports in the following years that "called for increased language study not only for its educational value but because having more citizens able to speak other languages is in the national interest" (Jenkins & Meyers, 2010, p. 8). Further, a series of reports from the Government Accountability Office documents how the lack of expertise in critical languages such as Arabic was affecting the United States' diplomatic relations, capacity to gather intelligence, and ability to further its policy objectives (Jenkins & Meyers, 2010). The ground was starting to shift, and the word *global*, which had seemed threatening to so many during the Cold War, was suddenly at the heart of educational dialogue.

> *Nearly every teacher I know is anxious to find a global partner—a classroom his or her students can work with to foster intercultural skills and see the world through a different lens.*

Why Foster Global Citizenship and Equity

Many scholars identify global citizenship and education as moral imperatives. While the term *citizenship* is a largely Western concept, related concepts of community engagement and responsibility are not. Harvard University's Fernando M. Reimers (in his work with Vidur Chopra, Connie K. Chung, Julia Higdon, and E. B. O'Donnell, 2016), describes a global citizenship curricula as providing the following:

> All students with effective opportunities to develop the dispositions, knowledge, and capabilities necessary to understand the world in which they live, to make sense of the way in which globalization shapes their lives, and to be good stewards of and contributors to the Sustainable Development Goals. (p. xx)

In an earlier work, Reimers (2009) emphasizes that schools must embrace the need to prepare students for the future, but he also points out candidly, that most schools don't prepare students for the future. There is no question that schools need to provide early opportunities for practice and participation, especially since "globalization impacts job prospects, health, physical security, public policy, communications, investment opportunities, immigration, and community relations" (Reimers, 2009, p. 4).

While developing a classroom partnership can be very labor intensive, it is one of the best ways to develop these understandings, knowledge, and skills. Global partnerships can take years of effort and false starts before reaching significant success, but they are among the most rewarding experiences you can create for students when you take the time to make them equitable and relevant. A powerful global partnership experience can change lives, career paths, and even our shared world in the long run. Whether you are talking about five-year-olds in San Francisco understanding and upholding children's rights through a partnership with students in Sierra Leone, a middle school class in Toronto sharing local mythology with students in rural Costa Rica, or high school students in Denver trying to understand the Israeli–Palestinian conflict through photography and poetry exchanges, directly connecting with real people in the world can help humanize your curriculum in powerful ways.

Direct connections with people are essential if you want to get students to a place of authentic citizenship, *which is when students can realistically understand or empathize with others' needs because they have met and collaborated with them personally.*

Direct connections with people are essential if you want to get students to a place of *authentic citizenship*, which is when students can realistically understand or empathize with others' needs because they have met and collaborated with them personally. Ian Davies's work (as cited in Evans, Hawes, Levere, Monette, & Mouftah, 2004) suggests that traditional attempts to transfer citizenship concepts such as tolerance, justice, and civic participation to students are nearly impossible using conventional teaching methods. Davies (as cited in Evans et al., 2004) finds that when students participate in inquiry with people worldwide, they are much more likely to become authentically engaged in *practicing* citizenship, both during and after the classroom experience. Julie Lindsay and Vicki A. Davis (2013) take this idea a step further, indicating that making personal connections with people around the world fosters open-mindedness and builds bridges. Pointing out that these connections are no longer optional for a better future, Lindsay and Davis (2013) write, "Students are the greatest textbook ever written for one another and will be travelers on this bridge" (p. 2).

Unfortunately, much of what global education has produced fosters inequitable thinking, particularly when the partnership projects originate in more developed countries (Kubik, 2012, 2016). Global citizenship is often translated in simplistic terms, becoming an endless fund-raising campaign in which students in the West do what's referred to as *saving the rest*. This is not meeting in the middle. This kind of global education does not foster true citizenship; instead, such experiences can dehumanize the people students seek to understand, turning them into empty vessels who can only survive with the outsiders' solutions, not whole people with multifaceted lives and their own ideas about how to improve their communities. At their worst, these kinds of global connections can exacerbate power imbalances and even cripple local industry.

Consider the example of a classroom in Canada partnered with a rural classroom in a coffee-producing region of Colombia. Students in Canada discover the deficits in their partner classroom, including a lack of school supplies, technologies, and flexible school furniture. Students in Canada run a fund-raiser for which they buy the cheapest Colombian coffee they can find, mark it up, and sell it locally to donate profits to their partners. It sounds reasonable enough, but the students' action actually exacerbates both the Colombian community's reliance on foreign aid and the root economic problems that are causing that reliance. If the students instead work toward fair market prices for Colombian coffee, or help their partner community connect with free trade networks to eliminate the middlemen who lower their profits, the impact would be more about empowering their partner's economic independence, thus improving their ability to solve their own problems. Making this shift means recognizing that their Colombian partners don't need handouts, but are complete, competent people who live in a complex system that doesn't consistently reward their hard work, and who can benefit from a collaboration built on mutual respect and recognition.

During one of the most powerful experiences I've had since leaving the classroom, I got to see five-year-olds at the Town School for Boys (www.townschool .com) in San Francisco, California, explore photos of children sent by their partner community in Sierra Leone through a see, think, wonder activity. Amid the usual *wonderings* (for example, I *wonder* what their houses look like; I *wonder* what their favorite animals are; I *wonder* what sports they like to play at recess) were a few difficult questions about how children in rural Sierra Leone live. When one little boy said, "I wonder if they're poor," the class erupted; the other boys insisted loudly that this was a rude question to ask. The teacher artfully unpacked the problem, asking the students why it felt rude. "What are we really trying to find out? How might we ask this question differently?" To my surprise, one five-year-old raised his hand tentatively and said, "I wonder if they have everything they need," and then another followed with, "And if not, I wonder *what* they need." This was a demonstration of deep empathy, a central tenet of global citizenship because of how deeply it motivates students to work toward a more fair and equitable world.

If that level of empathy—and the urge to respond—is present in five-year-olds who have personally connected with children in another part of the world, maybe all educators have to do is avoid crushing that hope and connectedness by developing humanizing global experiences. Maybe empathy and global citizenship aren't things to be *taught*, but to be *fostered*.

Maybe empathy and global citizenship aren't things to be taught, *but to be* fostered.

What Students Want From Global Education

Understanding what young people want from global education can help you engage them in more meaningful, relevant learning. Each year, the University of Wisconsin–Madison hosts a Global Youth Summit that brings together middle and high school students from across the state for activities and dialogue around global education. In 2013, student attendees identified four areas they would like to see addressed more consistently and authentically in their schools (Hill, 2013).

1. **Offer a diversity of world languages, with opportunities for authentic use:** Students recognize wide disparities among schools, many of which offer only French and Spanish, and most of which begin serious language study at ninth grade. As students point out, "If we start training for sports at a young age, why not languages? Can you imagine if a high school quarterback had to start freshman year? It doesn't make sense" (Hill, 2013). Students also call for using technologies to connect them with native speakers and teachers, enabling them to explore a broader array of cultural perspectives and to actually use world languages in authentic ways.

2. **Increase direct engagement through travel and exchange:** Students recognize that their most powerful global experiences take place because of exchange programs that bring international students into their schools and homes. They also emphasize the importance of developing scholarship opportunities for physical travel, noting that international immersion experiences are inaccessible for the majority of public school students.

3. **Connect with the world through technology:** Students emphasize the value of more and better technology use to integrate opportunities for nontravel international experiences. They would like their schools to develop long-term sister school relationships with other communities in the world—deep global partnerships between two school communities that include more than just a couple of classes connecting occasionally. Students point out that this is easily achievable through existing and

emerging technologies, citing the use of technology as a far less expensive and more convenient way to bring the world into the classroom.

4. **Foster open-mindedness; promote awareness and acceptance:**
   Students emphasize the importance not just of learning about the world but also of doing so in ways that develop a less nationalistic lens for engagement. For example, recognizing that most of their schools focus on national themes far more than international themes, one group notes, "Intolerance and ignorance of other cultures must be minimized. Get rid of patriotic egotism" (Hill, 2013). Students also recognize their own roles in spreading enthusiasm and open-mindedness within their communities, noting that young people need to get involved in global causes and be part of creating change in their schools and the world.

Hooking into students' existing urges and interests does not mean ignoring significant core content.

Hooking into students' existing urges and interests does not mean ignoring significant core content; it means creating a space for students to think and create for themselves within the context of our academic disciplines. It means recognizing that education is less about *covering* a breadth of knowledge and more about *uncovering* students' sense of passion and purpose; facilitating their voice and empowerment; and helping them see how disciplines matter across the patchwork of human experience.

Why You're Here

This book is for educators who want to find that middle ground—who want to develop equitable global partnerships based on trust, mutual respect, and a shared vision of global collaboration and development. Accessible for beginners, this book will help lead you through the process of developing project ideas, finding existing programs or partners on your own, designing and maintaining the collaboration, and evaluating your success. Also, to challenge more advanced global educators, this book invites conversations about how to handle more controversial topics in partnerships, build partnerships more equitably for all involved, and spread global thinking and engagement across the broader curriculum and school community.

This book will be helpful for teachers, instructional leaders, and administrators who strive to build direct global connections into the educational experiences they create for students in all disciplines and grade levels across the preK–12 spectrum (though many of these strategies would also work for higher education settings). It is also for specialists, after-school program leaders, camp counselors, and anyone helping foster global citizenship and the urge for collaborative action in young people.

In chapter 1, you will explore the concept and importance of global competency as a central facet of global citizenship, and you will consider how partnerships might foster that competency. In chapter 2, you will begin defining the kind of partnership you hope to build, exploring key elements to determine student learning priorities. Chapter 3 reveals several global partnership examples by age group, to help deepen your vision of what's possible when you connect your classroom to the world. In chapters 4 and 5, you will explore ways to find a partner, first through existing global partnership programs (chapter 4), and then through building a partnership on your own via online networking or travel (chapter 5). Chapter 6 lays out key strategies for communicating well with your global partner, as well as an overview of several useful technologies for live and off-line communication. Chapter 7 sets you up for an equitable experience by exploring some of the pitfalls to avoid in global partnerships, and chapter 8 helps you navigate challenges in partnerships that include controversial topics, offering strategies for building successful partnerships around social justice and human rights. Chapter 9 explains how you can assess students' growth and partnership success, and its last section on evaluating broader global programming leads into chapter 10, which explores how to build more buy-in and professional capacity around global learning across your community. Each chapter includes anecdotes from global education participants, practitioners, and leaders, as well as suggestions and a tool to help you build collaborative learning experiences. (Visit **go.SolutionTree.com/21stcenturyskills** to access live links to the websites mentioned in this book.)

I believe that tolerance is a low bar to set. I believe in the "shared world" evoked by poet Naomi Shihab Nye (2008) and in our potential to live a responsible, constructive, and engaged life as a global community (p. 163). I wrote this book with that shared world in mind. We are capable of building what poet Adrienne Rich (2013) calls "the dream of a common language," but we have to work at it collectively (p. 8). Every classroom and every student can make contributions to that better future, to "bending the arc of history" as Anthony Jackson (2015) puts it, so that we can meet in the middle and really understand each other. We aren't preparing students to be global leaders *after* they finish their education; we are creating the space for them to lead change *now*, from inside the classroom.

Whether you are a beginner or more experienced, I hope that this book provides the guidance and frameworks you need to build meaningful and equitable learning partnerships that help your students develop a more humanized sense of the world and their place in it.

CHAPTER 1

BUILDING GLOBAL COMPETENCIES VIA GLOBAL PARTNERSHIPS

The illiterate of the 21st century will not be those who cannot read and write, but those who cannot learn, unlearn, and relearn.

—Alvin Toffler

Before even trying to envision your global partnership ideas in action, it's important to ground your work in the goal of developing students' global competencies—communication, collaboration, humility, and empathy, to name a few. To do that, you need a starting place for trying to envision the world your students will graduate into, as well as the skills and knowledge they might need for that world. This chapter will explore the urgent rationale behind global competency development, some of the leading definitions of global competency, and the pedagogical approaches that help foster those skills as central facets of global citizenship and participation.

Educators want to see students not just *survive* the world they encounter but actually *thrive* within that world as constructive, innovative thinkers. No matter how they accomplish the goal, educators tend to share the common urge for vigor, motivation, and engagement in students as much as—or even more than—academic rigor. However, educators can't always agree on *what* students need to learn, what the right standards might be, and how to reach those goals in the classroom—particularly given that much of the world's population can find answers to knowledge-based questions on a smartphone. Linda Darling-Hammond (2010) notes that information is spreading so rapidly that "education can no longer be productively focused primarily on the transmission of pieces of information that, once memorized, comprise a stable storehouse of knowledge" (p. 4). Instead, she believes that education needs to focus on equipping students to be cognitively nimble (Darling-Hammond, 2010). Similarly, World Savvy co-founder and executive director Dana Mortenson believes that the only effective education in times of change is one that helps students "build skills and dispositions that make navigating change easier and more natural" (personal communication, October 28, 2016). Google chief education evangelist Jaime Casap suggests that instead of asking what students want to *be* when they grow up, we should ask what *problems* they want to solve, shifting students' thinking beyond traditional job fields and toward a problem-solving mindset that will serve them well in any career context (AZEdNews, 2014).

Starting From *Why*: Volatility, Uncertainty, Complexity, and Ambiguity

Since the tragedies of September 11, 2001, the U.S. military had described the world's state as a VUCA world, one marked by "Volatility, Uncertainty, Complexity, and Ambiguity" (Owens, as cited in Gerras, 2010, p. 11). Politics aside, the acronym is both accurate and useful as we think about what it means to equip students to thrive in the future. For educators, this acronym provides a challenge that may require redesigning many elements of education: How do we prepare students to thrive in a world of volatility, uncertainty, complexity, and ambiguity? Does the traditional view of what a student needs to know and be able to do by graduation provide the skills and knowledge needed to navigate that world? Will traditional instructional strategies get them there? And if not, what do graduates need to be successful in a world we can't even envision, in jobs that have yet to be created?

There is an urgency for global partnerships and engagement that goes beyond our curriculum and standards—though partnerships can be easily married to content, given that many global competencies are naturally content oriented to geography, history, and anthropology, to name a few; and our shared global challenges easily connect to science, mathematics, and world languages, as well as being reflected in literature, arts, and religion. (See chapter 2 on page 31 for more information about deciding on topics and educational goals.) To help teachers see the urgency of global citizenship and the accompanying competencies, I start workshops by asking teachers to identify the skills, knowledge, values, dispositions, and behaviors students will need to thrive in the VUCA world. Every time, no matter where I am in the world, the lists are incredibly similar. As the following exemplars from workshops in four different countries indicate, we have more goals in common than not.

MOUNT VERNON PRESBYTERIAN SCHOOL
Atlanta, Georgia, United States of America (2015 Workshop)

decodes, empathizes, thinks critically, is self-disciplined, is flexible, is resilient, resists judgment, expresses with or without approval, communicates, filters information, goes deep, is gritty, communicates value, listens, observes, gives and receives feedback, finds positive supports, has basic knowledge of disciplines, adapts, creates opportunities, self-assesses, self-reflects, collaborates, is socially and emotionally intelligent, reinvents, takes risks, is aware of action and inaction, creates

BUMPE HIGH SCHOOL AND VARIOUS NEARBY ELEMENTARY SCHOOLS
Bumpe, Sierra Leone, West Africa (2014 Workshop)

questions, dialogues, finds information, knows the difference between good and bad, lifelong learner, is decisive, demonstrates discipline, is accountable, is moral, is ethical, thinks creatively, is lawful, speaks out, is punctual, is time bound, is self-knowledgeable, motivates self, perseveres, is socially conscious, imagines, explores with curiosity, practices tolerance, is loving, solves problems, is honest, is proactive, collaborates, displays concern, teaches others, is result oriented, respects all, is authentic, leads, is responsible, thinks critically, overcomes fear, communicates, understands, empathizes, applies curriculum well

COLEGIO VALLE SAGRADO-URUBAMBA
Urubamba, Peru, South America (2013 Workshop)

integrates knowledge, writes, reads, understands, resolves problems (mathematical and in daily life), investigates, is technologically savvy, knows other world languages, is faithful, analyzes critically, knows and loves culture, loves, reflects, leads, lives in society, respects all (including the environment), resolves conflicts, makes choices, makes decisions, shows entrepreneurship, is proactive, controls emotions, shows solidarity, communicates, is sensitive to the needs of others, is reliable, is responsible, perseveres

COSTA RICAN REGIONAL EDUCATIONAL SPECIALISTS AND U.S. EDUCATORS
Sarapiquí, Costa Rica, Central America (2015 Workshop)

takes risks, resolves problems, makes decisions, discerns, thinks critically, leads, analyzes, engages, is flexible, practices patience, adapts, works in groups, empathizes, persists, loves country, has a sense of belonging, learns from others, informs, communicates, observes, is empowered, asks good questions, asserts self, is responsible, shows righteousness without impacting the rights of others, listens, participates, follows others, creates, is confident, innovates, respects others, shows self-respect, is proactive, appreciates everyone's talents, respects different perspectives, grows, practices digital citizenship, creates strategies

Source: Adapted from Project-Based Learning for Global Citizenship workshop.

These lists identify many of the same priorities for students and societies, and they hit on many of the goals of the new global competency component of the Programme for International Student Assessment (PISA), being developed by the Organisation for Economic Co-operation and Development (OECD) to begin in 2018 (OECD, 2016). As the OECD's work demonstrates, regardless of the field they choose, our students will spend their work lives collaborating across borders, whether geographic, political, racial, ethnic, socioeconomic, religious, or cultural. They will communicate with a wide array of stakeholders, who have complex and often conflicting needs and priorities. OECD (2016) thought leaders put it this way:

> The driving ideas are that global trends are complex and require careful investigation, that cross-cultural engagement should balance clear communication with sensitivity to multiple perspectives, and that global competence should equip young people not just to understand but to act. (p. 1)

Regardless of the field they choose, our students will spend their work lives collaborating across borders, whether geographic, political, racial, ethnic, socioeconomic, religious, or cultural.

Students who are successful in the new economy will be those who have global and intercultural competencies, and those are best developed by engaging directly with global issues and perspectives, whether inside or outside the classroom. As their teachers, we need the same global and intercultural competencies if we hope to be part of that journey. As Reimers (2009) cautions, "Those who are educated to understand those transformations and how to turn them into sources of comparative advantage are likely to benefit from globalization; but those who are not will face real and growing challenges" (p. 4).

Research suggests that global competencies are increasingly important alongside core knowledge, as technology and globalization have impacted almost every industry since the late 1960s (Zhao, 2012). Yong Zhao (2012) points out that global trends have changed the job market permanently:

> Technology advancement, globalization, and abundance of unemployed youth are all building blocks of a new economy . . . globalization and digitization together have created a new platform that helps create new jobs. This platform delivers a global customer base, a global capital pool, and a global workforce—all easily accessible. (pp. 59–60)

This new economy and all it entails will require a different set of skills than the more nationally bound economies of the past. To communicate and collaborate with a global customer base, capital pool, and workforce, students will need global competencies on very practical levels. In her article for *Harvard Business Review*, Erin Meyer (2015) makes the following claim:

> In today's globalized economy you could be negotiating a joint venture in China, an outsourcing agreement in India, or a supplier contract in Sweden. If so, you might find yourself working with very different norms of communication. What gets you to "yes" in one culture gets you to "no" in another. . . . In my work and research, I find that when managers from different parts of the world negotiate, they frequently misread such signals, reach erroneous conclusions, and act . . . in ways that thwart their ultimate goals.

From the ability to speak to a client in his or her native language to the ability to leverage the varied talents of key stakeholders with cultural savvy, the survival skills of the globalized business world are exactly the skills global partnerships develop. It is important to balance these skills with deep cultural and historical knowledge about other countries, plus the capacity to make collaborative decisions in intercultural settings. While I tend to approach this work from a social justice and equity orientation, I recognize that economic forces can do more to legitimize this work in many school communities. I encourage teachers to use this more practical argument as they build buy-in for new programs, particularly in school contexts where tying global education to students' futures in business might motivate change more effectively. Chapter 10 (page 177) provides more guidance about these kinds of efforts.

When we think about global skills in practice, whether in global business and economic entrepreneurship or in global development and social entrepreneurship, many of global education's supposedly soft skills actually qualify as metacognitive skills. Soft skills are allegedly the opposite of hard skills, which include easily demonstrable abilities such as mathematical calculation or specific technical proficiencies. Soft skills include abilities that are more difficult to prove or measure, such as emotional intelligence, adaptability, and critical thinking. However, thinking critically about how to meet the varied needs of diverse stakeholders, for example, requires extraordinarily complex, high-level reasoning that interweaves knowledge with social-emotional understandings (Critical Thinking Community, 2015). Far from being a soft skill, critical thinking across cultures elevates global competency to the metacognitive level.

Fernando M. Reimers (2009) suggests that the "preparation to develop these understandings, knowledge and skills must begin early in order to develop high levels of competence as well as help youth recognize the relevance of their education to the world in which they live" (p. 4). This means that global competency development is not just the work of high schools and colleges when the world beyond school looms most closely for students, but that global competency programs should begin early and intentionally build that sense of global and local relevance. Try the global graduate for a VUCA world activity in figure 1.1 with your colleagues to help build a sense of the skills a student needs and to determine when you might best foster them, being sure the conversation stays grounded in the age groups you serve and the competencies most important to the student's developmental needs.

At a faculty or all-school meeting, do the following.

1. Define VUCA: Volatility, uncertainty, complexity, and ambiguity (Gerras, 2010).

2. Do an initial brainstorm with the whole group by asking "What makes our world VUCA? What are the challenges our students will need to navigate—and potentially solve—in their lifetimes?"

3. Ask the following, ensuring participants explain the thinking behind their contributions: "What do our students need to know to face the future and thrive in a VUCA world?" If the group is large, split teachers into small groups and have participants share their answers with the larger group after small-group discussions. In other words, consider "What are the skills, knowledge, values, dispositions, and behaviors our graduates will need?"

4. Encourage all teachers to incorporate at least three of the competencies identified as educational goals in their course planning and assessments.

Figure 1.1: Global graduate for a VUCA world activity.
*Visit **go.SolutionTree.com/21stcenturyskills** for a free reproducible version of this figure.*

As you plan strategies for finding, developing, and maintaining partnerships for your students, being intentional about identifying the global competencies you want to address will ensure that integrations are meaningful and educational. In the case of the kindergarten students in San Francisco, for example, one of the teacher's explicit learning goals was empathy, so she developed her own rubrics to measure empathy's presence in students' discussions and classroom behavior. Given that global educators often feel isolated and need help creating buy-in across their communities, identifying specific, measurable global competencies and knowledge areas to intentionally teach, foster, and assess through those global partnerships can help legitimize efforts to potential naysayers. Some global competencies, such as research or negotiation skills, are easily measured; others, like empathy, humility, or resilience, are not

Being intentional about identifying the global competencies you want to address will ensure that integrations are meaningful and educational.

as easily measured. We will explore how you might approach assessing such immeasurables in chapter 9 (page 155), but you may find it useful to review your academic standards alongside a global competency framework, such as those we'll explore in this chapter, as you begin planning a new partnership.

Defining Global Competency

To teach and assess global competencies as central learning objectives in the classroom, you need to define those competencies, encourage practice and improvement toward mastery, and measure student performance over time. Global competencies tend to focus on several key learning areas, all of which an effective global partnership can address and foster, and most of which likely came up in the global graduate for a VUCA world activity in figure 1.1. Additionally, it is worth noting that global competencies have a great deal in common with the kinds of intercultural competencies emphasized by diversity and inclusivity practitioners such as Steven Jones, Rosetta Lee, and Glen E. Singleton. If your school is working on internal intercultural inclusivity as well as global education, and are trying to have deeper conversations about race and privilege, it is smart to align the two initiatives so they function in concert, rather than in isolation. The following competencies are the building blocks of global literacy and a good starting place for defining goals. The partnership strategies in this book are based on these sorts of competencies, and a successful partnership will nurture them intentionally.

- **Intercultural skills, especially communication and collaboration**, are needed in all fields. These skills are important for the increased diversity and complexity that human mobility creates within communities.

- **Empathy and humanizing the world** are necessary for building the kind of global progress that avoids conflict and meets the needs of the most stakeholders possible in an increasingly overpopulated world.

- **Inquiry skills** allow humans to adapt to and deal with uncertainty and ambiguity in our constantly changing global landscape. These skills are intrinsically connected to critical thinking, which is key to thriving as a lifelong learner.

- **Collaborative solution building and humility**, which we need because volatile change and equitable development require collaborative skills and the humility to value other people's priorities, not unilateral decision making.

Remember that this work does not have to happen *instead of* curricular goals; rather, global connections and partnerships help our students recognize that what they're learning has broad implications beyond the classroom, and that every discipline offers potential solutions to our most serious challenges. While it may be easier to run a partnership outside of the academic classroom, such as through clubs, after-school activities, or elective courses, a well-developed global experience that's grounded in significant content provides a rich opportunity to make that content relevant for students, just as the International Baccalaureate program has tried to do since 1968.

Global competency can be defined in various ways, and the criteria tend to depend on the particular educator's philosophical views. Reimers (2009), for example, believes that global competencies include the "attitudinal and ethical dispositions that make it possible to interact peacefully, respectfully, and productively with fellow human beings from diverse geographies" (p. 3). This definition suggests that a meaningful global partnership might address how our various disciplines can help solve global challenges, singularly and in concert, and that the development of "attitudinal and ethical dispositions" should be at the heart of our global efforts (Reimers, 2009, p. 3). Gabriela Ramos of the OECD believes that the "development of social and emotional skills, as well as values like tolerance, self-confidence, and a sense of belonging, are of the utmost importance to create opportunities for all and advance a shared respect for human dignity" (OECD, 2016, p. i). Finally, educational consultant Tim Kubik notes a distinction between *global competency* (which he believes implies a singularity, as though there is just one worldview to cultivate) and what he calls being *competently global*, a more pluralistic way of framing our goals (T. Kubik, personal communication, May 21, 2016).

> *Global connections and partnerships help our students recognize that what they're learning has broad implications beyond the classroom.*

While this multiplicity of definition can get confusing, many organizations have developed and redeveloped definitions of global competency into frameworks intended to support the work of educators. Three of the most important for this work include those from (1) Oxfam, (2) World Savvy, and (3) the Center for Global Education at Asia Society. Each provides a framework that offers a valuable lens for defining what global competency might look like. As you explore the following frameworks, consider which global competencies resonate for you, particularly in connection to the age groups and disciplines you teach, so that you can use them as learning goals in your global partnership design. As your school gets more involved in global education, you may even want to craft your own global competency matrix, capturing those elements that best mirror your school's guiding vision.

Oxfam

Organized around knowledge and understanding; skills; and values and attitudes, Oxfam's (https://oxfam.org) framework for global citizenship exemplifies the values of equity and social justice, the organization's core goals. See table 1.1 for a list of Oxfam's global citizenship components.

Table 1.1: Oxfam's Components of Global Citizenship

Knowledge and Understanding	Skills	Values and Attitudes
• Social justice and equity • Identity and diversity • Globalization and interdependence • Sustainable development • Peace and conflict • Human rights • Power and governance	• Critical and creative thinking • Empathy • Self-awareness and reflection • Communication • Cooperation and conflict resolution • Ability to manage complexity and uncertainty • Informed and reflective action	• Sense of identify and self-esteem • Commitment to social justice and equity • Respect for people and human rights • Appreciation for diversity • Concern for the environment and commitment to sustainable development • Commitment to participation and inclusion • Belief that people can bring about change

Source: Adapted from Oxfam, 2015.

The Oxfam framework emphasizes responsible global citizenship in particular, and the broader publication it comes from offers many useful classroom strategies for reaching these goals. While many learning objectives in the Oxfam framework, such as empathy or self-awareness, might seem challenging to teach and assess, this framework focuses on the kinds of immeasurables we most need students to develop. One aspect of the Oxfam framework worth spotlighting is the emphasis on conflict resolution, which is absent from the other two frameworks for global competency, as well as concern for the environment and commitment to sustainable development. Conflict resolution is a key element of building a more peaceful world, and many schools that use restorative justice practices find that such skills can be developed intentionally in teachers and students. (Visit **go.SolutionTree .com/21stcenturyskills** for a link to more information on restorative justice in schools.) Further, environmental stewardship and developmental sustainability, which are United Nations' (n.d.) sustainable development goals, are essential to long-term survival across the planet.

World Savvy

Alongside academic content foundations in core concepts that include history and geography, World Savvy (www.worldsavvy.org) emphasizes several hard skills like doing research and forming opinions based on evidence. This framework, which defines *global competence* as "the disposition and capacity to understand and act on issues of global significance," also emphasizes the importance of self-awareness when seeking to understand others (World Savvy, 2014).

World Savvy's framework is the only one that emphasizes becoming comfortable with "ambiguity and uncomfortable situations," exactly the sort of ambiguity VUCA identifies as a challenge of our times (World Savvy, 2014). I ask educators in professional development programs and diversity workshops to *lean into discomfort* so they can discover the power of confronting rather than avoiding the ambiguity and conflict that make us uncomfortable. To become comfortable with the uncomfortable, with the ambiguity that is constant in times of rapid change, we have to address what creates the discomfort. Many global cultures are nonconfrontational (Meyer, 2015), which means that they tend to avoid uncomfortable conversations about race, identity, and divergent perspectives—even though feeling discomfort signals the *importance* of such conversations. Globally competent young people who know how to lean into discomfort—and communicate effectively with those who lean away—are essential to success in any field impacted by globalization (Meyer, 2015). Also significant is World Savvy's emphasis on behaviors, which asks students to take global thinking and turn it into publicly demonstrated action. While deeper shifts in student behavior may take years to see and would require longitudinal studies beyond any singular classroom experience to measure, global educators have an important opportunity to help students learn to *act* on their values. See table 1.2 for a list of the attributes World Savvy considers crucial to being a globally competent student and educator.

> *To become comfortable with the uncomfortable, with the ambiguity that is constant in times of rapid change, we have to address what creates the discomfort.*

Center for Global Education at Asia Society

The Center for Global Education at Asia Society (http://asiasociety.org/education) commits to setting the standard for how to teach and assess global competency. Its framework blurs the lines between soft and hard skills by interweaving the social, emotional, and academic in powerful ways, making the four domains of global competency—(1) investigate the world, (2) recognize perspectives, (3) communicate ideas, and (4) take action—among the most respected frameworks for global learning in North America. (See table 1.3 on page 22.)

Table 1.2: World Savvy's Global Competence Matrix

Core Concepts	Values and Attitudes	Skills	Behaviors
• World events and global issues are complex and interdependent. • One's own culture and history are key to understanding one's relationships to others. • Multiple conditions fundamentally affect diverse global forces, events, conditions, and issues. • Historical forces have shaped the current world system.	• Is open to new opportunities, ideas, and ways of thinking • Desires to engage with others • Practices self-awareness about identity and culture, and sensitivity and respect for differences • Values multiple perspectives • Displays comfort with ambiguity and unfamiliar situations • Reflects on context and meaning of our lives in relationship to something bigger • Questions prevailing assumptions • Adapts and is cognitively nimble • Empathizes • Shows humility	• Investigates the world by framing questions, analyzing and synthesizing relevant evidence, and drawing reasonable conclusions that lead to further inquiry • Recognizes, articulates, and applies an understanding of different perspectives (including his or her own) • Selects and applies appropriate tools and strategies to communicate and collaborate effectively • Listens actively and engages in inclusive dialogue • Is fluent in 21st century digital technology • Demonstrates resiliency in new situations • Applies critical, comparative, and creative thinking and problem solving	• Seeks out and applies an understanding of different perspectives to problem solving and decision making • Forms opinions based on exploration and evidence • Commits to the process of continuous learning and reflection • Adopts shared responsibility and takes cooperative action • Shares knowledge and encourages discourse • Translates ideas, concerns, and findings into appropriate and responsible individual or collaborative actions to improve conditions • Approaches thinking and problem solving collaboratively

Source: Adapted from World Savvy, 2014.

Table 1.3: The Center for Global Education at Asia Society's Four Domains of Global Competence

Investigate the World	Recognize Perspectives	Communicate Ideas	Take Action
Students investigate the world beyond their immediate environment. • Identify an issue, generate questions, and explain its significance. • Use a variety of languages, sources, and media to identify and weigh relevant evidence. • Analyze, integrate, and synthesize evidence to construct coherent responses. • Develop arguments based on compelling evidence, and draw defensible conclusions.	Students recognize their own and others' perspectives. • Recognize and express one's own perspective, and identify influences on that perspective. • Examine others' perspectives, and identify what influenced them. • Explain the impact of cultural interactions. • Articulate how differential access to knowledge, technology, and resources affects quality of life and perspectives.	Students communicate their ideas effectively with diverse audiences. • Recognize and express how diverse audiences perceive meaning and how that affects communication. • Listen to and communicate effectively with diverse people. • Select and use appropriate technology and media to communicate with diverse audiences. • Reflect on how effective communication affects understanding and collaboration in an interdependent world.	Students translate their ideas into appropriate action to improve conditions. • Identify and create opportunities for personal or collaborative action to improve conditions. • Assess options and plan actions based on evidence and potential for impact. • Act, personally or collaboratively, in creative and ethical ways to contribute to improvement, and assess impact of actions taken. • Reflect on capacity to advocate for and contribute to improvement.

Source: Center for Global Education at Asia Society, 2005.

While most schools in the Center for Global Education at Asia Society's International Studies Schools Network use a variety of project- and inquiry-based instructional models, the four domains of global competency also provide a potential design structure for planning global partnerships and other global learning experiences, both inside and outside the classroom. Whereas the other two frameworks provide learning goals for skills, knowledge, and values, this framework provides potential steps for instructional practice—that we begin by investigating the world, for example, move into recognizing perspectives, come back to investigate more, recognize more perspectives, and begin communicating our ideas as we move toward taking action.

The next step is to apply one or a combination of these frameworks to specific pedagogical or instructional strategies.

Investigating Pedagogical and Instructional Strategies for Global Competency

In my experience, so-called *sit-and-get* pedagogies, what Cooper (2013) refers to as "DLR: drill, lecture, repeat," rarely create graduates ready to thrive in the world. Whereas DLR learning focuses on rote memorization and tightly controlled learning management, VUCA-ready graduates need to know how to think for themselves. While global education is not necessarily synonymous with *inquiry-based learning* (where students learn through investigating an issue), it shares one important feature: the best global education is based in student-centered instructional practices. This means that, with the teacher's guidance, students lead learning, making choices along the way, and enjoying opportunities to create something meaningful. The goal is to foster students' abilities to work across cultures, navigate complexity, and think for themselves about how to solve the world's pressing problems. Global education is about

> *The best global education is based in student-centered instructional practices.*

fostering our students' innovation, creativity, passion, and purpose; and their ability to collaborate globally to develop new solutions to issues such as poverty, disease, climate change, and global conflict (Mansilla & Jackson, 2011). These goals can't easily be fulfilled by using teacher-driven models in which students take notes on lectures, fill out worksheets, and regurgitate knowledge on tests.

As early as 1897, educational philosopher John Dewey (as cited in Kucey & Parsons, 2012) criticizes traditional modes of education for being too focused on issues of the past rather than on the process skills and thinking that help students thrive in their current and future worlds outside of school. Noting that it is impossible to know what the world will be like by the time students graduate, Dewey (as cited in Roth, 2012) advocates instead for the development of "habits of learning" in schools, including "plasticity . . . an openness to being shaped by experience," over the pure acquisition of knowledge. These habits, he insists, will outlive any era-specific content knowledge, providing students with the skills to navigate any reality they might encounter.

Paulo Freire takes these ideas further with his 1970 publication, *Pedagogy of the Oppressed*, in which he points out that the traditional *banking model of education* doesn't lead students to their own sense of personal conscience (Freire, 2000). Calling the problem with education "narration sickness," Freire (2000) explains the challenges of traditional education this way:

> The teacher talks about reality as if it were motionless, static, compartmentalized, and predictable. Or else he expounds on a topic completely alien to the existential experience of the students. His task is to "fill" the students with the contents of his narration—contents which are detached from reality, disconnected from the totality that engendered them and could give them significance. . . . Education thus becomes an act of depositing, in which the students are the depositories and the teacher is the depositor. Instead of communicating, the teacher issues communiqués and makes deposits which the students patiently receive, memorize, and repeat. (pp. 52–53)

Real conscience and an evolving sense of one's place in the world, Freire insists, require a dialogue between teacher and students. Global education movements are in sync with much of what Dewey (as cited in Kucey & Parsons, 2012) and Freire (2000) emphasize, and student-driven pedagogies are increasingly recognized as the best path to developing students' global competencies. Brandon L. Wiley (2014), former executive director of the Center for Global Education at Asia Society's International Studies Schools Network and chief program officer at the Buck Institute for Education, frames instructional tendencies this way:

> Schools that focus on developing global competence take into account the diverse learners in every class. Across the school, teachers use project-based learning, higher-order questioning, and inquiry-based instructional strategies and student needs, learning styles, interests and standards to guide them. Classrooms provide opportunities for students to learn and apply discipline-specific methods of inquiry. Woven throughout the curriculum are instructional strategies that enable students to demonstrate productive habits of mind, which include problem solving, creative- and generative-thinking skills, the capacity to analyze issues of international significance from multiple perspectives, and the ability to direct their own learning. (p. 138)

This instructional approach combines the global competencies outlined in the frameworks provided earlier in this chapter with student-centered pedagogies, and includes the disciplines, standards, and curriculum that most schools are required to teach. Wiley's (2014) image of a globally engaged school includes many layers of student-directed learning, as the student who thrives in a VUCA world knows how to manage his or her own knowledge acquisition, rather than waiting for a teacher for direction. He also emphasizes that these schools give equal time to the visual and performing arts as to core content areas (Wiley, 2014). His point is important. The arts can break down political and religious barriers in ways no other discipline can, as well as create an avenue for reflection and self-expression that students need—especially if they're studying controversial global challenges like conflict or human rights, as explored in chapter 8 (page 143).

Similarly, students need to develop their world language skills for global engagement in any career field—and increasingly, those language skills are important locally as well. Global partnerships provide an ideal forum for practicing a language through authentic, not contrived, communication. In my experience in the Spanish classroom, global partnerships that motivate students to learn about each other will naturally motivate language learning as well, since the ability to communicate is the whole point of language study. This is often a missing link for world language classrooms, and no number of videos or in-class exercises can parallel the experience of talking to a real human being in the target language, especially if that person lives in another country. In my own classroom, I saw huge leaps in student progress when I embedded opportunities to use Spanish authentically, particularly with other teenagers in Latin America. In this regard, global partnerships can allow world language teachers to develop not just their students' language competencies but also students' urge to *use* them, which takes language learning out of the textbook and into the world.

The arts can break down political and religious barriers in ways no other discipline can.

The following instructional strategies—project-based learning, problem-based learning, design thinking, understanding by design, and place-based education—are all appropriate for global partnerships. They are included here because they start from the premise that student-centered learning matters for student engagement and empowerment, and are a central ingredient for fostering students' problem-solving skills. Consider your own context and classroom, and identify the strategies you feel might work for your students as you read about the following approaches.

Project-Based Learning

Project-based learning has students choose a real-world challenge or question and investigate an answer, learning significant content through the process of addressing the challenge. Employing many strategies connected to design thinking and understanding by design (defined in later sections), project-based learning emphasizes a challenging problem or question, sustained inquiry, authenticity, student voice and choice, reflection, critique and revision, and public product creation, all with an emphasis on students gaining key knowledge, understanding, and success skills throughout the process (Larmer, Mergendoller, & Boss, 2015). This pedagogical approach is well suited to all forms of partnerships, as it puts students in charge of their own experiences, with a focus on producing something tangible or presenting an idea that is shared during the experience. The Canada and Colombia pairing mentioned in the introduction (page 1) could be run as a project-based learning experience, for example, in which a driving question, like How might we collaborate to improve our communities?, would allow students to work together, learn from each other, and develop actions and products they decide on together. The project might include connecting the Colombian community with free-trade networks, and the product could be a presentation or paper describing the impetus, process, and results.

> *A driving question, like How might we collaborate to improve our communities?, would allow students to work together, learn from each other, and develop actions and products they decide on together.*

Problem-Based Learning

Problem-based learning is incredibly similar to project-based learning in its student-centered design strategies and intentions. However, problem-based learning always includes engagement in solving a complex and authentic problem, whereas project-based learning can be problem focused but can also focus on inquiry explorations, creative productions, or design challenges that do not solve a core problem (Stanford University, Center for Teaching and Learning, 2001). This pedagogical approach is very well suited to engaging students in solving global issues, so it is particularly appropriate for partnerships in which two or more classrooms work together to build solutions—whether it's a design for a better water filter or an argument about how to address climate change. For example, eighth-grade algebra classes at the Town School for Boys partnered with rural Sierra Leone to explore the prevention of Ebola; in this problem-based approach, students worked on the question, How might we use mathematics to understand and help end the Ebola crisis in West Africa? Students used exponential equations to understand the disease's spread, explored and analyzed existing solutions through statistical analysis, and designed actions to educate their community about the problem.

Design Thinking

Design thinking focuses on the creation of a more tangible product, designed with the user's needs in mind. Tim Brown, David Kelley, and the IDEO team (Thomas, 2016) originally developed design thinking as a mirror of the processes used by real engineers and designers to solve complex problems. Blogger Parker Thomas (2016) describes design thinking as "a vocabulary for describing the process of making and improving." It includes unique facets such as specific empathy-building steps, in which students define users' needs on an emotional level, which provides the opportunity to incorporate multiple perspectives. Like project-based learning, design thinking encourages multiple phases of ideation, prototyping, and testing to achieve high quality. This approach (described at www.ideo.org/approach) is ideal for any partnership that focuses on building something better—a cook stove, a solar energy system, a bridge, or a better means of transportation for rural communities, for example. Because it incorporates the use of *empathy interviews*, used to understand the feelings and motives of the person or group being designed for, design thinking also creates opportunities for humanizing and understanding others' needs (Institute of Design at Stanford, n.d.). One of my favorite global partnerships using design thinking was the cook stove project, an eighth-grade science partnership that ran for several years between Brookwood School in Manchester, Massachusetts, the Forum for African Women Educationalists school in Kigali, Rwanda, and Colegio Bandeirantes in São Paulo, Brazil (Boss, 2013a). Each community worked with the materials most available to them locally, collaborating around their communities' specific cooking and efficiency needs, as well as their designs' environmental impacts.

Understanding by Design

Understanding by design, commonly known as UbD, is a planning structure and process intended to guide curriculum, assessment, and instruction with a focus on teaching and assessing deep, transferable knowledge and skills by focusing on long-term learning goals (McTighe & Wiggins, 2012). Understanding by design, a common concept in curricular planning, asks educators to begin with the end in mind and plan backwards (which is why understanding by design is also known as *backward design*). Understanding by design emphasizes authentic performance outcomes—tasks that require demonstrating learning beyond a multiple-choice test—and teachers serve as coaches in a largely student-centered experience, ensuring that learning occurs but refraining from directing it too overtly. For example, students in multiple locations might work together to co-create something to demonstrate their learning authentically—from a white paper on human trafficking to a Dream Flag Project (http://dreamflags.org) event that brings multiple cultures together. In many ways, the other strategies described here align with understanding by design because they begin with the end in mind, but the emphasis on authentic performance outcomes makes UbD particularly appropriate for global partnerships.

Place-Based Education

Place-based education focuses on deep explorations of heritage, culture, and challenges in students' own local communities. You can adapt it for partnerships in which two classrooms do deep local explorations and then share their findings with each other. Place-based education provides learners with ways to become active citizens and stewards of their local environment, and it often includes service learning experiences and hands-on, real-world problem solving (Sobel, 2005). Chris Harth (2010) explores similar strategies in his work on *glocal* learning approaches, in which students explore global issues but apply their learning by exploring and solving those issues in their local context. Place-based education is particularly useful in elementary partnerships because it makes global issues more concrete for young learners when they can see how these issues manifest locally. This approach also has the advantage of allowing students to do something about the injustices or challenges they discover, encouraging deep understandings of and engagement with their local communities. An excellent example of a place-based global collaboration comes from This Is Ours, an initiative of e2 Education & Environment (www.e2education.org). In This Is Ours, students in different parts of the world photograph and write about their local environment, identifying the plant and animal species that make it unique, as well as sharing how their environment impacts their lives. Any classroom can use the books of photography and writing each school produces for a deep understanding of place as an element of culture and identity.

A Few Concluding Thoughts

Arguably the most important element of global competency originates in the sense of purpose that making an authentic connection can develop in students. Yong Zhao (2012) asserts that "the most desirable education, of course, is one that enhances human curiosity and creativity, encourages risk taking, and cultivates the entrepreneurial spirit in the context of globalization" (p. 17). By connecting their learning to the world outside the school building, students can begin to envision themselves as change makers who can participate constructively, regardless of their age or capacity to travel. The more we get students thinking for themselves and pursuing sustained inquiry into topics of passion, the more likely they are to build their lives around such topics. Pedagogical and instructional approaches like project-based or problem-based learning, design thinking, understanding by design, and place-based education help students tap into their interests and make purposeful choices.

In addition to impacting student engagement—and creating the higher achievement that comes from improved engagement—global partnerships have the potential to develop a sense of purpose that researchers find improves emotional resilience, determination, and lifelong well-being (Damon, 2009). Psychologist William Damon's (2009) work suggests that connecting students with purposeful experiences throughout their education will help build many related strengths, including increased resilience from a "dedication to something larger than ourselves"

(p. 25), and the ability to make "a valued contribution to the world beyond the self" (p. 28). In that regard, a sense of purpose may well be the most important global competency we can develop in our students. Particularly as they begin to grapple with the volatility, uncertainty, complexity, and ambiguity of life in the 21st century, a deep sense of purpose—fostered through their connections with real people and experiences—will help them feel empowered rather than helpless.

Arguably the most important element of global competency originates in the sense of purpose that making an authentic connection can develop in students.

Global competencies are not about gathering data or proving that students think globally; global competencies are about students becoming people of good conscience who work with others around the world to create a more sustainably just and peaceful world. Our planet needs young people everywhere to become self-motivated global thinkers who care about all stakeholders' priorities, meaning that they work in partnership to find innovative ways to improve the lives of all people involved in or impacted by the global issues we explore, feel connected to others through a sense of common humanity, are curious about what is distinct in our cultural experiences, and are eager to learn from and collaborate with others. As you begin envisioning the sort of global partnership experience you'd like to create for your students, and which pedagogical and instructional strategies you want to embrace, keep these lofty goals in mind—but remember that first steps can be small as long as you connect students with perspectives and experiences that are humanizing and authentic.

CHAPTER 2

PREPARING FOR
GLOBAL COLLABORATION

*Knowledge emerges only through invention and re-invention, through
the restless, impatient, continuing, hopeful inquiry human beings pursue in the world, with the world, and with each other.*

—Paulo Freire

Which aspects of your curriculum might improve with the kind of humanizing
that comes from building connections and relationships? What kind of learning
experience do you hope to build for students through your global partnership?
What regions of the world connect to what your students are studying? How do
you envision partnerships playing out in your day-to-day classroom work? What
knowledge and skills do you hope your students will develop? This chapter will
explore these considerations and more, and help you establish your partnership
goals in concrete but flexible ways *before* you seek a partner.

It's up to you whether to join an existing project for partnership, which we explore
in chapter 4 (page 73), or whether you'd rather seek a partner and build something
from scratch, which we explore in chapter 5 (page 93). Both are viable means
of engaging, but building from scratch often requires more time. Some teachers
develop a collaborative project idea first and then invite other classrooms to join
in, welcoming anyone who likes their idea, while others start by finding a partner
and then building the project idea together. (Chapter 5 helps you navigate asking a
classroom to join yours.) You can work with one or multiple classrooms during your
partnership, or you might prefer to connect your students with a few individuals.
The key to building effective and sustainable international partnerships, according
to Yong Zhao (2012), "is mutual benefits and understanding. Learning to discover
mutual benefits and develop mutual understanding itself presents opportunities

to develop global competency" (p. 228). I encourage you to consider this your central goal as you begin developing your partnership ideas: How might you craft a partnership that leads students to discover mutual benefits and develop mutual understanding? What mutual benefits and understanding will you need to develop with your partner teacher in order to get students there?

How might you craft a partnership that leads students to discover mutual benefits and develop mutual understanding?

Building a global partnership requires an incredible amount of resilience, flexibility, and patience, regardless of design. If you go in expecting high levels of success in the first year, your experiences may be disheartening. If you are concerned that you don't have enough global competencies yourself and hold back from the elements that feel challenging, you may end up creating a superficial experience for your students. But if you can see yourself as a learner, can really embrace concepts like *failing forward* (because everyone fails, John C. Maxwell [2000] says what you do afterward determines whether you fail backward or forward), and are willing to be transparent with students as you hit the bumps, the partnership will be stronger in the long run—plus your students will have the important experience of learning *with you* more than *from you* (Freire, 2000).

Consider the following questions when contemplating the kind of partnership you would like to cultivate.

What Do I Want Students to Learn From Their Global Partnership?

The first serious consideration is the kind of learning experience you want to create for your students. If you consider the other classroom a true partner, and that's the goal, you should find a teacher you would like to work with and then make most of your decisions with your partner. (Finding partners is discussed in detail in chapter 4 and chapter 5.) Serious equity issues can emerge if you overplan the project before your first call, as doing so can make you less receptive to your partner's needs—and can even make you come across as dominating what should be a collaborative relationship. However, seeking a partner before clarifying some goals and hopes for the encounter can also be problematic. Even worse, failing to establish your readiness and needs, and then trying to coordinate your internal logistics *after* meeting your partner, can cause long delays in communication that can hurt your relationship with the other teacher.

It is important to ground your global partnership plans in significant learning goals that are fully relevant to your grade level and disciplines. The more you can ground your work in significant learning goals, particularly those that you can quantify through traditional assessments, the less resistance you will encounter from administrators, colleagues, parents, and students who might consider global learning "fluff" or see soft skills as less important than core content. William Kist (2014) notes that the necessary integration of technologies in global education exacerbates these misperceptions, as the use of new media often includes what Kist (2014) calls "the entertainment factor," and new technologies are often perceived as detracting from the "seriousness of school" and putting fun over rigorous learning (p. 62).

It is important to ground your global partnership plans in significant learning goals that are fully relevant to your grade level and disciplines.

You must balance the effort, however. While academic grounding and learning goals can help legitimize a global partnership experience within your school or district, remember that just getting to know students in another part of the world will matter to your students. Launching into too much significant content too quickly in a global partnership often results in initially unengaged students. It is worth taking the time to explore each other's lives (and not just at the lower-grade levels) to understand your partners as people before collaborating toward a specific goal. Sharing seemingly unimportant facets of life—such as students' family make-up, pets, favorite music, movies, or books—can help create the initial connectedness that will ensure meaningful engagement throughout a partnership. How much seemingly off-topic banter is acceptable? Kist (2014) notes that teachers often wrestle with how much to keep students on task during international communication:

> Most teachers in the global collaboration projects felt in the end that some amount of off-task chatter was acceptable and even desirable as students got to know each other. In the end, off-task conversation may help further the goals of global education projects in that students may learn more about other cultures through such informal conversations. (p. 61)

During a videoconference I facilitated between students at St. Mary's Academy in Colorado and Falastine Dwikat, a young poet in Palestine, a seemingly off-task question about what Dwikat was reading led to a surprisingly powerful conversation. It turned out that she had just finished a book all the juniors in the room were reading for class—and hating—at which point Dwikat spent five minutes convincing them that it was worth their time. Ultimately, controlling the conversation too much or insisting on significant content over building connections may result in missing a rich opportunity for more layered and meaningful learning and relationship building.

Along with leaving room for unplanned discussion, build plans that leave plenty of room for student choice on both sides of the partnership. Thematic frameworks, such as the Universal Declaration of Human Rights (http://bit.ly/2ho5QMO) or the United Nations' sustainable development goals (http://bit.ly/1VXvanH), can create space for both classrooms to participate in relevant and meaningful ways, and to make choices that ensure all students explore issues relevant to their lives. As explained in chapter 7 (page 129), it's important to come to partners with project ideas that can flex to the partner teacher's needs; thematic approaches often allow for more flexibility, creativity, and equity because both classrooms can focus on the same framework (the sustainable development goals, for example) but can focus in on the issues most relevant to each community (such as exploring how to ensure high-quality education for girls in one classroom, while exploring how to end poverty in the other).

Most teachers around the world specialize in one or two academic disciplines from fifth grade onward. However, some of the best global partnerships are inter-disciplinary. An interdisciplinary project can also make it easier to find the right partner teacher, as the project will be relevant to more potential partners. In fact, we do students a disservice when suggesting that each discipline exists in isolation. As a ninth grader at Parish Episcopal School in Dallas put it in his final reflections on an interdisciplinary global studies class, "It's very important to see the connections between multiple classes because it mirrors the way the world works. Nothing stands on its own and everything is connected in some way" (A. Jennings, personal communication, May 12, 2016).

Once you find your partner teacher, you can have a conversation about where your curricular priorities intersect. Consider your two classrooms as the two circles of a Venn diagram, and start your partnership conversations in the areas where your goals and course content overlap. But until you connect with your partner directly, it is more important to note where you can enrich your curric-ulum with the opportunity for primary-source investigations into global issues and perspectives through collaboration with people outside your community. Once you meet with your partner teacher, you can work together to identify your common learning goals and design a partnership experience that meets those goals. We will explore a wide array of global partnership examples in chapter 3 (page 49), all of which are tied to grade level–appropriate learning objectives in language arts, social studies, mathematics, science, and the arts across the K–12 spectrum.

Some of the best global partnerships are interdisciplinary.

How Can I Take My Students Beyond the Fs of Global Education?

It's easy and fun to engage with what many connected educators call the *Fs of global education*, but staying there often leads to superficial and less-than-humanizing partnerships. The *Fs* include topics like *flags, food, folks, fun, festivals,* and *fashion*—those elements of culture that are easy to see (Hall, 1976). Using Edward T. Hall's (1976) cultural iceberg model to understand this issue, it becomes clear that we miss approximately 90 percent of a culture or individual's identity if we only explore the Fs. According to the cultural iceberg model (Hall, 1976), we see only 10 percent of a given culture when we look at what's visible (such as fashion, festivals, and food). Below the waterline lies 90 percent of who we are, just as the majority of an iceberg is invisible. That is where we find the beliefs, values, and thought patterns *beneath* our behaviors, rituals, and rites of passage. It's not that we should avoid those surface-level Fs completely. In fact, many elementary and world language teachers spend a lot of time on them because topics like food and festivals help get kids excited and curious about different cultures and languages. But it's important to recognize that the Fs are only a starting point, and to find ways to intentionally take students beneath the waterline over the course of our partnerships.

Edutopia blogger Suzie Boss (2016), author of *Bringing Innovation to School*, suggests that too much focus on quick, superficial explorations relegates global education to "at best a sidebar to the regular curriculum," pointing out that "one-shot events or content-light programs do little to help students develop the global competencies that the 21st century demands of them." She quotes Harvard's Fernando M. Reimers, who fears that too many schools turn global education into an annual festival (Boss, 2016). Reimers claims, "Schools check the box and say, 'OK, we've done global,'" based on festivals and brief events that really have nothing to do with building deep global competency and citizenship (as cited in Boss, 2016). Perhaps even more problematic, superficially exploring a culture can more easily lead to cultural misrepresentation, a serious danger to watch out for in this work, as it can be more diminishing than humanizing, exacerbating stereotypes rather than nuancing students' understanding of the many layers of culture (Klein, 2017).

One way to move your students into a deeper experience is to use the Center for Global Education at Asia Society's four domains of global competency—(1) investigate the world, (2) recognize perspectives, (3) communicate ideas, and (4) take action—to provoke questions that require deeper cultural competency to answer. (See table 1.3 on page 22 for more on the domains.) Regardless of whether you explore the Fs initially, how might you ensure that students will have opportunities to investigate the world more deeply, recognize perspectives, communicate ideas, and take action (Mansilla & Jackson, 2011)? What might it look like to try to understand the reasons beneath what we see when investigating the world? Why do people in a given place hold the perspectives they do? Who do we want to communicate our ideas to, and how might we act to improve conditions? As soon as you start considering such questions, your partnership will build into an experience in which the Fs provide the appetizer to a more meaningful meal. For example, an exploration of a country's flag can lead to a deeper conversation about national and local identity, and even an opportunity to redesign a local flag in order to capture modern culture, as you'll see in the Global Partners Junior example in chapter 3 (page 56). All the Fs have a deeper cultural context, so make sure students dip below that waterline to reach more nuanced understandings of the places and people they connect with.

> *Why do people in a given place hold the perspectives they do? Who do we want to communicate our ideas to, and how might we act to improve conditions?*

PERSPECTIVES ON THE Fs OF GLOBAL EDUCATION: HOMA SABET TAVANGAR

Author of *Growing Up Global* and *The Global Education Toolkit for Elementary Learners*

I have a love-hate relationship with the notorious Fs—food, fun, and festivals. On the one hand, I rush to their defense when I hear them scoffed at. I have seen numerous instances where an international night, day, or week filled with the Fs brings school communities together, helps engage teachers who otherwise would not feel confident enough to incorporate various cultures or global perspectives, and draws in families from diverse backgrounds to showcase their experiences with pride. I've seen it build empathy among populations of recent immigrants and longtime locals, and serve as a springboard for deeper global learning, when teachers or school leaders noticed how engaged and creative their students and families could be, thanks to the Fs.

On the other hand, food, fun, and festivals might get one more F—*freak show*—tacked on, usually unconsciously, when cultures go on display in isolation from human experience, empathy, and humble learning; so these Fs can backfire. In isolation, a display of foreign food, fun, and festivals might create a single story, out of context and often distorted, and result in a great disservice to a complex culture, issue, or the experience of our neighbors. Rather than destroy prejudices, they could reinforce them. So, similar to the experience of technology use and social media, these Fs are not inherently good or bad. It's how we present them and utilize them in the process of facilitating learning. Whether it's a student-driven, personalized learning environment or a more traditional one, the role of teachers and school leaders can powerfully set the tone and facilitate authentic, empathy-building experiences—or not.

Source: Adapted from H. S. Tavangar, personal communication, April 30, 2016.

How Much Time Can I Put Into Crafting This Partnership?

This is an important question for any overworked educator. Realistically speaking, if you don't have the time to communicate consistently and craft something meaningful for all classrooms involved, you're better off going with an existing program, such as those explored in chapter 4 (page 73). Many are successful and provide excellent, ready-made projects with partners already in place. Because most existing programs have a set curriculum and standardized systems, they can lack the flexibility some teachers prefer, but as you make connections to partner teachers through existing programs, you can often develop your own innovations. If you're willing and able to put in more work to craft something from scratch, you can build a learning partnership that flexes to the curricular needs of all teachers. Chapter 5 (page 93) explains the process of finding a classroom or teacher partner for a from-scratch pairing. Neither approach necessarily comes with a better guarantee of success; partnerships succeed and fail in established programs as much as they do in homegrown projects. Which method you choose is really a question of the kind of educator you are; if you prefer established systems and programs, or have limited time to invest, go that route. And if you tend to struggle with existing structures, build something of your own. See the reproducible "Global Partnership Checklist" at **go.SolutionTree.com/21stcentury skills** for all the steps addressed in this book, both to help you be realistic about what you can take on and to help you stay organized as you progress.

I strongly recommend that teachers trying their first global partnership have at least a few of their regular duties assigned to another teacher in the first year, such as removing a few lunch, homeroom, or advisory duties, to provide more dedicated time for communication and collaboration with their partner teacher. Some school administrators even build global work into teachers' contracts and provide them with additional professional development and other support designed to help ensure success. Australian thought leader Julie Lindsay (2016) emphasizes the importance of a supportive administration, writing that the best global education leaders she's worked with are people who "instead of crushing new ideas, provided support through time release from the classroom, who provided funds for digital resources, and who listened with some understanding to my vision of the way things could be" (p. 72). While time release can be challenging, particularly in underfunded school environments, shifting even small responsibilities can make a big difference. Schools that have time delineated for collaborative teamwork can create a team for emerging partnerships, which builds in not just time but also community collaboration around addressing global partnership challenges. Regardless of whether you craft from scratch or join an existing program, you'll need time—and the support of your leadership—to make a new partnership work. Chapters 8 (page 143) and 10 (page 177) discuss more about the importance of administrative support.

With What Country or Region Do I Want to Connect?

Do you hope to connect with a different hemisphere, native language, or culture? Are there specific countries that connect to your current curriculum, or are you seeking to better understand topics that exist across multiple countries? While finding a partner without a specific country or community in mind can be much easier than searching with too many specific expectations, it's best to go in with a few ideas—and a lot of flexibility, should you find a committed partner in a country you hadn't considered. If a specific country is key to the curricular connections you want to make, however, then it's good to identify that from the start. For example, a language arts teacher studying Art Spiegelman's graphic novel *Maus* might prefer to partner with a school in Poland because of the book's focus and the insights Polish students can offer, whereas a language arts teacher interested in having students share their original poetry could partner with any country. On the other hand, if the teacher wants students to have equal footing as learners and experts, he or she might want two classrooms that are *not* in Poland to read *Maus*. It all depends on the kind of learning experience you want to create.

> *Language classrooms have an intrinsic reason to connect with native speakers, and language teachers use a variety of approaches to partner native speakers with nonnative speakers.*

For world language teachers, this topic is all the more complex. Language classrooms have an intrinsic reason to connect with native speakers, and language teachers use a variety of approaches to partner native speakers with nonnative speakers. In some cases, two classes study *each other's* language, and this can work well because both classrooms bring an expertise and an area for growth. I've seen this approach fail, however, when teachers didn't see their students' growth process the same way. (See chapter 9, page 155, for an example.) In other cases, teachers choose to partner based on the language being studied, so both classrooms are working toward mastery in the same target language. This removes the opportunity to hear authentic accents and fluent native speakers, but it can engender more risk-taking. In my mixed-level Spanish classes, for example, I found that non-native speakers were far more likely to practice and take risks with their Spanish when there wasn't a native speaker in the conversation. In fact, if students don't share a common language other than the one being studied, the partnership may create even more language fluency, as students will be motivated to use the new common language out of authentic necessity. Visit University of Minnesota's The Center for Advanced Research on Language Acquisition (http://carla.umn.edu/index.html) to learn more about instructional strategies for building motivation and risk-taking during world language acquisition, and the research behind those approaches.

Which Design Best Supports the Global Competencies I Want to Foster?

While many global competencies can be challenging to teach and assess, coupling academic goals with global competency goals will help ensure that students develop not just global knowledge but also the skills needed to act on that knowledge and engage with the world as active global citizens—and even leaders. Refer back to the global competency frameworks explored in chapter 1 (page 11) and think about your students' age groups and subject areas. Which global competencies best match your project ideas and topics? Which feel most developmentally appropriate for your age group? Keep in mind that students may use a wide array of global competencies in the course of a collaborative partnership, but it makes sense to choose just one or two to focus on most intentionally. Try to make sure those are competencies you can both foster and assess. For example, the critical thinking involved in gathering multiple perspectives on any given topic is fairly easy to teach and assess, while empathy or humility—central goals in many global partnerships—can be much more challenging to define, teach, and recognize in student work and behavior.

There are many design strategies for global partnerships, and your choices will impact which global competencies your partnership fosters. Before you find a partner (which is covered in chapter 4, page 73, and chapter 5, page 93), it's important to consider the following design strategies for how your students might engage with their global counterparts.

Classroom-to-Classroom Exchange

In a classroom-to-classroom exchange, students share or exchange the work produced in each classroom, often in relative isolation. Much like a physical student or teacher exchange program, many exchanges include sending students' projects to each other. For example, two music classes might create and share videos to teach each other songs and ask each other questions. In other cases, like the Teddy Bear Project outlined in chapter 3 (page 49), physical objects are sent from one class to the other and then back again. This design strategy is particularly useful with younger students who can't travel themselves, but also allows students at higher grade levels to share the work they're doing. For example, students in two countries might take photographs of what they see from their windows in their homes, dorms, or classrooms, ultimately sharing final photo essays with each other. This style of partnership is often more manageable than collaboration or co-creation, as most work occurs in the individual classrooms rather than requiring regular live connections between the two groups. This design strategy is all about sharing and learning from and with each other, and it is ideal when your goal is to build students' sense of connectedness with other people in the world.

Classroom-to-Classroom Collaboration

A classroom-to-classroom collaboration usually includes students working concurrently in two or more classrooms, perhaps on a local problem that impacts both communities, and sharing work regularly along the way. In this approach, students offer each other feedback on ideas and products, and sharing strategies and learning from each other becomes as important as addressing the local challenge itself. This approach is more complex than an exchange, as it builds in opportunities for students to see each other's thinking and help each other improve their work. As the example from Global Partners Junior (page 56) demonstrates, this approach helps students recognize that communities worldwide often share local challenges and themes, and it gives them the opportunity to learn from other communities as they craft solutions for their own.

Classroom-to-Classroom Co-Creation

While this is the most complex approach to global partnerships, it is often the most meaningful as well. In this design, students work together between two or more classrooms to produce one collaborative product. For example, students might work together to address a borderless global challenge, such as human trafficking or hunger, that affects both communities and requires collaborative efforts. In #Decarbonize, the project on climate change outlined in chapter 3, students work in multischool teams to co-create a white paper to bring to the Climate Change Conference of the Parties. However, a co-creation partnership doesn't necessarily require a solutions orientation; students could work together to create a piece of collaborative art, a music video, or a public service announcement to educate others, to name a few.

Nonschool Partners

Connecting with individuals doing global work on their own or through nongovernmental organizations (NGOs) can help fill gaps and bring meaningful global perspectives to your students, particularly while teachers are working to develop long-term partnerships with classrooms. Having a passionate individual connect with students is far less complex than collaborating with a classroom because you don't have to juggle as many variables with an individual, particularly in coordinating live connections. For example, an individual can often shift schedules to connect during class, regardless of time zone differences, whereas coordinating across two or more classroom schedules can be challenging. Also, global Skype (https://skype .com/en) sessions with individuals doing important work can have just as much impact on students' worldviews as connecting with other classrooms—and can even help students envision new career paths and avenues for creating change. In chapter 3 we explore several examples of nonclassroom partnerships, including those with an urban planner, a Navajo elder, and an international human rights lawyer, among others. The most important quality of a global speaker is his or her ability to make the topics students are learning about human, relevant, and real for their age group. Besides being easier for the teacher to coordinate, skyping in global speakers can often create high-profile learning opportunities, which increase community and administrative buy-in and get people excited about global partnerships without the expense of travel and speaker fees. Also, global speakers are usually one-off experiences that you can integrate into a larger global unit or project, which is part of why they're easier to set up, whereas global partnerships between classrooms are richer if communication happens repeatedly over time.

What Are the Ideal Duration and Timing for the Project I Have in Mind?

Partnerships can range from a month to the entire school year, depending on the teachers' needs and investment. Shorter projects tend to be more successful as you begin partnering with a new teacher, while longer, deeper projects can take time to develop. Many projects that start small grow into something significant, even in their first year, as the teachers get to know each other and learn to work together—and anything is possible when two or more committed partners move into their second or third year of collaboration. Often, it is best to start small, with the expectation of one or two *synchronous* (live) events, and one or two offline experiences, over the course of a month or two. See what might build from there.

While short projects can be meaningful, there is a difference between a global *activity* (one Skype call) and a true global *partnership*, which might include several calls and some collaborative, asynchronous communication in between. While global activities that make connections are still meaningful, you can dig deeper as you get to know each other better—and show students that global engagement isn't fleeting or episodic, but something to work at and grow with over weeks, months, and even years. This deeply engaged mindset is part of the key to retaining partners, too, as your partner teacher is likely to sense if your intentions are brief and episodic rather than deep and committed. In their essence, global partnerships are global friendships. They are global relationships that yield richer results—and develop more nuanced global competencies—as we find ways to dig deeper over time.

In their essence, global partnerships are global friendships. They are global relationships that yield richer results—and develop more nuanced global competencies—as we find ways to dig deeper over time.

You may be unable to control the pace of your partner's engagement, and I discourage you from forcing your priorities on your partner. Partnerships often take longer than expected to cultivate simply because communication styles are different, and teachers in different parts of the world often have vacations, national exams, and other demands at different times of the year. These complexities mean that building in more time for connecting than you estimate needing, and being flexible enough to allow global engagement to continue even after you've moved into new material, are paramount to your success. Most often, if one class has finished final products and needs to move on to new material while their partners are still working on theirs, reconnecting is just a question of circling back to share student work and celebrate the learning together. For example, in a mythology project done at Appleby College (Canada) and Paraíso High School (Costa Rica), classes work on products at totally different times of year because their school year calendars are so different. Teachers have learned to transition in and out of the projects as needed.

Creating the best timing possible means choosing a time frame that works well for you *and* your partner teacher. Flexibility is key to equity, as chapter 7 (page 129) explores, but sometimes curriculum sequencing or seasonal themes make it hard to move a topic to better fit the needs of a partner teacher. For example, many elementary teachers in North America explore reproduction in spring, when students will see evidence of animal and plant birth around them, so a partnership on this topic would need to occur in spring for both teachers—which means that a simultaneous partnership between Southern and Northern Hemisphere schools would be impossible. To avoid problems later in the partnership, be specific if you have time frame requirements (and be sure to *identify timing in your outreach by naming the months*, as seasons vary depending on hemisphere). Keep in mind that Southern-Hemisphere schools are on summer break during the Northern Hemisphere's winter, and vice versa, which means that connecting northern and southern schools requires timing partnerships from September to November and from March to May, when schools in both hemispheres are most likely to be in session simultaneously.

How Important Is the Opportunity for Synchronous Communication?

Synchronous experiences occur when students use live videoconferencing technologies like Skype or WebEx (www.webex.com) to connect in real time with their partner classroom. Asynchronous experiences are not live and occur, for example, via technologies like virtual classrooms, Google Drive (https://google.com/drive), and Edmodo (https://edmodo.com) spaces. In asynchronous experiences, students share work, ideas, or feedback when it's convenient for them, and the partner students see the work when they go online. How important is it that students have opportunities to talk to each other live, and how often? Ultimately, these answers depend on your goals.

These questions loop back to which countries you hope to partner with, but now the challenge is partnering between Eastern and Western Hemispheres. For example, if a teacher in Denver wants to partner with a teacher in Beijing, the two will have a fourteen- to fifteen-hour time difference that will make synchronous learning incredibly challenging. During daylight savings time switches, when different countries may or may not change their clocks on a wide variety of dates, planning a synchronous session requires paying very close attention to such changes. I always suggest that global educators find a reliable world clock application that allows accurate coordination across time zones, based on the engagement dates. Asynchronous communication can work really well with such a broad time difference, however, and teachers often describe high levels of excitement and engagement when students find work from their partners at the start of class each day, posted while they were asleep.

If synchronous learning is key to the project or experience you want to create, remember that even when time differences are small, school schedules may be vastly different, so it will still be hard to create live connections without disrupting the schedule. If your administration is serious about providing meaningful global learning experiences, that should include finding ways to flex the schedule or allow students to leave other classes for important live events. I've convinced teenagers, who are barely awake by 9 a.m., to show up at 6:30 a.m. to videoconference with teenagers in Palestine—all I had to do was bring the coffee and doughnuts. The experience's excitement and novelty drew in the students.

Regardless of your choices, remember that your goal is to humanize the people your students meet. You can improve asynchronous communications by having students share short videos of their homes, their families, and their ideas. In a second-grade music partnership between Hawken School in Ohio and the American School Foundation of Monterrey in Mexico, for example, students never met live but exchanged a total of six music videos over the course of a semester (three from each side). The experience was deeply humanizing. Likewise, synchronous experiences don't always humanize just because they're live; it requires skillful facilitation and the slow building of comfort and connection before students engage in meaningful dialogue during live experiences.

Remember that your goal is to humanize the people your students meet.

Do I Have Any Compatibility Non-Negotiables?

In chapter 7 (page 129), we explore more of the nuances of equity and compatibility in building global partnerships, but it's good to identify any non-negotiables before you start searching for your partner, which is tackled in chapters 4 (page 73) and 5 (pages 93). Common language use is often a non-negotiable for monolingual teachers, but the willingness to challenge yourself (and use translation tools as needed) will help build your own global competencies, as well as help students see you as a lifelong learner willing to struggle openly with something new. We will take a deeper dive into communication challenges and strategies in chapter 6 (page 107), as many educators work in communities filled with expertise in a diversity of world languages.

Other non-negotiables that impact compatibility might include timing needs for live encounters, common priorities for platforms and communication, and what you hope your students might gain from the experience. When we look at assessment in chapter 9 (page 155), you'll see that partnerships falter sometimes because the teachers use different pedagogical and instructional strategies, so it can be useful to search with your own teaching style and needs in mind as well.

Which Technological Platforms Might Be Best Suited to My Partnership?

This is a challenging question to answer before finding a partner classroom, as your partner's technology access could be very different. In the interest of equitable experiences it's important to choose a platform both classrooms can utilize easily. Your own tech savvy and comfort matter too, so choose a platform you either know already or can learn easily. The easier it is for you to use, the more likely it will work for your partner and students as well. The global increase in mobile technology means that the phone, or a mobile tool like WhatsApp (https://whatsapp.com) or Facebook for messaging and calls, is often the easiest synchronous option, even if the face-to-face nature of Skype or Google Hangouts (https://hangouts.google.com) can create more humanizing experiences.

Although traditional paper mail can take a lot longer for back-and-forth communication, giving students handwritten letters or other objects that they can hold, touch, and explore creates a visceral experience.

You might also consider minimizing the use of online technologies in your partnership, particularly if you hope to partner with a rural, lower-income school. Global education existed since long before the Internet, so consider 20th century options like traditional so-called snail mail. Although traditional paper mail can take a lot longer for back-and-forth communication, giving students handwritten letters or other objects that they can hold, touch, and explore creates a visceral experience. In chapters 4 (page 73) and 6 (page 107), we will explore the plethora of global programs and platforms that can take global learning into the 21st century, but it can be useful to remember that globally connected learning predates the Internet.

How Ready Are My School and Classroom for Global Partnerships?

There is little more frustrating than feeling like a team of one as you embark on such a complicated experience. Taking on a simpler project initially can help, but it's better to have support in your building and know how to leverage your on-site allies. Who are your potential allies and resources in your building, and how might they support your efforts? Who are your allies and resources in the broader school community, such as parents or partner organizations? Assessing readiness might also include sitting down with administrators and colleagues to think through how to ensure success. Use the Partnership Readiness worksheet (figure 2.1) to think through the elements explored in chapter 1 (page 11). You can complete some elements yourself, but others—such as the technology choices and curricular focus—require consulting your partner teacher.

The more details you can think through before seeking a global partner, the sooner you can move to engagement once you find that partner. Please be as specific as possible in your answers for the following questions, leaving blank any areas you prefer to develop with your partner. You may find it useful to fill out the majority of this worksheet during your first or second meeting with your partner as a way to develop common ground and begin the planning process.

- Do we have the technological infrastructures in place for synchronous videoconferences?

    - Sound system (incoming and outgoing):

    - Existing platform options:

    - Video system (incoming and outgoing):

    - Remaining challenges or concerns regarding synchronous technologies:

Figure 2.1: Partnership readiness worksheet.

continued →

- Do we have the technological infrastructures in place for asynchronous collaborations?

  - Existing platform options:

  - Permissions and school policies for students' online engagement:

  - Remaining challenges or concerns regarding asynchronous technologies:

- In which countries or regions might we seek a partner, given the nature of our ideas so far?

- Do we have on-site partners ready to support our needs?

  - Language experts (students, teachers, or parents):

  - Technology experts (students, colleagues, or specific IT personnel):

  - Intercultural experts (teachers, parents, or community members):

  - In-house partner teachers (interdisciplinary or grade-level team members):

  - Remaining challenges or concerns regarding on-site partners:

- What kind of learning experience do we want for our students?

- Which global competencies would we like to foster?

- Which instructional design strategies feel most appropriate to our current partnership ideas?

- Which topics or themes would we like to explore with our partners?

- Which educational goals or standards would we like students to develop?

- How do we hope to dig beneath the food, flags, and festivals of global education to engage on a deeper level? In other words, how might students investigate the world, recognize perspectives, communicate ideas, and take action through this partnership (Center for Global Education at Asia Society, 2005)?

- What is our desired partnership design? Note all that apply, and provide as much detail as possible.

  - Interdisciplinary (specify subjects):

  - Subject specific (specify):

  - Exchange (specify):

  - Collaboration (specify):

  - Co-creation (specify possible products and challenges):

  - Possible nonclassroom partners to draw in during gaps:

  - Remaining challenges or concerns regarding partnership design:

- Who are the allies in our community we might leverage for support?

- What are remaining challenges or concerns about our ability to develop and maintain a healthy partnership?

Visit **go.SolutionTree.com/21stcenturyskills** for a free reproducible version of this figure.

A Few Concluding Thoughts

As you do your initial planning around the topics, regions, competencies, and experiences you'd like to include, remember that this will be a learning experience for you as much as it is for your students.

As you do your initial planning around the topics, regions, competencies, and experiences you'd like to include, remember that this will be a learning experience for you as much as it is for your students. Sometimes, the best-laid plans don't turn out as hoped. Other times, loosely planned partnerships end up creating a series of happy accidents that create deep learning and connection. I meet teachers all the time who call their partnerships failures or question their value because, for example, they only communicated via Skype twice or never finished a final product. If you see each hurdle as a chance to learn more about each other, every accident is an opportunity for global learning and skill building—and even one Skype call signals success if you learn something from it alongside your students.

GETTING A FEEL FOR WHAT'S POSSIBLE

Borderless challenges must be addressed collaboratively, creatively, and constructively by multiple actors, especially those with the greatest stake and with the greatest capacity to effect positive change.

—Chris Harth

While it's important to come into your first conversation without too much of an agenda, envisioning what good partnerships can look like will help you enter the conversation with ideas about the shape your engagement might take. This chapter explores examples that demonstrate the various design strategies good partnerships might use, identifying a variety of age-appropriate ways of thinking about and designing global partnership experiences at the elementary, middle, and high school levels. While several of the classroom-to-classroom partnership examples come from existing organizations and programs, they are meant to reflect best practices regardless of who hosts or designs them—and you could easily recreate several in a different form with partners you find yourself, or adapt them to very different age groups. At the end of this chapter, we also explore examples of nonschool partners who can enrich your students' experiences in powerful ways.

Classroom-to-Classroom Partnerships by Division

The most common form of partnership occurs between two or more classrooms, and the individual teachers, a governing agency, or an organization usually run these partnerships. Organizations and agencies can help by providing *boots on the ground*, a phrase used by global educators and development organizations that means volunteers or personnel are on site to support collaborative learning. Some teachers just want one partner for a point-to-point collaboration, while others develop projects they hope many schools will join for more varied global perspectives and collaboration opportunities.

The following sections introduce potential projects at the elementary, middle, and high school levels. Specifically, you'll read about the Teddy Bear Project (elementary school), Global Partner Junior's annual theme (middle school), and the #Decarbonize project (high school).

Elementary Partnership: The Teddy Bear Project

In International Education and Resource Network's (iEARN) Teddy Bear Project, which is most appropriate for elementary classrooms, students send a teddy bear on a trip to the partner classroom and simultaneously receive a teddy bear from their partners. Both classrooms host their global guest teddy bear, photographing him or her at local landmarks, keeping a journal and photo album (usually written in English regardless of location), collecting souvenirs, and so on. The teddy bear stays for one night with each student in the host class and is photographed at the dinner table or during activities with the host family. After all students have hosted the teddy bear, they send it back to the partner classroom, replete with souvenirs, pen pal letters, a journal, and a photo album. Because young children tend to love stuffed animals, their sense of connection to the bear makes this a great project for developing students' urge to understand other places at an age when it's not easy to travel themselves. See table 3.1 for a project overview.

Table 3.1: Teddy Bear Project Overview

Characteristics	Description
Appropriate grade levels	PreK through grade 2
	Teachers can level up this project by making cultural explorations deeper and more complex, or by sending the bear with a specific goal (such as to understand local challenges and how they are being addressed, or to study specific local history and landmarks).
Timeline	Two to four-plus months, depending on transit time
Partnership design	Two-classroom exchange
Disciplines engaged	Language arts, social studies, geography, penmanship, writing, cultural exploration, and photography
Twenty-first century competencies fostered	Creativity, communication, and critical thinking
Global competencies fostered	Cultural literacy, empathy, cultural connectedness, and intercultural communication
Facilitating organization	iEARN
Guiding questions	How might we learn about the world through a stuffed animal? How might we learn about a culture without traveling there? How might we share what is most important about our own community?

Source: Adapted from iEARN, n.d.; M. Conte, personal communication, May 12, 2016 and May 16, 2016.

In many ways, iEARN's Teddy Bear Project (https://iearn.org/cc/space-2/group -94) is a perfect first global partnership for elementary teachers because it requires very little synchronous communication; most of the project is about facilitating the guest bear's experience in your community and exploring the artifacts your own bear brings home.

Some classrooms include a Skype session or two during the process, such as midway through the visit, to check on the traveling guests or after both classes explore the artifacts and have specific questions for each other. Since it doesn't require live communication, the Teddy Bear Project is easy to run between schools in vastly different time zones. However, it requires a deeply committed partner, as there is nothing worse for students' sense of connectedness than never getting their bear back.

It's important to note that actually sending a bear to the host community (as opposed to buying it locally) is essential, and students should help pack their bear to travel to the partner country. Although you and your partner teacher can save time and money by buying bears in-country, this shortcut removes the teddy bear as traveler concept and makes the project less authentic for students, who will have no attachment to the bear they receive and see in photos. Variations of this project include teachers taking a class mascot or Flat Stanley (see www.flatstanley.com/ find_host) on their travels and photographing them in different settings with the intent to help students feel connected to those places.

Particularly in the elementary years, global education often seeks to foster students' sense of empathy and connectedness. Partnerships designed to practice and deepen that empathy can do a lot to combat bullying in the early years of children's education, helping them feel a sense of connection to each other and belonging in the world beyond their classroom. The Teddy Bear Project also includes many opportunities to explore the Fs of global education (that is, the partner country's food, flags, festivals, fashion, and more), but astute teachers find ways to dig deeper by asking, "How do people live in the partner community today?", "What challenges does this community face, and how are they similar to our own?", and "What can we learn from their beliefs and practices that might change the way we think about our own lives and communities?"

Particularly in the elementary years, global education often seeks to foster students' sense of empathy and connectedness.

The Teddy Bear Project can easily develop students' knowledge and skills in a wide array of content areas, depending on the teachers' interdisciplinary design choices. Learning targets in K–2 often include understanding what a community is, roles in a community, systems of rules, and the services communities need, as well as map-reading skills, all of which you can target through this sort of place-based exploration of each other's communities. Science teachers could weave in targeted learning about local flora and fauna, and mathematics teachers could incorporate tallying and simple arithmetic by developing surveys to send with the bear. Most core to this project are the reading, writing, and other language arts standards that are easily fostered through writing the bear's daily journal, and weaving in the production of a video blog, or *vlog*, also allows teachers to foster technology-based filmmaking and creativity. Choosing local landmarks to share and exploring global landmarks the bear visits naturally build cultural literacy and critical thinking. By having students design the visiting bear's itinerary on a limited budget, teachers can also build their mathematics skills, map-reading skills, and knowledge of local landmarks, attractions, and geographic features. Finally, this project provides endless opportunities for creativity when students design the photo album and journal, and when they choose the artifacts to send back as souvenirs of the bear's journey.

Although iEARN suggests that all classrooms use English for the journal, native language use on other artifacts fosters an early curiosity about world languages. Consider visual literacy and critical-thinking elements when working with students to choose experiences for their visiting bear, which images and artifacts to send, and when understanding the received images and artifacts. Many classrooms do extensive *think, see, wonder* routines about the photos they receive prior to asking follow-up questions of their partners. For example, you might ask students what they *think* they already know about their partner classroom in China (which might elicit impressions and stereotypes students already have from cartoons and other sources, like all Chinese practicing kung fu); then what they actually *see* in the photos sent by their partners (different language characters, foods, clothing styles, buildings, landmarks, and forms of transportation); and then what they *wonder*

These routines offer an opportunity to build students' visual and cultural literacy skills, their inquiry skills, and their ability to think critically and break down assumptions and stereotypes.

(Why is there so much red in Chinese art? Why is a landmark important to the community? Why do so many people ride bikes? Why do they eat with chopsticks?). These routines offer an opportunity to build students' visual and cultural literacy skills, their inquiry skills, and their ability to think critically and break down assumptions and stereotypes.

Elementary teacher Maria Conte runs the Teddy Bear Project with her first graders at St. Rose of Lima School on Long Island, New York. During the 2015–2016 school year, her students sent out four teddy bears: two to a school in Taiwan (for different grade levels), one to Slovenia, and one to Pakistan. They received their boxes from the partner schools relatively quickly, each hand-packed in a different way; the one from Pakistan was in soft packaging that looked hand sewn, which provided additional opportunities for student learning. Writing a journal was familiar and fun, and most exciting was when students began to see connections between their partners' lives and their own, particularly with less familiar places like Pakistan. In addition to the physical bear exchange, students engaged in online learning and communication together. While many teachers run the Teddy Bear Project in the core classroom, Maria Conte runs a learning center that is considered enrichment, so she sees all grade levels and runs different iEARN projects with each (M. Conte, personal communication, May 12, 2016 and May 16, 2016).

PERSPECTIVES ON WORKING WITH iEARN: MARIA CONTE
Elementary Educator, St. Rose of Lima School on Long Island, New York

The Teddy Bear Project through iEARN has been a wonderful way for young students to learn about the world. My first graders were able to learn about children in different countries through the exchange of a soft toy. One of the most memorable moments for me was when we received our toy from Taiwan and the children were looking forward to reading the notes from the children. I gave each of my children a note from one of the students in Taiwan. One of my little boys began to cry because he had difficulty reading his. When I looked at his note, I noticed that the text was written vertically. That was a wonderful opportunity to show the children that our friends in Taiwan write their characters from top to bottom. We compared our alphabet with Chinese characters, and they were impressed that the children would be able to remember so many different characters. Students involved in this project also knew that they were the language experts, so they had to do their best to make sure that we were setting a good example for our friends who are just learning to write English.

My third and fourth graders worked on a project within iEARN's Finding Solutions to Hunger, Poverty and Inequality Project. We looked at our own nutrition so we could compare how the rest of the world eats. We shared food journals with students in Pakistan. When viewing a video from the Pakistani school, my students noticed that the Pakistani students were very much like them. There were foods they ate for lunch that were similar. While watching the video, at least one student in each class began to giggle when the class heard the first Pakistani student speaking with a heavy accent. I paused the video and knew it was a teachable moment. I asked if any of the students knew someone who spoke with an accent. Many students personally knew someone, and so I asked them if this person spoke another language. I used this opportunity to help the students understand that people who speak with accents are speaking at least two languages. So instead of thinking it's funny or that they are less intelligent, we should be very impressed that they understand and speak English, which is not an easy language to learn. My hope is that this little lesson will spill over into their lives, and when they meet someone from another country, they will see them in a positive light.

continued →

Teachers involved with iEARN around the world are passionate educators I can trust. There are many projects that can fit into any curriculum. With our educational system so focused on testing, many teachers and administrators are hesitant to delve into global collaborative projects. Teachers are pressured and feel there is no time for these types of projects, but no additional time is needed for a global collaborative project. When thinking about a project, you find ways to integrate it into what you already do in the classroom. There is no standard that will address a student's ability to be a socially responsible human being, so educators need to find a way to expose students to others around the world to promote a peaceful and sustainable planet. We have to help students understand that people everywhere have the same human dignity and that different languages, customs, and traditions are interesting, not "weird."

Being involved with educators around the world gives me many opportunities to learn as well as fine-tune my craft. It allows me to remain motivated and inspired to treat each day as an opportunity to make a difference in the lives of students.

Source: M. Conte, personal communication, May 12, 2016 and May 16, 2016.

Other Elementary School Partnership Examples

Following are some additional project ideas for elementary school partnerships, many of which I've seen in globally connected schools. All are meant to be slightly general and could be leveled up or down, depending on the specific standards. These examples are meant to provoke your thinking, as you and your partner will ultimately design your own focus based on the standards you need to meet.

- **First-grade students** participate in the Global Read Aloud (https://the globalreadaloud.com; also see chapter 4, page 73). Students read a storybook at the same time as students in schools around the world, and then share their reactions, insights, and ideas on platforms like Wikispaces (https://wikispaces.com) and Edmodo (https://edmodo.com), as well as through live Skype (https://skype.com/en) conversations. Teachers can encourage students to create and share their own illustrations or to co-create their own short storybooks with or for their partner classrooms. This sort of partnership hits a wide array of language arts and communication standards, and the book choice might also engage social studies or other disciplines.

- **Second-grade students** in the United States, Canada, and Mexico chart the migration of the monarch butterfly together. By understanding the route and the challenges along the way, students immerse in explorations of overdevelopment, urban sprawl, and other environmental conditions reducing milkweed proliferation—in addition to the science of butterfly life and migratory patterns. Teachers can invite students to identify and implement solutions along the route, such as planting milkweed or advocating against urban sprawl. Students might also create monarch-inspired art. Social studies teachers could incorporate parallels with early human migratory patterns and significant geography and map-reading skills, or could even explore immigration debates with students, especially between Mexico and the United States (which might level up the partnership a grade level or two). This partnership engages standards in science, social studies, and language arts, particularly reading (during investigations) and writing (in products and reflections).

- **Third-grade students** in two or more partner classrooms can chart and film what they eat, where it comes from, whether and how it's packaged, and how it's prepared, while learning to analyze the nutritional value and calories. This partnership works best when partners include an urban school and a rural school (in any country), and it can address many nutrition standards, health issues, and how the local environment impacts food sources, all of which help engage science and social studies standards. If students chart and track elements like calories or costs, or survey their peers' eating habits, they can engage mathematics standards, particularly around charting, tallying, and graphing. Students can share and compare films, photographs, and charts online, and then reflect on the differences and similarities they discover, perhaps sharing images of their most consistent lunch foods as part of a Global Speed Chat "Let's Do Lunch" (www.globalspeedchat.com) collaboration with additional schools. Students could also participate in a videoconference to celebrate food customs and new knowledge at the end of the project. This partnership engages science, social studies, and mathematics standards, and of course contains opportunities for language arts development in listening, writing, reading, and speaking.

- **Fourth-grade students** in Canada and Peru explore the displacement of indigenous populations with the arrival of European settlers. (This partnership can work among any two or more formerly colonized countries in any part of the world.) Students develop films or other artifacts to teach their local history to each other, and they share insights into the impact of colonization on cultural legacies. The project could culminate in a co-created celebration of remaining indigenous cultures in students' local areas, or a solutions-oriented product to support indigenous peoples' rights. This sort of partnership engages standards in social studies and language arts, as well as develops students' critical thinking and appreciation for indigenous knowledge.

- **Fifth-grade students** in two or more countries explore the history of human migration in their local regions, particularly the experiences of refugees. Students explore war and displacement complexities, as well as the social, political, and religious challenges in historic and current refugee crises. In culmination, students could co-create a guide to the effective support and integration of refugee populations, or develop and carry out an action plan for supporting their own local refugee populations. This partnership engages deep social studies standards around geography, human migration, and politics; and product development includes research and language arts standards as well.

Middle School Partnership: Global Partners Junior's Annual Theme

Each year, Global Partners Junior (http://gpjunior.tiged.org) brings together students from twenty-eight partner cities around the world to work on a different theme over the course of a school year. All U.S. participants are schools with 100 percent of the student body eligible for free and reduced lunch, or students who are engaged through community housing and outreach programs such as the Boys & Girls Clubs. The majority of international partner schools also have underserved demographics, as reaching underserved communities with rich global experiences is part of the philosophy of New York City Global Partners (2015), the broader initiative Global Partners Junior is a part of. See table 3.2 for an overview.

Table 3.2: Global Partners Junior Project Overview

Characteristics	Description
Appropriate grade levels	Grades 4 through 7
Timeline	Yearlong; different theme annually
Partnership design	Multischool; simultaneous local work; collaboration
Disciplines engaged	Language arts, art, gender studies, social studies, geography, science
Twenty-first century competencies fostered	Creativity, collaboration, communication, and critical thinking
Global competencies fostered	Intercultural communication, cultural literacy, empathy, and cultural connectedness
Facilitating organization	New York City Global Partners, Global Partners Junior

Characteristics	Description
Guiding questions	How can you best teach students in cities around the world about your city and community? How can you showcase the best of what your city has to offer? What makes your city unique? What can you learn about other cities based on student artwork from those cities? What can you learn from what other cities are doing to make your city a better place?

Source: Adapted from Global Partners Junior, n.d.; T. Hardy, personal communication, March 21, 2016.

Since after-school programs often manage Global Partners Junior, this project avoids some of the challenges of curricular alignment. However, each year's project provides rich opportunities for deep interdisciplinary explorations inside the classroom as well, and each theme is intentionally and carefully aligned with the U.S. Common Core State Standards for middle years education. Classrooms select a focus for final projects that can engage additional standards. Global Partners Junior has strong support networks in New York, and partner cities in Africa, Asia, Central America, Europe, North America, South America, and Oceania receive teacher training through Skype sessions.

Each year's project provides rich opportunities for deep interdisciplinary explorations inside the classroom.

Each year, the project is divided into four phases. The phases vary depending on the theme but always include local and global activities culminating in a student learning exhibition. While each year may engage slightly different academic standards for grades 4–7, there is always a strong foundation in language arts (reading, writing, speaking, and listening), social studies (geography, cultures, history, and politics), and artistic expression. A previous project, Colorful Communities for 2015–2016, included the following four phases (T. Hardy, personal communication, March 21, 2016):

Phase One: Art, Myself, and the World

> Students will critically examine a piece of narrative art to discover how art can tell someone's personal story and to develop their art literacy skills. They will reflect on their own identities, create self-portraits, and recognize that viewers bring varied experiences as they produce and interpret art. For the unit project, they will design digital flags that represent their communities.

The phase one guiding questions are How do others (from different cities or backgrounds) bring a different perspective to the same piece of art? What can we learn about an artist through her or his self-portrait? What can we learn about other cities based on the community flags that students designed?

Phase Two: Girls, Boys, and Stereotypes

Students will explore social media campaigns through film and online research, reflecting on what stereotypes people in their cities have about what it means to be a boy or a girl. They will research how colors, shapes, and toys influence gender identity, and film a performance or design digital poetry to defy gender stereotypes.

The phase two guiding question is How can art be used to challenge deeply held stereotypes?

Phase Three: Artistic Journeys

Students will listen to music and watch dance from global cities. They will research local musicians, artists, and dancers who have immigrated to their communities to discover how art moves and evolves across space and time. They will create a sound track that represents their city's diversity, recording their own music, languages, and urban sounds.

The phase three guiding question is When an art form moves from one city to another, is it static or does it evolve and incorporate local styles and traditions?

Phase Four: Final Project, Community Arts Exhibition

Students will select and research one of these old issues (kind and welcoming cities; gender equality; immigration) or a new issue (such as sustainability or disability rights) to explore locally and globally through the arts. They will design an arts exhibition for their community focused on telling a narrative around the issue they select. The exhibition may include original and borrowed artwork. They will use multimedia tools such as digital presentations, documentary video, and website design to present their work.

Students are invited to think critically about social issues of deep relevance, such as inclusivity and belonging, and to be actively involved in improving their communities.

The phase four guiding question is How can you continue using the arts as a means to improve your community in the future?

The Global Partners Junior curriculum has a deeply constructivist element, so students are creating repeatedly during the course of the school year as they investigate their communities and the world. Students are invited to think critically about social issues of deep relevance, such as inclusivity and belonging, and to be actively involved in improving their communities. Global partners provide insight, inspiration, and feedback along the way.

Another noteworthy element is the *glocal* orientation of Global Partners Junior themes. According to Harth (2010), *glocally* oriented experiences help students connect local and global issues in meaningful ways that help them make connections between cultures and find local avenues for relevant action. Harth (2010) writes, "Specifically, we need to cultivate glocal perspectives and attitudes in our students, including an awareness of our growing interconnectedness, an appreciation of cultures from all over the world, and a willingness to consider different viewpoints and opinions." Considering global perspectives in the improvement of our own communities is very different than imposing our cultural perspectives on the improvement of someone else's community. This is where Global Partners Junior really shines. The program focuses student action in their own communities but ensures that the ideas of their global counterparts inform those action plans. By framing the experience this way, Global Partners Junior ensures that all students engage believing that their partners have something to contribute, and it teaches them to take direct, tangible action in their own backyards.

PERSPECTIVES ON GLOBAL PARTNERS JUNIOR
Student and Teacher Reflections

"My city is full of people, just like in New York. I would love to know more!" —Nine-year-old student from Mumbai

"It makes me feel good when other people learn about my community." —Eleven-year-old student from New York City

"[This year I want to learn about] Warsaw because half of my family is Polish and I would love to learn more about where they came from." —Ten-year-old student from New York City

"[This year I want to learn about] Ho Chi Minh City because I want to see if they celebrate holidays and have different ways of transportation like us. I want to see if their lives are different from ours." —Ten-year-old student from New York City

"This year I want to learn about Paris and London because I want to learn about places that I don't have much prior knowledge about. I also want to learn more about New York City because it is good to know a lot about where you live." —Eleven-year-old student from New York City

"This program was one more step for [my students] believing that they matter and that everything they do in life affects others as well. . . . [The program] enabled my students to participate in such a positive, active, and responsible way." —Middle school teacher from Ljubljana, Slovenia

Source: T. Hardy, personal communication, March 21, 2016.

Other Middle School Partnership Examples

Following are some additional project ideas for middle school partnerships. As in the elementary section, several are projects I've seen in schools, with adaptations based on the grade levels and schools involved. Teachers can level these exemplars up or down, depending on the complexity of work and the academic standards most appropriate to the topic, and they are meant to help generate ideas and think creatively about the possibilities.

- **Sixth-grade students** in two or more countries write pen pal letters to each other and exchange photographs of family, home, and school. Letters might also include examples of popular culture (images from magazines, pieces of music, and games), and could be physically mailed or scanned and sent electronically. Students write letters in response, ideally exchanging with a partner at least twice. In a technology-enabled version of this project, you could invite students to participate in online discussion threads and private virtual classrooms where they could share photographs, video productions, and writing, or could blog and be each other's audience. They could exchange day-in-the-life podcasts as well, in which students create and share video chronicles of their day-to-day experiences, and both classrooms might have Skype calls with young photographers or film makers in different parts of the world as well. This sort of partnership engages standards in language arts, particularly in reading and writing, as well as having the potential to include technological literacies and social studies standards, depending on whether students are asked to address a specific theme (such as sharing something about their culture or history).

- **Seventh-grade students** in two or more rural communities collaborate to learn about each other's agricultural practices and related environmental challenges. Students learn about and share ways their own communities are addressing the use of harmful chemicals and the impact of present policies. Through science class, students at each school develop a garden (or improve an existing one), employing the best environmentally friendly practices they've learned from other parts of the world. Students in participating schools might also read the same short story or novel on indigenous farming practices, or read a piece of fiction about modern life in an indigenous community. This kind of partnership can engage many social studies standards, connecting into specific units on ancient and indigenous cultures, and it has endless possibilities in mathematics (such as geometry when students plot out the garden and decide on spacing) and science (making choices about what to grow and where, based on climate, elevation, water access, and sun exposure).

- **Eighth-grade students** in two or more countries look at the differences in how their textbooks and popular media present World War II in an effort to understand the nature of bias. This partnership can work in the case of any two or more countries that interpret a given conflict through a different lens, and can focus on any global conflict. Students explore their own cultural biases deeply and share learning with their partners. The project culminates with students co-creating a "real guide" to understanding World War II or another chosen conflict, bringing together a variety of different "truths" in order to create a more politically and culturally pluralistic interpretation of this period in history. This kind of partnership can foster significant critical thinking, but it also has direct connections to social studies units on WWII and to language arts standards for reading, writing, speaking, and listening. In adapted versions of this project, students might explore one specific event through three to five global media sources, something I did often when exploring the Israeli–Palestinian conflict, and which adds an element of media literacy students need as they are bombarded with information from often unreliable sources.

High School Partnership: #Decarbonize

The global partnership #Decarbonize: A Global Mobilization of Youth Perspectives on Climate Change (http://decarbonize.me) brings students together each year to confront climate change globally. With over ten thousand young leaders from every corner of our planet working together to synthesize the voice of over a million youth, the largest synthesis in advance of the United Nations Climate Change Conference, or Conference of the Parties (COP), held in a different city each December. This ongoing program, outlined in table 3.3, happens each September through December, and timing and topics are carefully aligned to the UN's COP events and concurrent student conferences.

Table 3.3: #Decarbonize Project Overview

Characteristics	Description
Appropriate grade levels	Grades 9 through 12
Timeline	Yearly; September through December
Partnership design	Thematic orientation; collaboration and co-creation
Disciplines engaged	Science, social studies, visual arts, and language arts
Twenty-first century competencies fostered	Communication, critical thinking, and collaboration
Global competencies fostered	Cultural literacy, empathy, cultural connectedness, intercultural communication and collaboration, and problem solving

continued →

Characteristics	Description
Facilitating organizations	The Centre for Global Education, TakingITGlobal
Guiding questions	How might we use our growing understanding of climate policy to identify the best actions in response? How might we collaborate with other young people to improve our shared planet's health?

Source: Adapted from #Decarbonize n.d.; T. Godwaldt, personal communication, May 12, 2016.

This project is appropriate for students who are addressing standards connected to environmental science, government, and advocacy, but it can also engage the arts and humanities as students develop and design their final white paper. It provides the opportunity for real voice and action on an issue of dire importance, and students engage in inquiry and dialogue with high-level experts as well as with other young people who care about the planet. A student-directed framework, with many of the trappings of problem- and project-based learning, includes science content (including carbon cycles and climate change, as well as political science's international agreements and diplomacy), opportunities for collaborative solution building, and constructive outcomes.

Each year, #Decarbonize focuses student collaborations on an element of climate change. Students engage with the Youth Climate Coalition or other local NGOs to prepare their nation's youth response and participate in research and online collaborations. The students' focus is creating an international white paper on climate change for their respective UN COP. Visit http://decarbonize.tigweb.org to see the most recent white paper. Three main issues were addressed across the project's three phases in 2015, tying into a wide array of science, mathematics, and humanities standards, plus governmental policy and advocacy objectives. Learning objectives depend on the country and grade level, which vary year to year.

- **Phase One: Climate Change in My Backyard—Our Current Context:** What changes are we seeing in our community? How does climate change affect other (local and global) communities and creatures? What is at stake if we fail to address the climate crisis?

- **Phase Two: Powering Tomorrow—The Energy Access Challenge:** What could energy in your community look like in 2030? How will you access energy for the services you need? How will the lives of your friends and family change?

- **Phase Three: A Climate for Change—Youth Driving Solutions:** How do we make bold action politically feasible? What can we do as individuals and as a global collective? How must we revision and remake our world to address this challenge? What are the first steps and the most important steps? What can we learn from previous challenges and influence our plans?

Canadian educators Gareth Thomson, executive director of the Alberta Council for Environmental Education, and Terry Godwaldt (2016), founder and executive director of the Centre for Global Education, point out their most important reason for running this project with young people: "In our work with tens of thousands of students, we've noticed that the ones who are actually doing something to help the environment are always the ones who are most hopeful about the future."

As a #Decarbonize facilitator and founder of the project, Godwaldt is convinced that programs like this one provide an important opportunity for students to see themselves through the eyes of their global counterparts (personal communication, May 12, 2016). He remembers an interaction between his Canadian students and a school in Nicaragua:

> The Canadian students were partnered with the Nicaraguan school. The Canadian schools were talking about the oil sands, which happen to be humanity's largest-ever industrial project, but also a huge part of the economy of the students who were connecting. The Canadians were shocked that none of the Nicaraguans had heard of the oil sands . . . and the Nicaraguans' response to the Canadians was, "In Nicaragua, we know we're not that important; but why do you in Canada think you guys are so important?"
>
> I can't provide that experience to my students through a YouTube video or through an essay assignment. I want my students to be able to look at themselves through the eyes of somebody else—look at the implications when it comes to globalization, when it comes to international agreements, when it comes to so many of these really difficult concepts that we want to teach students. We can't teach them these things—students need to experience it for themselves. (T. Godwaldt, personal communication, May 12, 2016)

It's important to note that this project includes significant opportunities for investigation and collaborative action aligned with many academic standards in science and the humanities. Reversing climate change requires a multilateral approach to reducing carbon emissions that considers the needs and perspectives of many different nations, so working with local schools and local students from a variety of socioeconomic backgrounds is key to gaining local perspectives from a multitude of countries. These kinds of high school projects help prove that academic rigor and high engagement are not mutually exclusive, as the best and most successful secondary partnerships accomplish both by addressing relevant topics and grounding the work in student voice.

These kinds of high school projects help prove that academic rigor and high engagement are not mutually exclusive.

PERSPECTIVES FROM THE CONFERENCE OF THE PARTIES 21
Student and Teacher Reflections

"I felt connected to people from all over the world because of our common interest. It was amazing to see and hear from people sharing my opinions from countries far from mine, such as India or Canada. You realize that at the end of the day we are not so different at all. Still, we all added a new perspective to the project, which was great." —High school student, Global College, Sweden

"I felt fully involved working in collaboration with students from different schools across the globe as one family." —High school student, Lincoln Community School, Ghana

"The best part was hearing from other countries during our live chats. Researching the information and doing various class activities was fun, as it widened my understanding and knowledge of climate change and its implications. I feel connected to the rest of the planet in ways I never would have imagined." —High school student, Lifeline Foundation, South City Central School, Philippines

"Before I felt kind of hopeless about the situation we are in today, and I felt like nothing I do really matters. After #Decarbonize, I feel that if we work together, we can make a difference." —High school student, Centro de Ensino Médio de Taguatinga Norte, Brazil

"This project made me feel that I was part of something bigger. I wish more youth could see the power they have when we all work together." —High school student, Queen Elizabeth High School, Canada

"This has been a truly fabulous experience. My students will never look at the world and their relationship to it the same." —High school teacher, Lincoln Community School, Ghana

"The process was indeed a great learning experience for the students, using 21st century tools and skills to collaborate and contribute. The whole programme has given the students an opportunity to take a deeper look at the broader perspective of climate change and address it seriously." —High school teacher, Yadavindra Public School, India

Source: *Conference of the Parties 21, 2015; T. Godwaldt, personal communication, May 12, 2016.*

Other High School Partnership Examples

Following are some additional project ideas for high school partnerships, several of which I've seen in schools. As with the elementary and middle school examples provided in this chapter, these are intentionally general to provoke your thinking—and can be leveled up or down through adaptations to match the grade level and content you teach. Ultimately, however, your projects will be most successful if you consider a variety of examples and then craft your own project that engages the specific standards you and your partner want to address.

- **Ninth-grade students** in two or more countries simultaneously view and discuss a cosmological event from different parts of the world or share images of nonsimultaneous viewings of the same cosmological phenomenon. This partnership can address learning standards in science, geography, and geometry, and could be adapted to any cosmological event, including yearly meteor showers, eclipses, Northern Lights, visible comets, and planetary sightings, which vary from location to location. It could also include explorations of the cosmological event throughout history, which adds the opportunity to address social studies standards.

- **Tenth-grade students** in two or more countries explore the Universal Declaration of Human Rights (http://bit.ly/2ho5QMO) together. Working in small, mixed-country teams, students focus on one human right under attack in a specific country other than their own—or a challenge common to both partner countries. If possible, student teams choose the country of focus or the right they most want to explore. The goal is to co-create a product (presentation, blog, online magazine, or something similar) that explores why the challenge exists and, based on their local and global knowledge on the topic, what they believe to be a viable solution. Ideally, students share final products with an international audience of real stakeholders, such as producing an argumentative podcast to uphold the rights of refugees and then ensuring it's seen by policy makers who are involved with laws connected to refugee rights. This project can address a wide array of social studies standards, including history and politics, and artistic and language arts goals, depending on what students produce.

- **Eleventh-grade students** in two or more countries participate in a community-oriented design challenge to build a new technology or other infrastructure for their home communities using local materials. Examples might include improved water filtration systems, greenhouse designs, bridge designs, clean cook stoves, or transportation devices, depending on the engineering, environmental, and physics standards the teachers want to address. Students could co-create in multischool teams, or they could create for their own communities and share ideas and feedback with their partners. The focus on design thinking should include empathy interviews in the impacted communities so that inventions address authentic needs. You can base design limitations on the science, engineering, and mathematics that you want to address through the project, or by the materials available in a given location.

- **Twelfth-grade students** from two or more countries work in small, multischool interest groups to develop short films that address the history of—and potential solutions to—the global challenge of their choice. (Teachers working on this project could use the UN's sustainable development goals [www.un.org/sustainabledevelopment/sustainable-development-goals] to provide those choices.) Ideally, this could be an interdisciplinary capstone partnership, in which students make relevant connections with the chosen global issues to science, mathematics, social sciences, humanities, and the arts. Students could act locally on one of the solutions (for example, volunteering at a local soup kitchen as a way to respond to local and global hunger and poverty), and could produce a final presentation or film to share in their community and with their global partners.

Nonschool Partnerships With Global Guest Speakers

While most people think of classroom-to-classroom connections when they envision global partnerships, connecting with individuals doing global work can serve different needs as larger partnerships develop—and can have a deep impact with much less effort because you are only coordinating with one person whose schedule is likely more flexible than that of another classroom teacher. International experts can help inspire new thinking and can also be helpful throughout the development of student products. For example, students working to invent a more efficient water pump for use in global development might have several Skype sessions with scientists and engineers involved in water access issues and pump designs for developing nations, asking questions and receiving feedback on their design prototypes. Similarly, students in photography courses might connect with young photographers in different parts of the world, to understand their motivations and goals, to ask questions about their work—and to discuss and share their own photography. For example, young Egyptian photographer Yasser Alaa Mobarak (www.flickr.com/photos/yasseralaa) has Skyped into middle and high school classrooms for many years, helping young people connect with Cairo's poorest and most disenfranchised populations through his photography, and the experiences have been deeply transformative for students. Connecting with such individuals exposes your students to people doing real, important work in the world and helps them identify jobs and roles they might be interested in working toward themselves. Such partnerships, though brief, help students become innovators, inventors, and social entrepreneurs who design with the world in mind.

Connecting with such individuals exposes your students to people doing real, important work in the world and helps them identify jobs and roles they might be interested in working toward themselves.

An *expert* in this context means anyone doing what the students are studying. That can and should include young people as much as older experts, as long as they've done hands-on field work or have other experiences connected to what students are learning. The classrooms in the following examples tapped into expertise on urban planning, Navajo culture, global change making, economics, and microfinancing.

Urban Planning

In a partnership I helped facilitate for Town School for Boys, students studied urban planning and collaborated to design their own city, engaging a range of second-grade standards for communities, roles, and services; in addition, language arts standards were engaged through reading, writing, speaking, and listening. During the project, students had a Skype session with Federico Cartín Arteaga, an urban planner from Costa Rica who lived for many years in Toronto, and who is leading Costa Rica's Rutas Naturbanas project (http://rutasnaturbanas.org) to reclaim the Central Valley region's watersheds. He told students about his projects and helped them understand some of the challenges urban planners face in Costa Rica that are different from—and similar to—places like Toronto and San Francisco. Cartín shared his vision for the future of Costa Rica, explained how urban planning might allow that vision to become reality, and answered questions from students about their own city designs.

Navajo Culture

At St. Mary's Academy in Englewood, Colorado, I helped facilitate a Skype session for the entire eighth grade with Benjamin Barney, a Navajo elder from Lukachukai, Arizona. Each class brainstormed questions in advance, mostly based on students' studies of Native American life, arts, and agriculture. Students voted on the best questions, and winners got to ask their questions during the live event. I was present for their Skype session the first year, and it was extraordinary. The students were totally focused on Barney, which is unusual for any age group but, in my experience, particularly for eighth graders. Barney was thoughtful and friendly, and he made students feel comfortable asking their questions. At one point, a student asked what Barney's favorite holiday was, and Barney said that it is birthdays. He went on to explain that the Navajo don't celebrate the day a child was *born,* however; instead, they celebrate the day a child *laughs* for the first time. The response from students was immediate and audible—the difference between birth and laughter, a sort of birth of self, was transformative for those eighth graders. This partnership was part of a larger unit on indigenous life and traditions, which engaged social studies, research, and language arts standards.

Global Change Making

In another nonclassroom partnership I helped facilitate, students in a ninth-grade introduction to global studies class at Parish Episcopal School in Dallas, Texas, have the opportunity each year to skype with individuals doing different global work. The course is an elective that serves as an entry point into Parish Episcopal School's Academy of Global Studies, a certificate program. (See more about global certification programs in chapter 9, page 155.) The course addresses a broad range of social studies and language arts standards, particularly in connection to the sustainable development goals, and students learn to do significant research, producing a major research paper and final presentation by the end of the course.

Each year, the students Skype with Hindogbae Kposowa, a young leader in southeastern Sierra Leone who led Ebola-prevention work across nearly 250 villages in the Bumpe Ngao Chiefdom in 2014–2015. As the grandson of a prior paramount chief and nephew of the current paramount chief, Kposowa worked tirelessly to bring hand-washing stations and education into every village, and to manage contact tracing, a system for monitoring all movement and contact with sick people in the region. In her final course reflections, one ninth grader noted the value of connecting with Kposowa, who goes by the nickname Hindo:

> The most impactful and inspiring element of this class for me was communicating through Skype calls, specifically the Skype call with Hindo in Africa. This call fascinated me because no matter how much you read about a topic in a book, it is always different when you hear a person talk about his own experiences. Hindo is a person who sees global issues, such as the need for education and health care, occurring on a daily basis. It opened my eyes to what some people have to go through to receive an education. Also, the young age that Hindo started to make a change in his community inspired me. Age really does not matter in making a difference. (A. Jennings, personal communication, May 12, 2016)

Parish Episcopal School students also connect each year with Kennedy Leavens, a U.S. citizen who started her own nongovernmental organization at the age of twenty-four to support the economic and social growth of weaving communities in the Peruvian Andes. (You can read her testimonial on page 194 in chapter 10.) Through these experiences, students in Dallas gained direct insights into the lives of people working in the global fields they were studying. One student remarked after meeting Leavens, "Now I know what an *NGO* is: it's what happens when someone becomes passionate about a particular issue or group of people, and then builds her life around that passion" (A. Jennings, personal communication, May 12, 2016).

Finally, Parish Episcopal School students also connect with David Akerson, a consultant and international human rights attorney who has been involved in the International Criminal Court trials in Sierra Leone, Rwanda, Kenya, and Lebanon, among others.

PERSPECTIVES ON PARTNERING WITH CLASSROOMS: DAVID AKERSON

Consultant and International Law Professor

People are interested and engaged all over the world. But most people don't live in major urban areas where international human rights organizations have a big presence. That is why it is important to speak to groups all over. I have spoken to groups in many areas, including Canada, Sweden, Germany, England, Kenya, Tanzania, Sierra Leone, and South Africa. The topics depend on the age group. For younger students, I focus on the atrocity and some of the factors that caused the tragedy. And I talk about victims and perpetrators of their age group to get them to see the conflict from the eyes of like-aged people in that region. I also try to paint the tragedy with some complexity, to try to get students to imagine what they would do if faced with being forced to participate in a mass crime.

For older students, I talk more about the institutions that work on the atrocities, such as truth commissions, tribunals, and reparations panels. I hope students learn that in the last twenty-five years, human rights has matured into an area of law that is holding some people accountable for crimes they have organized or planned. The system isn't perfect, but we have at least started down the road. I think students see and hear me; I seem pretty normal and as a result they can relate and can imagine doing this kind of work themselves.

Source: Adapted from D. Akerson, personal communication, February 22, 2016.

Economics and Microfinancing

Students in eleventh-grade economics at Appleby College had two Skype conversations I helped facilitate. Both conversations deepened their understanding of the human side of economics by hitting on a variety of advanced economics standards but also humanizing the topic in the process. (Economics is traditionally about systems and numbers, and economics teacher Dave Suchanek wanted his students to connect more deeply with the impact such systems have on people.) They had a Skype session with Beesan Ramadan, a young Palestinian who helped students understand the economics involved in the Israeli–Palestinian conflict. This experience gave students insights into how economics plays a role in the conflict, including the economic challenges created for Palestinians. As a boycott activist, Ramadan also introduced students to the Boycott, Divestment, and Sanctions movement, helping them understand how economic boycotts function as a nonviolent form of protest in the region.

Students also had a Skype session with Doris Köhn, former economic diplomat with KfW, the German version of World Bank. Köhn was overseeing microfinancing projects across Eastern Europe at the time, and she shared insights into the advantages of microfinancing in developing nations, particularly those whose governments have questionable track records for their development funding use. She was able to answer complex questions about the pros and cons of microfinancing versus macrofinancing as development strategies, from a long career doing a mixture of the two across the developing world. She also encouraged female students to consider economics as a career path, pointing out that many international fields are dominated by men and that an increased feminine presence could improve their efforts.

Again, a one-off session with an expert can offer humanizing and powerful insights for students, and often with less coordination. When you begin considering experts, the Brainstorming Global Speakers worksheet in figure 3.1 can help you pinpoint good candidates.

An easy way to start building partnerships and direct contact opportunities immediately is to bring global speakers into your classroom via technology (or local individuals in person if their work has global relevance). Spend some time brainstorming potential speakers as specifically as you can, ideally with your grade-level or disciplinary team. Do not stop to judge or overthink your ideas.

- With which local and global organizations are we most interested in seeing our students connect?

- Which expert* voices would we most like our students to hear?

- With which youth perspectives would we most like our students to connect?

- What connections do we already have for bringing these voices into our classrooms?

- What connections do we need to make this happen?

*An *expert* in this context can mean anyone doing what the students are studying. That should include young people as much as older experts, as long as they have hands-on field work or other experiences connected to what students are learning.

Figure 3.1: Brainstorming global speakers worksheet.

*Visit **go.SolutionTree.com/21stcenturyskills** for a free reproducible version of this figure.*

A Few Concluding Thoughts

The examples in this chapter—appropriate for elementary, middle, and high school students—are only a tiny cross section of the kinds of creative, innovative partnerships constantly emerging from public, private, and parochial schools around the world. Chapter 4 (page 73) explores organizations running successful projects that any educator can join, many of which include or can be connected to specific Common Core State Standards and other academic benchmarks. Ultimately, a project's shape—multischool or classroom-to-classroom, collaboration, or co-creation—depends on the students' and teachers' passions and needs. When students in both classrooms help determine the shape, global partnerships are most successful. Whether you join an existing project or create something new, global partnerships provide the opportunity to co-create learning and understanding; address our borderless problems creatively and constructively from multiple perspectives (Harth, 2010); and break down the barriers that too often separate us.

Ultimately, a project's shape—multischool or classroom-to-classroom, collaboration, or co-creation—depends on the students' and teachers' passions and needs.

CHAPTER 4

FINDING EXISTING PARTNERSHIP PROGRAMS THAT WORK

Great social forces are the accumulation of individual actions. Let the future say of our generation that we sent forth mighty currents of hope, and that we worked together to heal the world.

—Jeffrey D. Sachs

The significant growth and popularity of global education have spawned a plethora of organizations offering platforms, communities, and projects. Rather than creating a project of their own, many educators find that joining existing projects can save a lot of time and work.

While several are fee-based organizations, since having boots on the ground in multiple communities requires maintaining local salaries and infrastructure, many teachers find that access to existing networks, simple partnership structures, existing communication platforms, and ready-made projects is more than worth the costs. It can be useful to check a partnership organization's track record, particularly if it charges, to make sure that fees go straight into the support services you need, not into elaborate administrative systems. This is easy to do through Twitter, for example: use the hashtag #globaled to search what other global educators have experienced with that organization. You may find a partnership opportunity through an organization focused specifically on building global partnerships for learning, and you may successfully partner through an organization that targets a specific issue, such as peace building, and whose side benefits include global partnerships.

Connected educator and global education thought leader Silvia Rosenthal Tolisano (2014), born in Germany and raised in Argentina, points out, "It's important to be careful and not just invite anyone into your classroom, so it is a great idea to join a pre-established community or network of video-conferencing educators"

It can be useful to communicate your plans to parents, preparing them for and involving them in the conversations that arise during your partnership.

(p. 41). Especially if you work with early elementary students or fear that challenging topics might arise, working with an established program can provide a slightly more predictable experience. It can also be useful to communicate your plans to parents, preparing them for and involving them in the conversations that arise during your partnership, and many teachers develop a permission slip for sharing images and video of children between classrooms. This chapter explores several outstanding organizations and projects teachers can join easily, with the recognition that because global education is in an era of rapid growth and experimentation—led predominantly by nonprofits that rely on donations to survive—programs appear and disappear constantly in this field.

Established Partnership Programs

An established partnership program can't guarantee success, nor can it remove all the challenges. However, such programs often have well-established networks or run global events that classrooms can join easily. Some, like iEARN, have offices around the world that support partnerships at the local level in different communities. Others, like TakingITGlobal, have a global community of online volunteers ready to do whatever they can to support global learning.

New partnership programs appear whenever motivated educators find formulas that work, and I know hundreds of teachers who have started their own small projects that other teachers can join. Middle school mathematics teacher Kristen Goggin (http://kristengoggin.com), who has become known for her sixth-grade microfinancing project with Kiva (www.kiva.org), runs several global partnership projects inviting any global educator to join and making all of her work public on her blog. Similarly, projects and programs disappear when leadership changes or teachers move on to new initiatives or schools. There may be several new programs worth exploring by the time you read this, and some of the projects listed here may be defunct. Visit **go.SolutionTree.com/21stcenturyskills** to access live links to a list of global partnership organizations.

Some organizations are specifically created with global education and partnership as their intent. Those included in this section (iEARN, TIGed, CGE, WorldVuze, and Global Read Aloud) are well established and work specifically toward helping students and classrooms around the world connect, with an emphasis not only on global competencies but also on creating solutions for real-world problems.

iEARN

With over thirty thousand schools and youth organizations participating from 140 countries, iEARN (http://iearn.org) is arguably one of the oldest and best global educational organizations on the planet, pioneering online school connections around meaningful educational projects since 1988. The organization maintains over 150 projects every year, all teacher- and student-designed, and facilitated to meet teachers' curricular needs and schedules. Rather than partnering just two or three schools, iEARN projects tend to include multiple schools and countries, and all projects include teacher or student facilitators who are available to advise along the way. Some projects attract the participation of over one hundred classrooms (typically with smaller groupings or pairings for the exchanges themselves), while others coordinate through smaller groups of four or five classes. Most important are the iEARN centers, country representatives, and country contacts, as they provide boots-on-the-ground support for participating teachers in their specific region.

Besides the Teddy Bear Project described in chapter 3 (page 49), another iEARN classic is the Tulip and Daffodil Project (http://bit.ly/2pdEKZi), where students plant the same flowers in different countries and collect data on parameters such as latitude, longitude, sunlight, and temperature, as well as track when the plants blossom. This project, which is ideal for upper-elementary or middle school science, allows students to learn about how soil conditions, water quality and access, and other issues impact plant growth in different parts of the world. It is an excellent entry point for discussing native and nonnative species, why certain plants flourish in different regions, and the environmental impacts of invasive species. It also provides an opportunity to gather, share, and do comparative analysis of mathematical data sets.

Even if you want to develop your own project, spend twenty minutes looking through iEARN's project database. It offers myriad creative ideas for partnering and shaping collaborative projects. Newer projects include building kites with messages about a better world, understanding the importance of Hiroshima and Nagasaki, and developing and collaborating on local environmental projects for students' local communities. Sixth-grade language arts teacher Maile Black involved her class in iEARN's Our Story Book project (http://bit.ly/2qy5tDU) at Brookwood School in Manchester, Massachusetts. According to Black, the experience was exciting for her and her students because they received chapters from places like Moldova and Indonesia. "Some were handwritten in perfect, tiny script; many were illustrated beautifully," reports Black (personal communication, February 22, 2016). Students enjoyed synchronous communication with students in Kaohsuing, Taiwan, while using Google Earth (https://google.com/earth) to see photographs of the area.

PERSPECTIVES ON iEARN: ED GRAGERT

Former Executive Director, iEARN-USA, and Interim Global Coordinator, Global Campaign for Education–US

iEARN's core philosophy is that students will (1) learn their curriculum subjects better if they interact and learn with and from peers globally; and (2) become global citizens, equipped with the tools to collaborate on global issues facing the planet. In order to achieve these two objectives, the iEARN Collaboration Centre enables student-to-student interaction (in any of ninety languages with instant translation) within each of the teacher-designed and facilitated projects. Rather than giving teachers a canned curriculum to teach across 140 countries, educators adapt an online project to what they are teaching through a bottom-up process. Further, as part of the project-design process, teachers complete a template with a series of questions designed to give enough information for educators worldwide to decide whether to participate. One of these questions is, How will this project make a meaningful improvement in the quality of life on the planet? Therefore, from the outset, for every project (whether political, musical, cultural, mathematical, historical, or artistic), teachers and students plan how they will address a global issue on their journey to becoming collaborative global citizens.

Since none of us can achieve exponential accomplishments on our own, global partnerships are critical in both experiencing and respecting differences, and in creating a movement to truly effect global educational change. Without global partnerships, neither the individual student transformation that accompanies global education work, nor the ultimate goal of education and peace for all, will be achieved. Collaboration works.

Source: E. Gragert, personal communication, May 22, 2016.

TakingITGlobal for Educators

TakingITGlobal for Educators, or TIGed (www.tigweb.org/tiged), is a social media platform that includes a global community of more than fifteen thousand educators from over five thousand schools in 150 countries (TakingITGlobal for Educators, 2015). TIGed's project database includes many teacher-driven projects you can join, or you can post your own project and use the platform to find partners. The network allows teachers to find partner teachers based on their country of origin and subjects taught, and TIGed's educational space also includes private virtual classrooms for synchronous and asynchronous learning. TIGed's parallel site for students, TakingITGlobal (www.tigweb.org), is the oldest social-networking site designed for collaborative global learning, offering a wealth of user-driven content on global topics from young people worldwide. Read more on TakingITGlobal as a partnership communication tool in chapter 6 (page 107).

TIGed is centrally involved in hosting several global partnership projects, many in coordination with the Centre for Global Education (http://tcge.tiged.org; see more on page 78). One of the largest is the DeforestACTION project, which schools from the Asia-Pacific region began in 2010, and which is ideal for students studying science, especially biology or the environment. It also has myriad applications in mathematics (geometry for tracking illegal logging via satellite) and the humanities (persuasive writing). This project focuses on the goal of ending deforestation in Borneo by uniting youth in education and action around the world (DeforestACTION, 2012). Christopher Gauthier, originally from Canada, is working toward the ability to partner local schools in Borneo with his students in Australia.

PERSPECTIVES ON DEFORESTACTION: CHRISTOPHER GAUTHIER
High School Teacher and Lead Teacher for Global Education,
Cleveland State District High School in Brisbane, Australia

Originally (our experience with DeforestACTION) was very insular. It was our students doing their own thing. It wasn't until we started getting connected in the webinars that our students started realizing they weren't alone. They were missing that connection with peers and sources of inspiration. Seeing students their own age, and seeing the projects that they were doing, gave some fuel to the fire to keep them going. We got involved in the global webinars; from that, one of our students was selected to be in the Promethean Education Fast Forward debate. She ended up representing Australia on two different occasions for that debate. And that really set her off; she's now a young activist. She was running the Australian Youth Climate Coalition in Queensland, running their school program, and going to thousands of classrooms a year.

The connection (for virtual partnerships with schools in Borneo) is not where we want it to be because Internet connectivity is a massive issue. But we connect through the teachers. We might get a Facebook message or a WhatsApp message once or twice a month. We could go up to six months without hearing something; it's just the nature of the beast there. We've got contacts in the embassy in Jakarta. We're looking at trying to get an Internet tower for the village, to try to improve that. We've put in an application but are still waiting to hear. As you can imagine, that would just drastically enhance the connections that are possible—if we could actually connect in real time.

As they say in Australia, teachers should just "give it a go." Try connecting your classroom. Often, we get caught up in what we've done before because it's easy—it's what we know. For me, it sort of happened accidentally. It was through meeting Michael Furdyk (of TakingITGlobal) at a conference. It really triggered for me, like, "Wow, I really do have such a diverse network and experiences. I should be pulling this in more." It's those opportunities that never would have happened if I didn't give it a shot. And I'm not saying it's always going to happen. But if we don't step outside and challenge ourselves to do things in a different way, then we could be potentially robbing our students of those opportunities that we never realize are possible.

Source: Adapted from C. Gauthier, personal communication, June 11, 2016.

The Centre for Global Education

The Centre for Global Education (CGE) is a small nonprofit organization based in Edmonton, Alberta. Founder, executive director, and former mathematics teacher Terry Godwaldt, who is deeply involved in Alberta's global education initiatives, runs one or two videoconferences every week throughout the school year. Each of these global encounters includes a handful of participating schools, which means students can be seen and heard throughout the conference. These spots are in addition to an endless number of observing locations, which allow participants to ask questions through Twitter. Each event also includes a couple of expert voices from different parts of the world—usually young people working on the topic being discussed in the videoconference. Videoconferences explore global topics that engage language arts, social studies, science, health, religion, and environmental learning through discussions of peace and conflict, child soldiers, girls' rights, the body system, poverty, environmental stewardship, and more. Students participate in asynchronous online curriculum before, during, and after live conferences, all designed as project-based learning experiences and facilitated in the virtual classrooms of CGE's central partner, TakingITGlobal for Educators.

Videoconferences explore global topics that engage language arts, social studies, science, health, religion, and environmental learning through discussions of peace and conflict, child soldiers, girls' rights, the body system, poverty, environmental stewardship, and many more.

Rather than trying to cater to the individual needs of multiple classrooms, CGE's global encounters take place at set times and explore set topics, putting the responsibility on participating schools to make that timing work (again, an important indication that globally connected schools need flexible schedules). Read chapter 3 (page 49) for an overview of CGE's annual #Decarbonize project for high school students, which includes a creative combination of synchronous and asynchronous experiences in large and small groups.

I am involved in the Centre for Global Education's Middle East in Transition events, and I cohost Resistance Art: Poetry of Witness videoconferences each semester that connect high school students to young writers and artists in the Middle East who are trying to create change through their work. By also including authentic North American voices, such as slam poets Andrea Gibson, Sonya Renee Taylor, and Franny Choi, we help students recognize the power of the arts for creating connections and change in any society.

**PERSPECTIVES ON BUILDING GLOBAL DIALOGUE:
TERRY GODWALDT**

Founder and Executive Director, Centre for Global Education

The Centre for Global Education was created because as a classroom teacher, I want my students to have an opportunity to hear from the people who are being affected by what we are encountering in the classroom curriculum. At a primal level, human beings are not meant to read *about* each other. . . . We're meant to sit around a campfire and experience our stories together. We're meant to enter into dialogue; we're meant to have a personal connection—and by having these facilitated events for my students . . . I'm connecting them at the most fundamental level I can, which is in a conversation with the people that we're learning about and we're reading about.

I remember that Omar Barghouti (founder and leader of the Palestinian Boycott, Divestment, and Sanctions movement) commented about how often teachers hear the phrase, *What does this have to do with me?* Barghouti said, "What it has to do with you now is that you have met me. Our circles have crossed; we have spent this time together, and now when you go home, this isn't about some faceless mass in Palestine; this is about a person that you have spoken with." I cannot create that any other way than through having my students come into these personal encounters.

Source: Adapted from T. Godwaldt, personal communication, May 12, 2016.

WorldVuze

WorldVuze (http://worldvuze.com) is a nonprofit platform that provides a safe forum for kindergarten through grade 12 students to share and explore a wide array of perspectives on pressing global issues. Students, the staff of nonprofit organizations, and experts from anywhere in the world can pose and answer questions, and the site allows students to engage in deep, authentic investigations of local and global issues that matter to them. In the process, WorldVuze allows students to break down stereotypes and open themselves to different ways of thinking, developing students' *pluralism* by providing extensive and varied perspectives. It also helps develop the problem-solving skills students will need to address complex issues in their own communities. While the development of a more pluralistic worldview through recognizing multiple perspectives is a hallmark of global education and not unique to WorldVuze, this particular project brings together those perspectives through a unique and interesting crowdsourcing strategy.

The development of a more pluralistic worldview through recognizing multiple perspectives is a hallmark of global education.

Rather than trying to help teacher pairs or trios develop sustainable global projects, WorldVuze creates a larger learning community by connecting classrooms worldwide. Students from any school can question students, experts, and nonprofit leaders, and students from any school or partner organization can respond, eliminating the need for two partners to follow through consistently. While this approach may not always lead to long-term, deep relationships, it provides an easy way to ensure your students are able to communicate with people from beyond your community.

You can easily track students' participation through a backchannel designed to meet educator needs. (A *backchannel* is a tool that allows for communication in the background of a partnership, such as teachers being able to monitor student participation in an online forum or teachers being able to exchange messages during a live videoconference or workshop. It can even include students sharing questions and insights during classes or calls through a synchronous platform such as TodaysMeet.) The ability to filter questions and answers by topic and region makes WorldVuze an easy tool for enriching perspectives in the classroom. For example, students studying water in a middle school science class in Toronto might ask others around the world about their water access.

PERSPECTIVES ON BUILDING A GLOBAL NETWORK: JULIA COBURN

Cofounder and Executive Director, WorldVuze

Our goal is to . . . open students' minds to new ways of thinking. The greater the number and diversity of perspectives, the better. We see WorldVuze as a tool that can integrate into other global collaboration projects quite easily and are expanding our partnerships to do just that. We believe it's absolutely critical for young people . . . to directly connect with other young people around the world and also in their own communities. In a world with more cell phones than toilets, it is quite astounding how truly disconnected we can be from one another. For example, danah boyd's (2014) research of how teens use social media finds that their online environments are just as racially and socioeconomically homogeneous as their day-to-day lives.

Our vision is to see a generation of critical global citizens. These are informed and curious investigators; critical thinkers who thoughtfully engage with the world; and people who are comfortable with complexity, open-minded when faced with diversity and uncertainty, and empathetic with different cultures and points of view. This, we believe, develops through ongoing connection and dialogue, with the purposeful mix of pedagogical practices that enhance these skill sets in young people.

Source: Adapted from J. Coburn, personal communication, January 22, 2016.

Global Read Aloud

Pernille Ripp began the Global Read Aloud (https://theglobalreadaloud.com) in 2010 with the goal of using one book to connect the world. Since it began, the Global Read Aloud has connected more than one million students around the world by offering simultaneous reading choices each fall (based on Ripp's interests and participant input) for lower-primary and upper-elementary grades. Teachers decide on the time commitment and global partnership experience they want for their students; while some teachers connect with just one other classroom, others connect across multiple classrooms for a wider array of perspectives. With reading choices for different age groups, from authors like Lauren Castillo, Roald Dahl, Sara Pennypacker, and Gary D. Schmidt, the project focuses on the idea of connecting through reading—not just with the book and its characters but also with partner readers. With a wiki to facilitate dialogue, the Global Read Aloud is quickly becoming a global community of dedicated teachers who want to expose younger students to book-based collaboration and dialogue. You can read more about it in Ripp's (2017) *Reimagining Literacy Through Global Collaboration.*

Teachers decide on the time commitment and global partnership experience they want for their students; while some teachers connect with just one other classroom, others connect across multiple classrooms for a wider array of perspectives.

Elementary educator Maria Conte has participated in the Global Read Aloud and has seen a notable improvement in her students' literacy skills and classroom engagement as a result:

> I've done the Global Read Aloud for the past two years and have connected with students from South Africa, Australia, Kazakhstan, and Canada. Collaborating and communicating via Edmodo made my students more conscientious about their own work, knowing that it was being shared with other students. I've had students who were not motivated to review and revise their work in the past ask for advice and help from their peers. Through this project, many students who are reluctant to participate in an open discussion in class were very active in the Edmodo groups they were part of. It was wonderful to see these normally shy and reserved children open up and become an active part of the collaboration process. In addition, the children who were reluctant readers became very interested in reading and so were able to be active members in the discussions and collaboration. (M. Conte, personal communication, May 12, 2016 and May 16, 2016)

Flat Connections Project

Global education thought leader Julie Lindsay is the founder and CEO of Flat Connections (www.flatconnections.com), based in Australia. Flat Connections provides online global projects for kindergarten through grade 12 teachers and students.

Educators and students who join Flat Connections learn how to build futuristic global online classrooms without walls, helping learning to become personal, collaborative, and challenge based. Lindsay and other educators implement and manage the online global projects, collaborative experiences that last ten weeks and engage core content areas of language, mathematics, science, and social studies, as well as dipping into arts and technology. Students in upper-elementary, middle, and high school projects are put into mixed classroom teams and learn how to connect, communicate, and co-create products that will impact the world in some way. Online digital technologies support synchronous and asynchronous learning activities.

One example is the A Week in the Life project, where students in grades 3 through 6 study global issues and share ideas and solutions through co-created digital artifacts. A Week in the Life is based on design thinking for better collaboration, and incorporates interdisciplinary concepts, including "how we live, how we communicate, cultural understanding and global awareness" (J. Lindsay, personal communication, June 22, 2016).

Another example is Global Youth Debates, where student debate teams from different schools and countries join together for formal debating using the online tool VoiceThread (https://voicethread.com) to facilitate asynchronous responses. Students research and debate issues such as climate change, and a global educator group judges and offers feedback for completed debates. The debate series culminates in finals, where top teams debate live online to an international audience (J. Lindsay, personal communication, June 22, 2016).

PERSPECTIVES ON TECHNOLOGY-BASED GLOBAL CONNECTIONS: JULIE LINDSAY
Founder and CEO, Flat Connections

It is important that students connect with peers and others beyond the immediate classroom. Modern learning is not about textbook learning; it is about making authentic connections that lead to collaborations.

The main goal should be to learn *with* each other and not merely *about* each other. Other goals include intercultural understanding, global competency through interaction and learning about other lives, and digital fluency—using online technologies to forge synchronous and asynchronous learning modes.

Early on (twenty-plus years ago), I experienced the power of global connections and the enhanced learning that takes place when the world is brought into the classroom. This goes beyond any and all jargon surrounding online global learning—bringing learners together for shared understanding and collaborative work is one of the most exciting areas in education right now. Unfortunately, most educators have still not taken those first steps to connect the learning. I see my role as a vital global connector and someone who can support designed and managed global collaborations to produce successful outcomes for all learners.

Source: J. Lindsay, personal communication, June 22, 2016.

Global Classroom Project

Michael Graffin cofounded the Global Classroom Project (http://theglobal classroomproject.org) in 2011, and it quickly drew a network of global educators looking for partnerships and projects. Hosts of the #globalclassroom weekly Twitter chat for four years, Global Classroom Project participants enjoy a blog that anyone can submit project ideas and articles through and opportunities to come together in person at international conferences. The projects range from mathematics to science to technology.

Fifth-grade teacher Heidi Hutchison has been involved with the Global Classroom Project for several years, and she values the community and platform it provides for participant-driven project development and finding partners. Recognizing that most partnership challenges originate in how effectively teachers collaborate, she has had both successful and challenging experiences. Regardless of what does and doesn't work in a given partnership, Hutchison recognizes the need for a central platform that's driven by teachers' own project ideas: "To have a space where people can post their projects is huge, and Global Classroom [Project] is free and pure and clean and simple" (personal communication, May 20, 2016).

One thing Hutchison has found through her work with the Global Classroom Project is that her students' experiences can be rich, and can include diverse perspectives, even when they're only able to connect with cultures locally. The most important element of a successful project isn't the distance between you and your partner; it's the willingness to collaborate, explore, and learn together. So even when she doesn't find true global partners, or her partnerships fall through, Hutchison is always helping her students connect to different stories and perspectives, even those which originate inside her own community.

The most important element of a successful project isn't the distance between you and your partner; it's the willingness to collaborate, explore, and learn together.

PERSPECTIVES ON THE GLOBAL CLASSROOM PROJECT: HEIDI HUTCHISON

Fifth-Grade Teacher, Global Classroom Project Leader, Friends School of Baltimore, Maryland

I tried to do a new project called Revolutions 101 in 2014–2015. So that year, I created the driving questions and worked with these teachers. Project sharing can be messy, and it can feel like we aren't going to learn anything or it isn't going to go anywhere. But it always does go somewhere. So that was unsuccessful because I was trying to do it *with* everyone and *for* everyone. I'm not the constant there; you have to turn over control to these teachers—and some are ready to do that while others are not.

continued →

I ended up doing it again in 2015–2016, but mostly with local partners. My driving question was How can we, as investigative journalists, create an online magazine to help others learn about revolution? To launch the project, we had a Spanish teacher who lived through the revolution in El Salvador speak about her experiences and she gave a whole presentation. They (students) were hooked from that moment on. The second person we had come was our first-grade teacher, whose mother happens to be a princess from Afghanistan. Her mother lived through the revolution but her mother's brother, in addition to thirty-eight members of their family, were killed. She lived through that and was able to tell her story about what it was like to live in a modern revolution.

We did our need-to-know list of questions as journalists online. What kinds of revolutions should we talk about, since there are all kinds of revolutions? The students decided we should just talk about the political revolutions because we were all going to learn about the American Revolution. So we started getting into the causes of the American Revolution, and I taught content that was on their (students') list of need-to-know questions. It was the cleanest global project I've done so far. I got some of the content in, and then kids chose. After deciding what part of the world they were interested in, students picked the revolutions they wanted to investigate. Somebody learned about the Singing Revolution in Estonia, another the Cuban Revolution. We were able to see the connections between revolutions—not just connections to the American Revolution but to other revolutions that kids were learning about.

Source: Adapted from H. Hutchison, personal communication, May 20, 2016.

The Wonderment

The Wonderment (http://thewonderment.com) is a global network created by the nonprofit organization Kidnected World (http://kidnectedworld.org). These educators, students, and parents share the goal of creating a better world through multimedia production. Content areas include arts (such as painting and music), gaming, reading, sciences (including biology and environment), history, religion, and world cultures. Educators can start *paths*, or new avenues of inquiry. According to its educator resources, every interaction helps students gain confidence that their voices matter: "As kids see their ideas, creations and interactions contribute to projects happening around the world, you have opportunities to support and strengthen their awareness and sense of belonging in a global community" (Wonderment, n.d.). Take a look to see existing topics and projects, or create your own path based on your students' interests.

Global Nomads Group

The Global Nomads Group (http://gng.org) notes that less than 3 percent of young people travel during their K–12 academic careers. The Global Nomads

Group (n.d.) has reached over a million students on all seven continents since its founding in 1998. Including an extensive application process, teacher interviews, and the requirement of at least four live videoconferences yearly to stay active in the program, the organization partners schools for dialogue; and while it provides a curriculum to help build conversation and trust, the topics that the participating classrooms explore depend on students' and teachers' needs and interests.

Arnetta Koger, social studies senior teacher lead and International Studies School Network (ISSN) coordinator at the Denver Center for International Studies at Montbello (DCISM), had an excellent experience in her partnership through Global Nomads in 2015–2016 (personal communication, May 17, 2016). DCISM has 850 students in grades 6 through 12, and between seven and ten languages are spoken in the building in any given year. With 70 percent of the students eligible for free or reduced lunch, Koger's ethnic studies class needed a low- or no-cost option that provided direct connections. Partnered with a girls school in Jordan, her class's first goal was to create relationships and learn about each other, so students shared about their homes, schools, and day-to-day lives, as well as asked each other questions about popular culture and personal interests. Then, each school chose one issue that was most relevant to their local community and taught their partner classroom about how that issue affected teens.

Students shared about their homes, schools, and day-to-day lives, as well as asking each other questions about popular culture and personal interests.

In Koger's case, the Jordanian students focused on prevalent drug use, particularly heroin, in their community. DCISM students reciprocated by offering statistics on teen drug use in the Denver area, so that their Jordanian partners would understand what students deal with in their community. The DCISM students focused on Flint, Michigan, investigating water-quality issues there and in Denver. The Jordanian students provided insights into water challenges in their community to help inform the DCISM students' work. The two classrooms had four live videoconferences plus continual asynchronous connections, and both classrooms focused on creating awareness-raising campaigns in their local communities as their final action projects.

Koger incorporated several Common Core State Standards into the project, particularly around high school–level persuasive and informational writing, as her students wrote a position paper that wasn't part of the Global Nomads Group curriculum. Her students' choice to focus on water meant that some of their research included science benchmarks as well. The partnership also engaged a variety of social studies standards connected to social challenges, race, culture, and religion. Koger noticed that students' reflections suggested they learned a lot about the stereotypes they held about Muslims and people from the Middle East, and that the opportunity to break down those stereotypes was incredibly meaningful.

PERSPECTIVES ON PARTNERING THROUGH GLOBAL NOMADS GROUP: ARNETTA KOGER

Social Studies Senior Teacher Lead and ISSN Coordinator, Denver Center for International Studies at Montbello, Colorado

What my students have taken away from this live interaction through our partnership with Global Nomads Group is that we all have so much in common—so much more in common than we have different. My students have learned ways to help build their leadership skills and their ability to take action and spread awareness about issues that affect their community, as well as other communities around the world. They have realized that we may have some of the same issues going on and not even know about it.

We live in a world in which our young people are so much more connected than they were in the past because of the use of social media. However, I think the opportunity for a structured partnership is really meaningful and productive because students can engage, talk about, brainstorm, and work on some type of issue or concern that they have, that they feel they can make an impact on and do something transformative about, be it a social, a cultural, or an economic topic. It's what we do in our school; it's part of our mission—not only the traveling part but the global citizenship part (of global education). To be global citizens, students have to connect with people in different parts of the world.

I think that providing these opportunities to connect with organizations like Global Nomads Group or any other has nothing to do with how much money your school has. It's about being creative, being innovative, being intuitive. It's about learning—it's part of the learning process as a human being, and should have nothing to do with money. We want our students to be critical thinkers, we want them to be socially aware, to be socially involved. We want them to think globally and act locally, and if they have the opportunity to act globally as well, so be it. I think it is something that we're all entitled to as part of our rights as human beings, as citizens of this world, to be a part of the world and to teach our students how important their voices are—and to find ways for them to learn to make their voices heard.

Source: Adapted from A. Koger, personal communication, May 17, 2016.

Level Up Village

Level Up Village (www.levelupvillage.com) offers global online courses that connect teachers and their classrooms in different parts of the world. Level Up Village promotes design thinking and collaboration, targeting students' global communication and collaboration skills through project-based learning experiences that emphasize a variety of disciplines, including science, technology, engineering, arts, and mathematics (STEAM). Level Up Village makes it easy to globalize the classroom by providing the technology, training, curriculum, and global partner management at a low cost.

In one partnership between New Canaan Country School in Connecticut and Kenya Connect in Wamunyu, Kenya, classrooms participated in Global Inventors, the Level Up Village 3-D printing course. In Global Inventors (www.levelup village.com/global-inventors), upper-elementary and middle school students learn 3-D printing to engineer solutions to real-world issues. Students learn how to use computer-aided design software to create and modify a series of designs; in the final project, students and their global partners from a developing country make a solar-powered light source (E. Dowd, personal communication, October 19, 2016).

In another partnership around a course called Global Conversations (www.level upvillage.com/global-conversations), students in middle school language arts at St. Margaret's Episcopal School in San Juan Capistrano, California, partnered with Masoom night schools in Mumbai, India, and Gayaza High School in Uganda. In this course, students engaged in a literature and culture exchange. Students read *I Am Malala* and discussed its important themes. U.S. teacher Heidi Galloway and her students participated in this project, and she found the experience transformative:

> I could see that young, impressionable minds on both sides of the camera were becoming informed about world issues . . . and their goals for the future were changing . . . Level Up Village extended what we could learn from a book into real life. Meeting our global partners, seeing them in their modest classrooms, hearing their voices and observing their dress and mannerisms was [*sic*] inspirational to my students. Here were kids who in so many ways, were just like them, but for whom education was a privilege, something to both seek and fight for. This experience underscored the power of the written word and the human voice to bridge geographic and cultural divides, connecting us to one another and revealing our common humanity. (H. Galloway, personal communication, 2016)

Know My World

With a specific focus on building an inclusive world by fostering social-emotional learning and cultural awareness, Know My World (http://knowmyworld.org) uses digital exchanges to connect young people of all ages, but specializes in primary and secondary learners and multigenerational learning relationships. (Their cross-grade projects, which are not common in the global education arena, have been very successful.) The organization matches classrooms with partner schools from its network, and works with other kinds of learning communities, including after-school programs, home-school groups, international schools, and major institutions. All projects are designed under a philosophy called T.R.A.C.E., which focuses on transformation, responsibility, awareness, connectivity, and experience (Know My World, n.d.).

Created by teachers for teachers, Know My World focuses on the experiential processes of communication and cultural understanding. Its twice-yearly digital exchange scholarship program offers a cohort of teachers the opportunity to be coached through a multi-week digital cross-cultural exchange experience with the teachers' classes. A Know My World facilitator supports teachers while they locate a match, plan a project to suit their individual classroom needs, and reflect on learning outcomes for students, as well as teacher professional growth. The international team also offers dynamic intercultural, and social-emotional projects, an online project-development webinar series, and in-person professional development workshops.

PERSPECTIVES ON THE FOUNDING OF KNOW MY WORLD: LISA PETRO

Cofounder, Know My World; Curriculum Development Specialist

Our goal is to increase the kinds of social-emotional skills and attitudes needed for an inclusive world, such as open-mindedness, flexibility, empathy, and respect. Without baseline social and emotional skills, students struggle with cultural and global competence. You can have a student who speaks several languages, has traveled to many countries, or studied the history of the world, but that does not necessarily mean the student can be culturally sensitive or build meaningful connections to others.

Our methodology at Know My World is based on our own experiences as global citizens and educators. In 2012, the founders of Know My World, Genevieve Murphy and I, were both living and teaching between Japan and Nepal. Through our work training teachers in the whole-child approach, we realized that there are many committed educators and students in the world who do not have resources or access to programs that promote cross-cultural learning. We decided to begin an international teacher exchange using digital technology and the Internet for our teacher friends to work together.

In the first year of our pilot, we discovered that the exchange experiences were falling apart. The most common reasons: time management, communication skills, and ability to be flexible, among various social and economic differences in resources. We devised a method of facilitation to coach teachers in the digital exchange experience to provide them with the base skills needed to increase probability of successful experiences. We focused on helping them see the successes when an exchange did not meet their expectations and to seek SMART (specific, measurable, attainable, relevant, and timely) outcomes. We decided that the emphasis of all our learning experiences would be relationship building and utilizing the practitioner knowledge first before standardization. This is our distinction: a staff of educators and practitioners who have experienced and are experiencing similar challenges in the classroom and who can help teachers find attainable real-world solutions.

One of our most memorable moments included a multigenerational exchange with a twelfth-grade senior art class in Canada and a first-grade grade primary school class in Japan. With relationship building as the main goal; students were able to exchange across a collaborative project to locate favorite local architecture in their respective areas. The seniors researched the structures and built models; the first graders took photos. This accumulated from a series of social and emotional inquiries about each other's cultures over a private Google community. For example, Where is your favorite place and why? How does it make you feel to be there? Students then sent each other care packages with the information, representations, and diary responses. The result: truly enlightened seniors who connected to a renewed sense of inquiry, and empowered first graders who learned their point of view matters in the world.

Source: L. Petro, personal communication, March 18, 2017.

Purpose-Based Organizations

Another way to connect with partner classrooms is through organizations that focus on a more specific topic or mission, such as peace building or the environment, and bring together teachers for global partnerships within that context. Each of these organizations works from a deep sense of passion and purpose; they don't exist for the sake of building global partnerships, but for a broader philosophical vision, generally unique to their organization, in which global partnerships play a vital role. Consider the following examples.

Another way to connect with partner classrooms is through organizations that focus on a more specific topic or mission.

Narrative 4

A powerful example of a purpose-based organization is Narrative 4 (www .narrative4.com), born out of the 2012 school shooting at Sandy Hook Elementary School in Newtown, Connecticut, with the express philosophy of using stories to build humanizing connections. With the goal to create "fearless hope through radical empathy," the core methodology focuses on story exchanges in which individuals listen deeply to each other's stories and then retell them in first person to a larger group (Narrative 4, 2015). Using Chimamanda Ngozi Adichie's (2009) idea of moving beyond a single story, Narrative 4 combines the exchanges with writing and visual arts, and its work has expanded to include more and more schools partnering for international story exchanges.

Narrative 4 keeps its main focus on local work in predominantly underserved public schools around the world, facilitating exchanges within a given community and training local teachers and leaders to carry on the story exchanges after they leave. Narrative 4 also focuses on helping ensure all facilitators use best practices around developing safe spaces for open dialogue. Global partnerships are established only after extensive local groundwork, and Narrative 4 is also developing a network of *hubs* (physical spaces in a variety of cities where students and teachers can find all the necessary technology, spaces, and facilitators for such partnerships). In one powerful example, a virtual story exchange between Newtown High School in Sandy Hook, Connecticut, and the American School in Tampico, Mexico, brought together two schools that have experienced violence in their communities—and students worked together on gun control legislation after the story exchange (L. Keylock, personal communication, May 13, 2016).

PERSPECTIVES ON THE POWER OF THE STORY: LEE KEYLOCK
Director of Programs, Narrative 4

What is the highest aim of storytelling? It's been around since the cave paintings on the wall, so that's what we have to think about. And we never deviate from that power. So then what happens is students put empathy into action in the field in certain projects, which in turn generates another story for them to tell at another time. So it's this exponential growth thing. For us, storytelling is power; it's the ultimate democracy. As Colum McCann would say, it's the "currency of the world."

We don't turn schools away. Every school needs it; there's no need higher than another need. But I think that in some underserved areas, kids feel like their stories aren't heard, like they're not valid, they're not being told, and actually there's only one narrative coming out of a lot of those neighborhoods, so we're in there to rewrite the script with them.

Source: Adapted from L. Keylock, personal communication, May 13, 2016.

LINEglobal

LINEglobal (www.lineglobal.org) is a nonprofit organization based in New York that facilitates long-term professional partnerships among educators in the United States and India, including physical travel. With the goal of creating dialogue, sharing perspectives, increasing understanding, and encouraging empathy, LINEglobal connects teachers for authentic collaboration through a learning process that incorporates professional inquiry and personal introspection. While LINEglobal's mission focuses on professional development collaboration between U.S. and Indian teachers, classroom partnerships frequently emerge from those interactions. LINEglobal focuses on in-person, immersive experiences that shape teachers' global competencies first and foremost, but virtual engagement continues after in-person travel to ensure that learning partnerships continue to benefit teachers and their students.

Founder Rekha Puri asserts, "Educators learn about each other, from each other, and with each other. We are not imposing our agenda, we are not 'saving' anyone, but rather empowering ourselves and our partners" (personal communication, October 20, 2016). In one particularly successful classroom partnership, Emily Schorr Lesnick, a LINEglobal fellow from Riverdale Country School in Bronx, New York, partnered with the Avasara Leadership Fellows Program, an after-school program for underprivileged girls in Mumbai, India. Lesnick and her partner connected face-to-face in Mumbai and worked together online. Focusing on empowering girls through theatrical experiences, they share theater resources and ideas, and they work together to individualize and personalize students' collaborative experiences (R. Puri, personal communication, October 20, 2016).

Thinking of partnerships as reciprocal is important.

LINEglobal exists for philosophical reasons that extend beyond classroom partnerships. Puri writes, "We are committed to shifting age-old paradigms by finding common ground to collaborate and engage with respectful reciprocity" (personal communication, October 20, 2016). Thinking of partnerships as reciprocal is important. That is what equitable global partnerships work toward, and LINEglobal provides a powerful example of what's possible when educators approach the work this way. See the Partnership Idea Generation worksheet in figure 4.1.

Spend some time exploring the project databases of the organizations you're most interested in. Find project examples that might work well in your classroom or administrative role, and spend a few minutes reflecting on what you find, as well as on any new ideas your explorations generate.

- Which organizations did you find most interesting? Why?

- Which specific partnership projects did you find most resonant? Why?

- Which project examples might work in your own community or classroom? Sketch out any remediations you might need to make based on your context (grade level, discipline, school culture).

- Which partnership examples would not work well for your discipline or grade level? Why?

- What other project ideas are starting to emerge for you? Brainstorm as many ideas as possible, without judging any of them.

Figure 4.1: Partnership idea generation worksheet.

*Visit **go.SolutionTree.com/21stcenturyskills** for a free reproducible version of this figure.*

A Few Concluding Thoughts

While partnerships that you create yourself often appeal to innovative educators more than ready-made partnerships, the realities of teaching make existing networks and programs extremely valuable. Many of these organizations, such as the Global Classroom Project, strive to create collaborative learning teams where participants work together to build new initiatives rather than relying on a central leadership committee to create partnerships for them. All function as professional learning networks at the very least, with multiple forums for professional growth, dialogue, resource sharing, and feedback. As discussed more deeply in chapter 10 (page 177), connecting into these networks has an added benefit: beyond helping find partners for specific global learning projects, the networks can help offset the feeling of isolation that many innovative teachers express.

CHAPTER 5

FINDING A GLOBAL PARTNER ON YOUR OWN

Friends and partners do not just fall from a tree in one's backyard. They become friends and partners only through interactions in various occasions when mutual interests, respect, and understanding are uncovered and developed.

—Yong Zhao

There is no perfect formula for finding a global partner on your own, but several strategies can help you find committed, serious partner teachers. The point is to find a teacher whose goals complement your own and to develop a collaborative experience in which students on both sides experience significant learning and connect authentically.

This is not easy to do in any educational setting; teachers are busy people who often work over sixty hours per week. It can take a year or two before a partnership functions at its full potential, and even the most successfully partnered teachers experience frustration and challenges along the way. The bottom line is that both partners have to be equally committed—and equally communicative and flexible—for meaningful collaborative learning to occur. Long-term partnerships are a marathon, not a sprint, and even short-term partnerships need careful nurturing.

Most partnerships almost appear as happy accidents because open-minded, flexible teachers reach out for unique resources and allow classroom visitors to reach in. The more you run a connected classroom, both literally and figuratively, the easier building partnerships becomes. Try to embody what Australian inquiry educator Kath Murdoch (2014) calls being *hunters and gatherers,* and become the kind of educator who is always looking for ways to connect his or her classroom to the world. Similarly, Silvia Rosenthal Tolisano (2014) points out that global educators can make "Connecting with, talking to, and collaborating with colleagues in other countries or continents and across oceans and time zones . . . as commonplace as speaking to your colleagues in the same building" and such interactions should include "calling on experts, eyewitnesses, or volunteers at a moment's notice—that teachable moment in your classroom prompts" (pp. 42, 48–49). Tolisano's mention of the teachable moment is particularly apt in global education because a sort of fluidity with events, opportunities, and communication in general leads to a richer experience for both teachers and students—but it requires comfort with looser lesson planning than some educators prefer.

> *A sort of fluidity with events, opportunities, and communication in general leads to a richer experience for both teachers and students.*

Consider, too, the thoughts of Adam McKim, cofounder of the Global Goals Educator Task Force (www.teachsdgs.org) and editor of *The Global Times*, a monthly current events publication for students:

> In 2010, a world traveling guest speaker plopped a genuine crisis into my world issues classroom. The ensuing Skype-fueled relationships with Ugandan learners changed the course of my professional and personal life. The power of integrating the current event of climate change, the live visuals of the garden we funded, and the talk from locals about unusually dry conditions, was probably the most impactful teaching moment of my career. (A. McKim, personal communication, October 28, 2016)

Truthfully speaking, there is no accident involved in what McKim describes; it was his willingness to open his door to the world through a traveling visitor, and to engage his learners with real current events beyond the classroom walls, that created the opportunities he's built so much on since.

Prior to this chapter, complete as much of the Partnership Readiness worksheet (figure 2.1, page 45) as possible without your partner; once you find a potential partner, be sure that you answer the worksheet's curricular questions together. (Chapter 6, page 107, will explore strategies for how to handle those initial calls with your partner.) This chapter offers a variety of strategies for finding potential partners through social media; in-person and online conferences; personal, professional, and community networks; teacher professional and personal travel programs (both grant-based and fee-based).

Social Media

One of the cheapest and easiest ways to find a potential partner teacher is to use existing social media networks. Though a handful of governments such as China and Kuwait block a few, like Facebook and Google+, many have a global membership and can be a good starting place for advertising your interest in a partner. (Even in heavily regulated countries, such as China, creative teachers are often able to use virtual personal networks [VPNs] to work around network blocks.) Facebook, Instagram, Google+, and LinkedIn can help teachers network to find other teachers, and can serve to share student work between classrooms, depending on your privacy restrictions for online engagement. (See more in chapter 6, page 107, on choosing the best technological platforms.) As long as the social media network extends beyond your borders, it has the potential to help you connect with global educators.

One of the cheapest and easiest ways to find a potential partner teacher is to use existing social media networks.

Hashtags make it easier to find the *right* potential partners by focusing your requests, and they work on most social media sites. On Twitter (https://twitter.com), the popular hashtags #globaled, #globaledchat, #globalclassroom, #connectededucator, and #globalpartnership can help you connect with teachers from other parts of the world seeking partners. It's good to include an issue-specific hashtag in your posts, too; hashtags like #malariaprevention or #humanrights can help you find like-minded partners interested in the topics you want to explore. If you include the Twitter handles of global educators you know—including me—we can help push your request out to our networks as well. If you create a classroom Twitter account separate from your personal account, make it easily searchable by including the grade level in the name—and use the same strategy for finding teachers of your grade level. For example, if you type *third grade* into a Twitter search, hundreds of third-grade classrooms around the world appear. Through such connections, global partnerships often emerge organically through shared interests or age groups, both of which are strong starting points.

There are regular Twitter chats of relevance to the global educator, including the increasingly popular #globaledchat. Educators worldwide attend these chats. They are a great way to connect with a network experimenting with global connections in their classrooms.

In-Person and Online Conferences

Conferences that draw an international audience are great for connecting with like-minded colleagues. The following conferences are particularly useful for building global partnerships.

The International Society for Technology in Education

The International Society for Technology in Education (ISTE; https://iste.org) has diverse international attendees at its U.S.-based conference every June, including ministers of education and thousands of teachers and school leaders. If you choose the sessions you attend with a potential partnership in mind, you can often make initial connections with educators who are working toward similar goals or teaching similar themes. ISTE always includes a Global Education Day at the preconference, a networking and collaboration event, run by global education thought leaders Lucy Gray and Steve Hargadon, that brings together between 250 and 500 global educators in any given year. The opening poster session and reception also focus on global collaborations, making that first preconference day key for anyone seeking global partnership opportunities.

GlobalEdCon

GlobalEdCon is the common nickname for the online Global Education Conference (www.globaleducationconference.com). Founders Lucy Gray and Steve Hargadon facilitate this conference each November. While GlobalEdCon is one of several online conferences Gray and Hargadon run, it remains one of the best for finding global project ideas and partners. With presenters and participants from around the globe, GlobalEdCon is as close to being a fully equitable and accessible conference as exists in global education to date. The only prerequisite for participation is a computer with Internet connection. The Global Education Conference network also maintains a Ning (https://ning.com) social networking site for the GlobalEdCon community to continue communicating and collaborating throughout the year. Connected Educator Month Reports (www.connectededucators .org/briefs) are also worth a look, as are the annual Connected Educator events. With multiple smaller groups and forums for dialogue and resource sharing, the GlobalEdCon community is an excellent platform for seeking like-minded partners who already have technology access. (See chapter 10, page 177, for more on professional learning through the Global EdCon network.)

Personal, Professional, and Community Networks

Your chances of finding an invested partner are sometimes improved by working through your school's existing networks since someone you know—even two or three times removed—may be more likely to follow through. However, stay vigilant if things begin to go downhill. Sometimes people connected to your community will say *yes* out of a sense of obligation instead of a true sense of engagement, and it's disappointing and disruptive to discover an imbalance of passion late in the process. While personal networks may produce more individual guest speakers than teacher partners, both are equally valuable for student growth.

Partners from your professional and community networks might include former students, teachers, administrators, or parents who have done international work. For elementary and middle school students, just meeting someone their age who has lived in another country or is doing work outside the students' country is enough to impact their thinking and worldview. For high school students, meeting a graduate who has gone on to do interesting global work can often inspire them toward new fields of study or even new career paths. Previous community members often have a vested interest in contributing to your school, and that means you can rely on them to take the students' experiences seriously and volunteer their time.

Partners from your professional and community networks might include former students, teachers, administrators, or parents who have done international work.

Partners from governmental and nongovernmental organizations might include individuals working in the fields students are studying, as in the examples explored in chapter 3 (page 49). While many such organizations are often understaffed, their personnel maintain a deep sense of passion and purpose, having dedicated their lives to the global topics that most concern them. Such purpose-driven individuals are often anxious to see young people become passionate about the same topics, especially if they have a personal connection to your school community. Additionally, scheduling a Skype session can be much easier with nonclassroom partners, as their schedules are often more flexible than those of partner teachers.

Also, think about where your school already travels and about the extended global community you already strive to be part of. If your school supports any international student travel, colleagues who have led programs can help you connect and engage with those communities, particularly if your school travels to the same communities often. It is valuable to extend the relationship by building classroom partnerships and connecting travel experiences to the academic curriculum. This sends an important message to students and parents alike that global engagement and active global citizenship happen throughout the year, not just during summer vacation or spring break. Further, it helps ensure that global education has deep foundations in and connections to academic content, and that travel experiences are crafted with a deep sense of purpose. See the Outreach Planning for Finding Partners worksheet in figure 5.1, designed to help you identify existing networks and consider how you might engage the connections you already have.

Gather a team of administrators, capacity builders, teachers, and student leaders to brainstorm existing global connections you already have in your community. Before beginning the brainstorm, set the following norms.

- Don't stop to judge ideas; generate as many ideas as possible and discuss feasibility later.

- Capture all ideas in writing, either through individual sticky notes or large chart paper and a group scribe.

Figure 5.1: Outreach planning for finding partners worksheet.

continued →

- If the group is large, like a full faculty, have members brainstorm in smaller groups of four to five, with each group generating a written list that can be shared.

Use the following questions to brainstorm, dedicating five to ten minutes for each. Then, discuss the following questions.

- Where does our school take students in international programs? What connections do we have in those countries that could help enrich experiences inside our classrooms?

- Where does our school hope to take students in the near future? How might we connect those destinations to the academic curriculum?

- Do we have alumni who work internationally and might love to connect with their old school to show current students what their education can lead to?

- Where were our teachers and administrators before they came to us? Where have our teachers and administrators gone after leaving us? Have former administrators moved on to international posts? Have any teachers gone on to teach in different parts of the world?

- Where have our students' parents lived or worked previously? Where do they have deep connections with organizations, schools, or individuals? Which parents work in a national role with an international focus, or internationally themselves? What experiences might parents have to share?

- What organizations in our local area focus on international topics or glocal challenges (Harth, 2010)? How might they help us partner with the countries and topics they focus on?

*Visit **go.SolutionTree.com/21stcenturyskills** for a free reproducible version of this figure.*

Teacher Professional and Personal Travel Programs

One of the most effective ways to find a viable partner is by visiting schools and educational communities outside your home country. While international professional development travel may feel out of reach for many educators because of the expense, there are solutions—and there is no better way to find the right partner than to enter a school in another country and converse face-to-face with teachers about the collaborative learning experiences you might build together. There are myriad programs discussed in this chapter, many supported by grants and foundations that allow teachers to engage with the world at no expense.

One of the most effective ways to find a viable partner is by visiting schools and educational communities outside your home country.

Tolisano (2014) uses the term *global fluency* to describe an individual's "ability to move effortlessly between local and global connections for his or her own ongoing professional development and for the benefit of his or her students" (p. 48). Globally connected teachers have that sort of fluency, but its formation is generally far from effortless. Most spend years building networks, experiencing setbacks, and making and learning from intercultural mistakes. If you think of global fluency as your goal, inspiration has to lie at the core; global education can't just be another initiative on your already full schedule, another ball to juggle simply because your administrators told you to. Like students, it's important that *you* practice toward global competency with an open mind—and there's nothing that will build your inspiration and motivation like engaging directly with the world.

Grant-Based Teacher Travel Fellowships

Travel is expensive, and so grant-based teacher travel fellowships are one solution. Many global educators I know—from both public and private schools—haven't paid for their summer travel in decades because they know how to find and earn travel grants. Among the best are the following programs; however, each year new organizations appear, offering both grant- and fee-based professional development programs that include international travel. Search online by *travel grants for teachers*. Edutopia (https://edutopia.org) and other educational organizations also catalog new travel grant opportunities each year, and even offer tips for writing a strong proposal (Davis, 2016).

PERSPECTIVES ON FINDING GLOBAL PARTNERS THROUGH TRAVEL: SUSAN LAMBERT

Founder and Director, Away 2 Be

In the classroom, I don't think finding a partner is much different than in life, in the sense that we are all connected. If we hypothetically look at a classroom of twenty-five students and a teacher, all of those students have families, and all of those families have connections. The teacher has a lifetime of experience, and a local community that also has connections and experiences. So when you ask how to make something virtual more personal, I think you depend on the personal. We look at our life stories and experiences. I've spent the last ten years going back and forth from Nicaragua as a liaison for the Casa Materna, a home for at-risk pregnant women. So, what I was able to do with my classroom is connect my family in Nicaragua with my students. Because of my life experience, I had students wanting to come with me to Nicaragua. That wasn't necessarily the goal, but because of my connections, students were able to write letters back and forth, and have phone conversations with people in Nicaragua because they are my family.

All of the students who came with me to Nicaragua ended up getting scholarships for college. I ran into one of them who is doing global engineering work, another one is in Argentina right now, and another who went to Guatemala. So I think those personal relationships are the foundation. Personal relationships evolve into global relationships.

Source: S. Lambert, personal communication, May 22, 2016.

Fund for Teachers

Fund for Teachers (www.fundforteachers.org) is one of the only organizations offering travel grants based on teacher-formulated needs and locations (Fund for Teachers, n.d.). This approach makes Fund for Teachers an incredibly flexible travel grant when it comes to where teachers go and what they choose to investigate. Fund for Teachers allows educators to plan experiences that are 100 percent relevant to their classroom and instructional needs, and to travel to countries that might not be supported by governmental programs.

Jeanne Boland, a former Denver-area teacher with Odyssey Middle School, spent a summer in Israel/Palestine through Fund for Teachers, participating in a wide variety of experiences and projects to enrich her humanities classroom (personal communication, May 9, 2016). She had almost no experience with or knowledge about the region and conflict previously. This region is politically complex when it comes to finding government-sponsored travel grants, and Boland found extraordinary value in the inside perspectives she gained by going to the region. Some of the complexities of Boland's subsequent global partnership work on the Israeli–Palestinian conflict are explored in chapter 8 (page 143).

IREX's Teachers for Global Classrooms Program

IREX's Teachers for Global Classrooms Program (https://irex.org/project/teachers -global-classrooms-program-tgc) is a yearlong professional development opportunity for U.S. elementary, middle, and high school teachers to develop their skills in global education and become global ambassadors in their classrooms, schools, and broader communities. Participants do this by collaborating with U.S. and international colleagues to promote mutual understanding; experiencing professional development that equips them to return to their schools as catalysts for global engagement; having international field experiences; and developing curriculum focused on "global competency, technology integration, and cross cultural communication" (www.irex.org, n.d.).

The Institute of International Education

The Institute of International Education (IIE) administers several Fulbright grant programs, including the Fulbright Distinguished Awards in Teaching Program. This program and others provide educators with international professional development experiences through travel abroad, with a focus on classroom enrichment and authentic curriculum development. All are programs for building global connections and partnerships, and all cost nothing for educators (but include a competitive application process).

The program allows teachers to work with equally committed global partners to develop strong, authentic collaborative curricula for classrooms in both countries.

According to Holly Emert, who leads the professional exchanges unit where she manages K–12 teacher exchanges at the IIE, these teacher exchange programs are about building relationships:

> These programs connect people to one society from another. This is what's keeping us from destroying ourselves. I firmly believe that. When you see teachers in the Fulbright program and how they relate to each other, they are all hugs and kisses at the end. And it's because we're people, and we get that chance to connect over three to six months. (H. Emert, personal communication, May 20, 2016)

The Fulbright Distinguished Awards in Teaching Program (http://bit.ly/1r2AN2H) provides grants to U.S. and international teachers to immerse abroad to observe, study, and create a project. The program is open to K–12 educators, including administrators, who either hold or are currently enrolled in a master's program. Program destinations include Botswana, Greece, Finland, India, Israel, Mexico, Morocco, the Netherlands, New Zealand, the Palestinian Territories, Singapore, South Korea, Taiwan, United Kingdom, and Vietnam.

The Japan–U.S. Teacher Exchange Program for Education for Sustainable Development (www.iie.org/Programs/ESD/About) offers an annual travel exchange that focuses specifically on developing programs and partnerships for teaching sustainable development. Through travel and immersion experiences for a cohort of Japanese and U.S. teachers who connect with each other in both countries, the program allows teachers to work with equally committed global partners to develop strong, authentic collaborative curricula for classrooms in both countries.

The Fulbright-Hays Group Projects Abroad program (www2.ed.gov/programs/iegpsgpa) provides grants to support overseas projects in training, research, and curriculum development in modern world languages, and area studies for teachers, students, and faculty engaged in a common endeavor. Projects may include short-term seminars, curriculum development, group research or study, or advanced intensive language programs. Projects must focus on the humanities, social sciences, and languages, and on one or more of the following areas: Africa, East Asia, South Asia, Southeast Asia and the Pacific, Central and South America, Mexico, the Caribbean, East Central Europe and Eurasia, or the Near East.

Colorado Academy English teacher Betsey Coleman, who has participated in several Fulbright teacher programs, discovered the power of starting global partnerships from the programs' in-person connections and has had success with a variety of global partnership projects.

PERSPECTIVES ON GLOBAL PARTNERSHIPS: BETSEY COLEMAN
Fulbright Distinguished Awards in Teaching Recipient,
Colorado Academy, Denver

The purpose of the project I created in 2015–2016 was to cross global borders by sharing stories of empowered South African youth in an under-resourced rural school, and to teach U.S. students about the possibilities of leadership inherent in all young people, regardless of race, class, or nationality. This project included an international exchange of stories—stories from students in South Africa back to youth in a U.S. high school in Denver, Colorado—as well as the building of digital skills with South African youth, necessary for higher education and the global marketplace. Through this exchange, cross-pollination promoted the internationalization of U.S. youth and furthered the digital development of at-risk South African youth, bridging the digital divide. Through a process of exploring storytelling, U.S. and South African secondary students created new identities. The highly personal nature of these narratives served as powerful acknowledgment of an individual's role and voice—an opportunity to be seen and heard as a voice to cross borders.

The project included a weeklong workshop in South Africa and several weeks in the United States. The South African students and the Colorado Academy students developed narratives of identity and explored brainstorming, writing, editing, and revising around transcending limitations. They recorded two- to three-minute final narratives into a soundtrack. Students learned photography and videography skills, and a software program for digital storytelling. Students downloaded and uploaded photos and completed a multimedia narrative with audio, visuals, music, transitions, and title and end slides.

Students exported their stories, showcasing their narratives with their school community, with their larger community, and the partner school. Colorado Academy students wrote responses, to be shared with South African students, to the South African stories. This globalization project was shared locally through Colorado Academy's school and family community, and in South Africa. The results crossed both the digital divide and the global divide by developing understanding across cultures through shared authentic stories of transformation and youth leadership.

Source: Adapted from B. Coleman, personal communication, January 15, 2016.

National Geographic's Grosvenor Teacher Fellow Program

The Grosvenor Teacher Fellow Program (http://nationalgeographic.org/education/programs/grosvenor-teacher-fellows) is a National Geographic Society professional development experience. Exemplary educators are recognized for their commitment to geographic education and given the opportunity to travel aboard the Lindblad-National Geographic fleet. Canadian, Puerto Rican, and U.S. educators for K–12 are eligible to participate in the program, which focuses on geography and environmental sustainability, and they commit to serving in a leadership role for two years.

Fee-Based Teacher Travel Programs

While the idea is to find fully funded travel whenever possible, all schools have a professional development budget, and many designate a portion for teacher-initiated professional development experiences such as conferences or travel. Fee-based professional development travel programs can often qualify for such funding as well. Many such programs offer immersive travel and curriculum development opportunities in a variety of countries. The following are well established.

All schools have a professional development budget, and many designate a portion for teacher-initiated professional development experiences such as conferences or travel.

World Leadership School

World Leadership School (www.worldleadershipschool.com) facilitates only two or three small professional development programs each year to its partner communities. Schools can send a group for a school-specific program, which allows the facilitation of long-term planning and global program development during an immersive stay in a rural community. For example, in 2015, I led a small team of elementary teachers from The Berkeley Carroll School in Brooklyn, New York, who traveled to rural Costa Rica with the goal of developing new global projects for their classrooms. In the process, the group ended up defining what global educational programming might look like across the elementary grades and developed ideas for several schoolwide global themes and experiences. Because school-specific programs like these bring educators together outside of their usual routines, teachers bond and think in a different way than they can during strategic planning sessions inside the school building, and the immersive setting encourages new ideas about what global might mean for their schools.

Teachers can also join open enrollment programs through World Leadership School that focus on project-based and purpose-driven global learning. All of these programs include authentic school and homestay immersion experiences with teachers from a variety of schools, where participants live for at least five days with a family and immerse in the family's daily life. The curriculum builds a rich cross-pollination opportunity among teachers from different schools, disciplines, and grade bands. All programs include project development, so teachers can take their learning back to the classroom, and the school visits and community dialogues often lead to long-term global partnerships. While building classroom partnerships is not a central goal in these programs, World Leadership School's philosophy of sending student groups back to the same communities and including significant homestays in all programs helps ensure that students and teachers build friendships that benefit their broader school communities and last beyond the limits of physical travel.

Global Exploration for Educators Organization

Global Exploration for Educators Organization (GEEO; www.geeo.org) is a nonprofit organization that encourages teachers to travel abroad and share their experiences with students. GEEO strives to turn teachers into goodwill ambassadors by enabling them to have intercultural and volunteer experiences in educational communities around the world.

While GEEO doesn't supply funding for teacher travel, it is committed to accepting all interested teachers into its programs, regardless of resources, and then supporting teachers in their search for funding. According to founder and executive director Jesse Weisz, GEEO works continually to find funders to subsidize the costs for teachers, and its access to humanitarian-rate airfares and low-cost insurance helps keep costs to a minimum. GEEO has its own curriculum; teachers develop an action plan for how they want to incorporate their travel into the classroom, and during the trip they encounter academic and thought leaders. The goal is for teachers to come back with a presentation they can give in a variety of classes and settings and customize as they wish (J. Weisz, personal communication, April 11, 2016).

A Few Concluding Thoughts

However you begin the relationship, remember that developing a global partnership on your own will require more work—and will repeatedly test your own global competencies. The next chapter explores communication strategies and technology solutions. Try to be patient with challenges, flexible to shifts, willing to take risks, and optimistic about what you can craft together. Always advocate for time release if you craft something from scratch; even a removed duty or two each week can open up the extra time you'll need to build your partnership intentionally and thoughtfully. The How Much Time Can I Put Into Crafting This Partnership? section in chapter 2 (page 31) can help you navigate that issue.

Developing a global partnership on your own will require more work—and will repeatedly test your own global competencies.

CHAPTER 6

CHOOSING STRATEGIES FOR SUCCESSFUL COMMUNICATION

Learning has never been as fluid as now. A mobile device in conjunction with ubiquitous wireless network access literally means we can learn anywhere, anytime, from anyone.

—Julie Lindsay

While it may seem obvious, communication challenges are the biggest reason partnerships fail. Whether caused by limited Internet access, overworked teachers who don't answer emails, key people dropped from email threads, or lack of a common language, the challenges are fairly easy to address and avoid. Start by focusing on building a relationship with simple, personal, and consistent communication—and an open mind. Lean into, or embrace as a growth opportunity, any language differences you might have with your partner teacher. From there, choose the right synchronous and asynchronous communication platforms. This chapter can help ensure that your partnership is successful.

Build Relationships First

The most important element of a global partnership is the relationship between the teachers. It is the foundation needed to forge relationships among students. If there is no trust, communicating can feel flat and unimportant—even when technologies are working. Consider the ideas of activist and educator Mark Thomas (formerly Turner), creator of the documentary film *Ripples Cross*, who spent many years connecting students in Palestine with students in the United States and Canada through the initiative:

Ultimately, as educators, we have to determine critically what we do with technologies. Putting technologies in front of students has not demonstrated itself to improve learning outcomes; technology in and of itself is not an avenue toward better achievement in schools nor better human connections. Can you use Twitter effectively in the classroom for allowing young people a voice? Sure, absolutely you can, but not in the absence of genuine human connections. Because those technologies are so accessible, we are inclined to vest our hopes in them to forge connections. If we don't see critically, then we might forget that those connections are based on trust and human relationships, not voice and video streams. I think a technology needs to be wielded critically by educators who share real human connections and the trust that drives learning. If you can do global education that way, it can be the most powerful experience in the world for those young people. But you shouldn't be surprised that it's just another television show that they rapidly forget if they've not established any real relationship through the process. (M. Thomas, personal communication, May 8, 2016)

Real connections require building trust and developing a common vision for our students' learning.

As Thomas indicates, just tweeting doesn't automatically build relationships between students or teachers; real connections require building trust and developing a common vision for our students' learning.

Harry T. Reis and Phillip Shaver (1988) explain that intimacy begins when someone reveals something about him- or herself and, in response, the listener is supportive and empathetic. Having global competencies and students' global education at the heart of your intentions, and sharing your vision of what the partnership might do for students, will go far in establishing that intimacy with your partner teacher. Zhao (2012) takes this thinking further, recognizing that such relationships are essential in business partnerships as much as in educational ones:

Finding and working with international partners is in itself a challenging task. Understanding and managing cultural differences, different expectations, and different ways of conducting business are a must in creating successful international partnerships. As well, sustaining international partnerships requires expertise in languages and cultures, mutual respect, and empathy. Furthermore, international partnership means "joint-venture"—taking risks together, which requires a deep appreciation for each other's situations and demands. (p. 221)

Certainly, any class-to-class partnership will require a sort of joint-venture risk taking as you establish goals and work toward them together, and many of the challenges Zhao (2012) describes are just as salient in classroom partnerships. As you begin your communication with a potential partner, remember that your first goal is to connect and build the kind of trust that will lead to mutual respect, understanding, and the willingness to take risks together, so that you can work to build a culture of trust and connectedness among your students as well.

Global educators develop the capacity to collaborate and communicate in increasingly effective ways, but everyone stumbles along the way. A friend in Palestine once insisted that the best passport in intercultural settings is a smile, and I remain grateful for his insight. By smiling through the challenges, I encourage my partners to see me as fallible and human, but also willing and eager, friendly, and kind.

PERSPECTIVES ON GLOBAL PARTNERS: SUSAN LAMBERT
Founder and Director, Away 2 Be

Building global relationships is all about what you're already doing and what you're already passionate about. What is it that you're already interested in? Teaching aside, is your family from Ireland? From a place that's had conflict? Does that interest you? Are you interested in women's health? Are you interested in music as a vehicle to connect with others? You have to connect on an individual level. I don't think a teacher's global experiences necessarily matter; it's more about connecting with the personal passions or interests. It may or may not seem to connect to what you're teaching, but there's always a link you can find.

Knowing personal interests, you can then connect with others with similar interests, and that's where the projects start to develop. This is not to discount normal, everyday questions you might ask a friend, like, "How are you? What are you interested in? Who is in your family? What are you excited about in life?" Then if that aligns, just like a relationship, maybe you take it to the next step. You have a second date. But if you don't connect, find someone else—they're out there! Keep asking. I think teachers have to go through the experience they hope their students will go through.

Source: Adapted from S. Lambert, personal communication, May 22, 2016.

Lean Into Language Differences

The fear of working with a partner teacher who doesn't share a common language has derailed many excellent partnership opportunities and left many schools on the periphery of global educational movements, particularly those where the primary language is a nondominant language internationally. To build more inclusive global networks and partnerships, it's important for teachers to take the leap to establish partnerships with good, motivated teachers, regardless of language. One of the partnership's goals is to develop your own global competencies—and to demonstrate adult learning to increase students' willingness to take risks. Because of that, there is actually more to be learned from partnerships that do *not* share a common language.

Leaning into language differences means making regular use of online translation tools as much as tapping into the skills of local language speakers, and that brings up concerns in many schools. World language teachers are rightfully worried about students' use of online translation tools, given that the goal of world language study is to develop a level of fluency that requires no tools. Reliance on such tools can be problematic in a language classroom, as can using them to cheat, but they can be incredibly helpful during global partnerships. Students will encounter many more languages than they could learn to master in their lifetimes, so knowing how to use translation and other navigational tools will be important skills *in addition to* becoming a fluent speaker in at least one nonnative language.

> *There is actually more to be learned from partnerships that do* not *share a common language.*

Tools like Google Translate (https://translate.google.com) don't generally craft language as well as they translate existing text. Therefore, communication through translators is most effective if teachers and students write to each other in their native language and then use translation tools to understand what they receive. The inquiry work of understanding a pen pal letter or student video introduction in a different world language is a great experience for students. Rather than avoiding it, there is more value for students in embracing such complexity as part of the partnership experience. Such experiences also encourage students to study world languages with more intention, as the urge to communicate is key to engaged language learning.

Using translation tools doesn't work as well during live experiences. This is when local community partnerships come in most handy. If there are students in your school who speak the language in question, ideally those students can serve as language experts for their peers, even interpreting live events such as videoconferences. This approach has the added benefit of turning world language proficiency from a perceived detriment into a gift, empowering English learners to use their native languages for the benefit of all students. There may also be parents, teachers, or other staff who speak the target languages. I facilitated a partnership in which teachers at Town School for Boys asked a janitor to help interpret during a third-grade partnership on bird migration with a school in Mexico. As a result of this powerful experience, students came to see the janitor in a whole new way—as someone with talents they would not have otherwise known about. It permanently changed the way students interacted with him.

International schools have a huge advantage when it comes to having available interpreters, as do particularly diverse schools in regions with a high immigrant population. Appleby College near Toronto, whose student body represents between thirty and forty countries in a given year, has worked to make intercultural and interlanguage skills an intentional part of the work it does in residence halls and classrooms, building global dialogue through more authentic inclusivity within its own community. If your school isn't particularly diverse and the language speaker you need isn't inside your school building, poll parents and try outreach across your broader community. Particularly in urban areas, there tend to be pockets of world language use, and most of these communities would love to help educators and have others see their native language as an asset.

Start From Simple, Personal Communication

Email communication can get tricky very quickly, and even teachers with easy access are often too busy to communicate regularly. Based on monitoring partnerships I've helped initiate over the years, many potential partnerships die in the first few months because one partner isn't replying to emails or someone forgets to choose Reply All and include the entire team. Email initially only to set up a Skype session or phone call, so that you can introduce yourselves in a more personal way and have a real conversation about the goals and ideas you bring to the table. If you need help with language on a live call, invite a student or colleague to sit with you for the call and help with interpretation.

Remember to be flexible about the means of communication; even social media messaging can lead to better dialogue than email because the former tends to lead to shorter communications with more back and forth. While Skype has its limitations, it is by far the most widely used synchronous communication tool outside of North America. Facebook Messenger (https://facebook.com/messenger) and WhatsApp (https://whatsapp.com) have become my favorite tools for quick and consistent communication with many partner teachers and students. Like Imo in parts of Latin America and WeChat in China, these are the messaging platforms where global networks are *already* communicating. All have call or audio recording features, which makes them a tool for free international phone calls when the user is on a WiFi network. Data charges may apply when using cell connectivity, and those charges vary, so ask your partner. Do not assume anything. Working with the technology your partner teacher feels most adept at—and can best afford—helps start your partnership on strong, equal footing.

Working with the technology your partner teacher feels most adept at—and can best afford—helps start your partnership on strong, equal footing.

Start the first call with a little personal sharing. Explain how many years you have been a teacher, and in what grades. What are your passions? Tell your partner about your family, where you live, and what makes you want to start this partnership. Ask your partner teacher questions about himself or herself.

Be sure your first call addresses logistical concerns as well, so that you end with plans for your next call and a solid sense of how you will communicate with each other in the meantime. For example, I facilitated a partnership between an elementary school in Denver, Colorado, and a network of urban schools in Freetown, Sierra Leone. I loved that the first question from the U.S. school was about whether the Sierra Leonean grade levels matched its in terms of student ages. The U.S. teacher included a full list of grade levels and relative ages for her school in that first email, which kept them from having to go back and forth several times to get a full picture. As soon as her partner replied with his list of ages and grade levels, which he did in his first reply, they were on the same page. The first contact is also a good time to talk about time zones and determine best meeting times. It may seem silly to bring up such details before agreeing on a project, but they are consequential in a global partnership.

PERSPECTIVES ON INTERCULTURAL COMMUNICATION: HOLLY EMERT

Lead, Professional Programs, Global Education and Training Programs Department, Institute of International Education

I work with multiple countries and multiple sponsors on a daily basis, primarily through email. We all are busy, we all have a thousand things we're doing every day, but you have to consider the appropriate communication style. A simple example is that every once in a while, my colleagues from the United States will say, "Oh, I see you put *PhD* in the signature line," and part of me thinks, "Yes, I worked very hard for that." But another reason—and I like to say this to people on the team—is that I'm thinking about how in Asia, status is important.

We work with partners in Singapore, India, Vietnam, and Taiwan, to name a few, and that doctorate ascribes me a status. It lets them know I'm in a position for a reason; I have the qualifications. And it also helps others understand the hierarchy of things. So there's an element of culture in putting that degree there. If I'm writing to a colleague in Washington, DC, it's signed *Holly*, not *Dr. Emert*. Culture plays a key role when you're thinking about global connections.

Source: Adapted from H. Emert, personal communication, May 20, 2016.

Talk About Project Ideas With an Open Mind

Many inexperienced teachers make the mistake of starting their first partnership conversation with too much information about their own goals and courses.

Complete the less-curricular elements of the Partnership Readiness worksheet (see figure 2.1, page 45) before meeting, but plan to complete the curricular elements together. Keeping an open mind is most important. If you send your syllabus or other significant documentation in the first email exchange, for example, this can have two negative effects: (1) it will suggest that your priorities matter most, and (2) it will create significant reading homework for your partner teacher, who may not share your native language or be able to make sense of your plans. Teachers who start their communication this way rarely hear back from their partner teachers. Keep in mind that you want to build a partnership that's valuable for both teachers—that helps you both reach concrete educational goals that match the demands placed on you. It is useful to start the conversation with ideas, but with a tone of flexibility and curiosity about your partner's needs as well. In other words, try to come to the table with an empty plate, so that you can fill the plate together with your partner.

Try to come to the table with an empty plate, so that you can fill the plate together with your partner.

Then, ask questions. Ask a lot of questions about your partner's classroom, about his or her subject areas, about his or her goals for global collaboration. Listen for connections to your own curriculum. Talk about the connections you hear and the ideas that come from them. After your potential partner teacher shares his or her ideas, it's appropriate to share your educational goals and hopes, particularly as you see them connecting to your partner's interests.

Thought leader Tim Kubik, principal consultant at Kubik Perspectives, also stresses the importance of beginning with questions as you build a global partnership:

> I would like to know from [a partner] teacher what they think they can get out of a conversation with kids from Northern Colorado. What is it that you hope to understand? And I would like to begin to question what cultural assumptions are being made by both groups of teachers. I'm with a group of teachers from Colorado, and they're a group of teachers from Sierra Leone. And the Sierra Leoneans are saying, "We want to learn a lot more about entrepreneurship and economic growth and that kind of stuff, because we think that's important." Well that's a pretty interesting cultural assumption about what America is, right? They're making a cultural assumption about me and my students—that we all get business—that I want to start unpacking. And I'm probably making cultural assumptions about them, like, "We want to understand how you coped with the Ebola outbreak," which was a very real issue in Sierra Leone and Liberia. And there's something interesting to be learned

there, but that's also making a cultural assumption that the only thing interesting that's happening in West Africa is an exotic disease. (T. Kubik, personal communication, May 21, 2016)

As you ask questions and unpack the answers together, remember that you don't have to figure out the whole project on the first call; connect with your partner as a person first. Trying to do too much can easily end up causing major delays, as many teachers put off the first opportunity for student contact until the whole curriculum is developed. Instead, try to share initial ideas in the first call. Decide on the first steps both classrooms can take, even if it's as simple as having students write to introduce themselves and deciding on a platform for sharing the work. End every call by scheduling the next one, as finding common meeting opportunities across time zones can cause the most significant communication delays. Such scheduling is better done live.

End every call by scheduling the next one.

The collaborative portions of the Partnership Readiness worksheet in figure 2.1 (page 45) are best filled out during your next couple of conversations with your partner. Start by identifying the topic or theme you want to explore together, making sure it will fulfill the academic demands you both face. Figure out the collaboration's design structure (such as classroom-to-classroom exchange, or co-creation), the best technologies to use, the goals, and the possible end products students might create. Remember to use the *month names*, not seasons, when you talk about timing, and create as much timing flexibility as you can. Talk to your students, too; in the best student-centered global learning, students are involved in setting many of their own global learning goals and may even decide on collaborative products together with their partner classroom.

Communicate Consistently and Then Step Aside

The most important quality of a good partner is his or her willingness to communicate consistently and often; take your time to find the technology that makes communication quick and easy for both of you. Try to be patient and responsive even if you can only let your partner know that you need more time to work on a given issue or request, and always try to reply to his or her communication within forty-eight hours to show you still care. Make sure your partner knows when you go on vacation. Again, always set your next appointment at the end of every call. Copy everyone even marginally involved in the project when you send emails, so everyone with a vested interest knows where you are in the process and can support you. Establishing these norms early in a partnership will make communication much smoother—and your collaborations more successful—in the long run. The more complex the partnership project, the better the communication between partner teachers has to be.

Teachers can easily manage all communication, but in the long run this approach removes key opportunities for students to engage as leaders and learners. Once things are moving along with your partner teacher, encourage student voice and leadership as much as possible. Students' global competencies only develop when adults create the right conditions—building initial relationships and identifying curricular focus—and then get out of the way and allow students to take the lead.

Once things are moving along with your partner teacher, encourage student voice and leadership as much as possible.

For example, middle and high school students might be involved in setting the agenda for interactions, choosing the questions for collaborative discussions, handling interpretation of a world language that is used, and running live calls. In schools with a focus on student-led technology initiatives, students are often involved in choosing and managing logistics and technology choices as well. Even at the earlier grade levels, putting students in charge of communication creates less work for teachers and more direct engagement for students. Elementary students can choose the discussion focus, create discussion questions, and ask those questions during the live call. While incorporating student-led conversations can lead any age group into tricky ground that requires the teacher's intervention, this is still a better approach than having teacher-controlled interactions that quickly become passive learning experiences for students.

Students' first videoconference experiences may feel awkward and unnatural, particularly when the partnership is in its infancy. Creating the conditions for more intimacy includes preparing students for the videoconference. This might include brainstorming questions in advance to increase confidence, or letting students get used to being on camera before connecting with your partners. That said, preparing too much in advance can also create challenges; if students are reading their questions from a scripted list, they may not really hear the answers or interact in an authentic, conversational way. Encourage students to have questions in hand but to use them only when they feel a new subject is necessary, always keeping back-and-forth dialogue as their first goal. Creating a culture of comfort and informality helps students take more risks during live events—and that includes sharing your own potential discomfort with the camera and working with students to strategize ways you might all become more comfortable during live calls.

Even at the earlier grade levels, putting students in charge of communication creates less work for teachers and more direct engagement for students.

Choose the Right Communication Platforms

You can choose from a plethora of technological tools, platforms, and online communities for your global partnership. Most are free or low cost for education, or are already integrated into the hardware found in many schools. Tolisano's (2014) concept of *global fluency* includes choosing the right "tools for specific tasks, such as videoconferencing, wikis, backchannels, and synchronous and asynchronous communication without feeling paralyzed when unforeseen situations arise" (p. 49). Less tech-savvy educators find their way through global partnerships by their willingness to be proactive, investigative learners. You may have to put significant effort into practicing with new technologies, but it can be a great opportunity to model adult learning and let your students lead the way.

Most classroom partnerships use a combination of synchronous and asynchronous technologies. As explored in chapter 2 (page 31), the extent to which you can realistically manage live connections will depend on the time zones you're working with. Understanding your partner teacher's technological capacity goes a long way to making the most equitable choices. (See chapter 7, page 129, for more about this topic.) In several countries, governments block particular tools, such as Skype and Facebook, and in other places, economics and infrastructure are barriers to equitable access. As you explore technologies, remember that it is more important to meet your partner where he or she is. Focusing on people more than tools will help you build a meaningful experience, and that can happen even if you only ever use the telephone or traditional (snail) mail. As Tavangar and Mladic-Morales (2014) point out, "It's ultimately about meaningful connections, not amassing apps and web links" (p. 113).

Focusing on people more than tools will help you build a meaningful experience.

Assuming that you will be using 21st century technologies in your partnership, look for ways to blend synchronous and asynchronous experiences. Most globally connected educators use a combination of tools such as Skype, Twitter, Google Apps, and wikis (a collaboratively contributed and edited information repository) to support a combination of live and asynchronous interactions, and WhatsApp makes messaging accessible to teachers in regions with expensive cell-based texting. Asynchronous tools allow students to communicate and engage at any time of day or evening, helping extend the learning and connections beyond the walls of the school building. Wikis (https://en.wikipedia.org/wiki/Wiki) are particularly useful for tracking students' participation across the history of a collaborative document. Asynchronous artifacts like vlogs can allow students to "meet" each other in a deeply humanizing way.

Peppering in a few live experiences may increase students' engagement and excitement, but trying to set up too many synchronous experiences may lower your enthusiasm for global partnerships. They are a lot of work, and there are alternative ways to create deep human connections. For example, in the music exchange I helped facilitate between second graders at the American School Foundation of Monterrey in Mexico and Hawken School in Ohio, second-grade students shared videos in which they taught each other local songs and asked their partners questions. They exchanged six videos over the course of a semester, and although they never had a live experience, the videos created most of the humanizing elements we seek from a synchronous connection.

If you are uncomfortable with technology, remember that testing systems in advance will help alleviate problems on the day of a live event. Another safeguard is to have your school's IT support person present the first time you connect, just in case challenges arise. It's valuable to involve students as technology leaders, depending on their ages; even when students don't know a given technology well, younger people tend to be digital natives who understand new technologies more quickly. Have students teach and support each other—and you—with those new tools, and have them teach your partner classroom as needed (or choose a tool your partner knows better and let his or her students teach yours). Letting students lead the technological work can make for a more meaningful partnership, as it allows the teachers to focus on the partnership content and students to learn and lead using authentic 21st century tools.

The following sections explore several prominent synchronous technologies, as well as ways educators can build meaningful, humanizing connections through asynchronous technologies—or through no technology at all. We will explore communication tools for both partner teachers and students in the partner classrooms. Remember that technology is a rapidly changing industry; what is popular today will be gone tomorrow, and even long-standing technologies evolve with different looks and functionalities. Because of that evolution, using the Technological Needs Assessment worksheet in figure 6.1 (page 118) can help you choose based more on function and compatibility than on a tool's popularity or age. With your partner teacher and educational technology director, identify the tools that meet your partnership's priorities, and be sure firewalls are open as needed to allow those technologies to work. Be sure to include your partner teacher in the technological needs assessment conversation, since his or her needs may be different from your own, and remember that business-oriented technologies may also be worth considering, as long as the higher costs are manageable. Finally, embrace what technology specialists call *device-agnostic* programs and platforms, meaning those tools that function on different types of devices. (For example, iMovie is an Apple-only tool; MovieMaker only works on Windows computers. Those are proprietary.) It is unlikely you and your global partner will be using the same operating system or hardware.

With your partner teacher and educational technology director, identify top priorities and specific needs on both sides of the exchange. Note that completing this worksheet without your partner could lead to proprietary or high-broadband choices your partner has limited or no access to.

Teacher Communication

Consideration	Challenges and Specific Needs
Accessibility Will your broadband speed support the tools you want to use? What are the limitations inside the classroom? Will the platforms require lowering firewalls?	
Cost concerns or limitations What is your budget?	
Privacy features and compliance with school policies for Internet safety What can ensure your platform choices address your local requirements for safe teacher Internet use?	
Translation tools needed If your partnership will include multiple languages, what translation tools or supports will you need and when?	
Other considerations What are other specific features you would like from your teacher communication tools?	
Final tools for partner teacher communication	

Figure 6.1: Technological needs assessment worksheet.

Student Communication

Consideration	Challenges and Specific Needs
Privacy features and compliance with school policies for Internet safety What can ensure your platform choices address your local requirements and that you understand any legal limitations on student participation online?	
Accessibility Will your broadband speed support the tools you want to use? What are the limitations inside the classroom? Will the platforms require lowering firewalls?	
Cost concerns or limitations What is your budget?	
Translation tools needed If your partnership will include multiple languages, what sorts of translation tools or supports will you need and when?	
Other tools needed What kinds of interactions do you hope your students can have? Are discussion threads enough, or do you want students to design and take polls or quizzes, share photos or art, work on collaborative documents, or have other kinds of interactions?	
Tracking student participation How important is the ability to track student participation and interaction? How well do the platforms allow access to students' communication?	

continued →

Consideration	Challenges and Specific Needs
Grouping Do you want to create small-group and large-group breakout configurations for student interactions? Do you want subgroups to have their own discussion threads or wikis?	
Ease of student registration Can students easily register and log in?	
Other specific features you would like from your student communication tools Do you want instant messaging or discussion boards?	
Final tools for student communication	

*Visit **go.SolutionTree.com/21stcenturyskills** for a free reproducible version of this figure.*

It's a great idea to find out which platforms your students enjoy using, as their enjoyment is directly related to their engagement. I often had students generate a list of platforms they were interested in trying, and I backfilled with a few of my own favorites at the end of the brainstorm. Then, their homework was to explore those sites, and the next day students would make the case for their favorites and we would decide on the final platform together. If such a process can be done with your partner teacher and their students, all the better; the more voice and buy-in your partners and students have, the more likely the platform will be a good choice—and get lots of student use. Norwegian educator Ann S. Michaelsen (2013) took student voice in technology to its logical conclusion by having her ninth-grade students create a book about connected learning, *Connected Learners: A Step-by-Step Guide to Creating a Global Classroom.*

Michaelsen's students used SkyDrive (https://onedrive.live. com/about/en-us) and OneNote (www.onenote.com) to write about "Quadblogging, iTunes University, Twitter, Skype for Education, gaming for learning, Facebook. . . They also wrote chapters on digital literacy and 21st century skills" (Boss, 2013b). "The book includes stories, advice, and how-to articles designed to help high school teachers and their students shift from classrooms that are isolated and teacher-centered to digitally rich environments where learning is student-driven and constantly connected to the global Internet . . . . Teachers can use the book to set up their own global classroom[s] where learners are connected to the world. Show your students the importance of connecting. Thin the classroom walls and let learning spiral out into the larger world."

Platforms for Synchronous Communication

Synchronous communication occurs in real time, as it would with a telephone call or video chat. While synchronous connections are often a goal, time zones and class schedules can make live connections challenging. The videoconferencing market also changes constantly. The most important qualities of a live global education platform have to do with how well the tool functions in low-speed broadband situations, as live communication is best when students can see and hear their partners clearly. Understanding accents requires an unacknowledged amount of lip reading, for example, so the minute you can't see the person talking, it becomes much harder to understand what's being said. Choppy video can also interrupt sound.

Anything you can do to improve the broadband speed in your own building, and that of your partner teacher, will certainly help. Compare different providers to find the best speed available, and rewire networks and update routers, when necessary, to speed up connectivity. Some schools create a separate network for global video-conferences that exists only for these events. Talk to your partner about his or her limitations, too, even if your partner has relatively good Internet. In many cities with decent broadband and cellular data service, like Cairo or Shanghai, the Internet is barely functional at certain hours because of heavy use. In rural Costa Rica and Sierra Leone, heavy rains often limit Internet speed—and it's rainy season at least half the year in tropical zones. Conversations about accessibility—and potential local partners who could help improve the odds of a good connection—should happen before going live with students. For example, many global partnerships rely on stronger connections and higher-quality equipment at local universities or business offices that utilize videoconferencing and are willing to be partners for live events. In several cases, like the Education Fast Forward (www.effdebate.org) youth collaborations, videoconference companies like Polycom (www.polycom.com) and Cisco (www.cisco.com/c/en/us/index.html) have allowed partner organizations and school groups to use higher-quality videoconferencing suites in their offices around the world.

The following sections discuss these synchronous communication software and programs: Skype; Google Hangouts; Blackboard Collaborate; and WebEx, RealPresence, GoTo-Meeting, and Zoom.

Working with an internationally popular technology is often the easiest choice.

Skype

Given that coaching your partner teacher on the other side of the planet to use a new technology can get a little complicated, working with an internationally popular technology like Skype (www.skype.com/en) is often the easiest choice because it remains the most dominant synchronous option outside of North America. The technology is free when connecting two sites with audio and video; with a paid subscription, the host can connect up to five video feeds, allowing connection offsite interpreters or additional classrooms. Skype has challenges with the broadband speed required for good video, however, and even audio can be interrupted by low-broadband connections, so be prepared to turn off video if sound is poor.

Google Hangouts

Many educators swear by Google Hangouts (https://hangouts.google.com) as an easy tool for connecting multiple sites with lower-broadband connectivity. Entry into a hangout can appear differently on different computers, depending on the participant's browser and connectivity, and anyone with multiple Google accounts may struggle to get into live calls through the right account. However, if the more tech-savvy teacher is using Google Apps for Education (https://google.com/edu), you might as well try Google Hangouts for a videoconference. Google Hangouts has far fewer challenges with broadband requirements and poor video, but can be trickier to enter, as it's not always clear to participants how to do so; be sure to test and practice entry at least twenty-four hours before any live event with students. Like Skype, Google Hangouts has the capacity for a discussion thread, and multiple audio and video connections at once.

Blackboard Collaborate

I taught online courses for many years on Blackboard Collaborate (http://bit .ly/1NFZDGM), formerly Elluminate, and I loved it. For group interactions from a wide array of locations, it's a great platform with an interactive whiteboard that allows sharing slides and computer screens—up to five live video screens at a time— and a running discussion board. The video resolution is based on a user's broadband quality, and this robust educational platform includes tools like document sharing, breakout rooms, and polls. While only a few people can be live on video at a time, Blackboard Collaborate allows for hundreds of audiovisual participants, depending on the size of the classroom it's purchased for. (Pricing depends on the number of participants and features required, and Blackboard Collaborate is among the more expensive options in education.)

Blackboard Collaborate is designed for connecting multiple sites simultaneously and does not emphasize large video windows the way a traditional videoconference tends to, so it may be less ideal for a two-site conversation (although an advanced user can enlarge the video screens). On the other hand, integrating an interactive whiteboard with the ability to upload slides is ideal for sessions when students are presenting for each other, and the smaller breakout room configurations work well for large programs like the #Decarbonize project described in chapter 3 (page 49). The Global Education Conference network consistently employs Blackboard Collaborate for GlobalEdCon and other events, so you can experience the tool by participating in one of its live events. While Blackboard Collaborate is one of the more expensive tools available for educational videoconferencing, it comes closer to being a true educational tool than any other synchronous platform I've encountered.

> *Integrating an interactive whiteboard and the ability to upload slides is ideal for sessions when students are presenting for each other.*

WebEx, RealPresence, GoToMeeting, and Zoom

The business world continues to lead in live videoconferencing technologies, and tools designed for business can work beautifully in an educational setting—although the price point isn't always accessible for schools. If you use a paid technology, be sure that the school with more resources pays for the host account. Web-based software like Cisco WebEx (www.webex.com) and Polycom RealPresence (http://bit.ly/2pEQdAZ) provide all the needed tools and can run from any laptop with a webcam. GoToMeeting (https://gotomeeting.com) and Zoom (https://zoom.us) are similar in that they work from any laptop and the host shoulders all costs. While these platforms don't integrate all the same educational tools as Blackboard Collaborate, they do include many useful functions, such as screen sharing, slide sharing, document sharing, multiple video screens, and discussion threads.

Platforms for Asynchronous Communication

Asynchronous communication does not occur in real time. Instead, communication takes place by messages or posts that are seen by partners when they go online. More asynchronous platforms are emerging as connected learning gains popularity, and these platforms vary in design and approach. If you prefer to monitor all student engagement, go for a tool that allows you to do so; if you prefer to allow students more autonomy, try others. Some teachers prefer to group students into small teams online, while others use a central discussion wall where all students can contribute their ideas in one space, much like a private group does on Facebook. Choose a platform that your partner teacher knows how to use and can access easily. Sometimes, the decision comes down to school culture and norms. If you teach in a school using Google tools in other contexts, Google Classroom may be your easiest solution. But if your partner teacher needs to learn Google Classroom and his or her students don't use Gmail (https://google.com/gmail/about), going that route may hurt your partner's ability to facilitate contributions from his or her end.

It's worth emphasizing the importance of *focused* discussion in asynchronous collaborations. Discussion threads left wide open for students to start conversations rarely work well, except with older students who have experience interacting with their global counterparts. For most students, an open, unfocused thread is as scary as it gets and will probably only lead to silly, superficial interactions (like the thirteen consecutive "Hey . . ." posts I encountered between two middle school classes who hadn't been given any direction). Instead, give students something specific to explore together to focus the dialogue—even two or three prompts or questions a week will help. In an ideal scenario, discussion prompts should come from the students themselves, with teachers reframing the questions only slightly to make curricular connections. Having students from both sides generate and post open-ended discussion questions will lead to deeper engagement, dialogue, and connectedness.

The following sections explore the asynchronous communication methods TakingITGlobal, Edmodo, and Google Apps for Education, and various social media applications.

TakingITGlobal

A nonprofit based in Toronto, the student-focused end of TakingITGlobal (http://tigweb.org) led early movements of social media with a focus on social media for social good, and was specifically designed to unite youth to solve global challenges. Under the slogan of "Inspire, Inform, Involve," the platforms of TakingITGlobal connect well over five hundred thousand youth globally for the exploration of global issues through writing, the arts, and digital media (TIG, 2016). With user-driven resources and content in thirteen main languages (Arabic, Chinese, Dutch, English, French, Italian, Portuguese, Romanian, Russian, Spanish, Swahili, Swedish, and Turkish), the site is carefully designed to be safe for students and accessible regardless of broadband quality. This means that the site is carefully protected from malicious hackers, contains no advertising, and even keeps students from sharing personal information with each other, like physical addresses, phone numbers, or even email addresses. (Students can communicate only through the site, which has filters to keep language appropriate.)

TIG's parallel site for teachers, TakingITGlobal for Educators (TIGed; www.tigweb.org/tiged), is designed for classroom use more than social networking, with a focus on supporting teachers' needs and creating private spaces for more focused partnerships. While registration can be a bit challenging, depending on how the virtual classroom is set up, TIGed's virtual classrooms feature file upload and folder management, discussion threads, and spaces for sharing project documents and bookmarking online resources. The virtual classrooms are private, user-friendly spaces for global collaboration that allow easy student participation monitoring. You can customize features to suit your needs and students' needs, including low-broadband video chatting, instant messaging, map features, and several integrated Google tools. Students can submit and answer questions in multiple discussion threads, use the student writing wiki to share ideas with their partners, and use the gallery to share project videos, photos, and other digital work.

PERSPECTIVES ON FOUNDING TAKINGITGLOBAL: JENNIFER CORRIERO
Cofounder and Executive Director, TakingITGlobal

My motivation started as a high school student who grew up in a time when advertisements from companies promoted the possibility of global connectivity, though I did not feel like I was part of it. In founding TakingITGlobal, it was our hope to create a global community that would foster intercultural exchanges. As my professional knowledge and experience have grown, I see that with all of the technology access that exists, there remain major gaps in classrooms. Building global partnerships is still not a common practice, as educators face challenges with curriculum integration or sufficient technology access in their classrooms. As the parent of a young child, I feel a growing sense of urgency in building global partnerships. The nature of the global challenges that are pervasive in our world today requires widespread expertise in global collaboration skills. It begins in classrooms and extends into workplaces, across sectors and boundaries.

Our understanding of the world is rooted in our life experiences and personal connections with people. When we have opportunities to expand our horizons beyond our typical daily surroundings, we become more aware and inspired in our thinking and daily actions. Direct global partnerships are about providing students with access to perspectives that will expand their curiosity and empathy . . . . Global partnerships are beautiful illustrations of experience-based learning that allow students to guide their inquiry and exchange with others to make a difference in the world.

Source: J. Corriero, personal communication, February 5, 2016.

Edmodo

Designed to look, feel, and function much like a social-networking site, Edmodo (https://edmodo.com) offers safe, well-designed private spaces for managing student work and online dialogue, as well as student engagement with partner classrooms. While it is a simpler and less robust tool than some, Edmodo's user-friendly interface, easy registration process, and broad use by teachers around the world makes it an important option to consider. Edmodo does not have an intentional global orientation, nor does it provide spaces for broader community conversations the way TakingITGlobal does, but inside each virtual classroom are a plethora of education tools. Edmodo uses a central wall for community posts all students and teachers can see, and teachers can create subgroups for small-group discussions. Students can post and respond to questions, turn in assignments, and take quizzes inside this virtual space. Teachers have easy file upload and folder management, document sharing, and the ability to post texts, photos, links, videos, quizzes, polls, event announcements (such as live chats or videoconferences), and documents.

G Suite for Education

Google may dominate your platform conversations simply because it is more easily integrated in schools already using Google. With G Suite for Education, you can create private spaces with controlled membership, including a central wall for discussions, events announcements, and photograph postings. This tool may be more flexible and robust than other options because of the articulation between Google's various apps for education. Because many schools and districts give students Google-based email accounts, this also simplifies the registration process.

The Google Classroom (https://classroom.google.com) feature offers a private space for managing assignments, data, and other elements of student work. Though it is more common for a single teacher to use it for his or her own classroom, you can adapt it for global partnerships in which more than one teacher and student group connect. That said, it is important to ensure that your partner teacher's school is also using G Suite for Education; otherwise, there may be significant obstacles or expenses for your partner. It is also important to note that the Chinese government blocks Google entirely; while Google restricts access to some of its tools in certain countries or regions, such as Crimea, Cuba, Iran, North Korea, Sudan, and Syria.

Social Media Applications

Many young people worldwide already use global education tools in day-to-day communication, and most are more popular than email for their affordability and ease of access from mobile devices in regions where computers with Internet are scarce. As noted earlier in this chapter, WhatsApp and WeChat can go a long way to improving communication between partner teachers because they are relatively inexpensive and easy to use from any mobile device, and their use is incredibly broad around the world. Students can also use other social media applications like Facebook, Instagram (https://instagram.com), Snapchat (https://snapchat.com), and Twitter to share ideas and products during a project.

Using such tools in the classroom can help make the partnership more relevant, particularly if you work with teenagers who are already using these tools in their daily lives. Just be sure you know in advance whether the firewalls in your school building will keep students from accessing these forums during class, as you can easily waste class time if you assume students will have full access to a forum your school is actively blocking. Remember, too, that social media trends change quickly, so ask your students before assuming a site is relevant to them.

A Few Concluding Thoughts

A plethora of communication and social media technologies offer educational tools that allow for the kinds of communication global partnerships most rely on. Some are free, some are educationally focused, and others cost and are business based. Some allow synchronous events, and others focus on asynchronous communication. Be mindful of your partner teacher's facilities and what your mutual goals are when choosing technology. Consult your on-site IT staff, and make sure you're working within the school's policy and broadband limits. And finally, keep in mind that while 21st century technologies have improved the speed of global exchanges and made live interaction significantly easier, there are 20th century tools such as traditional mail at your disposal if you want to partner with schools that aren't equipped for virtual connection. Remember the story of Maria Conte, in chapter 3 (page 49), whose students received the beautifully hand-sewn package from Pakistan, and of Maile Black's mention in chapter 4 (page 73) of handwritten stories in tiny script. Remember what it felt like, during your own childhood, to hold a handwritten letter and see the penmanship and personalized drawings. The abundance of technology in use means that students are missing out on these more visceral and humanizing experiences, and research is even suggesting that students need less screen time and more time without technology at home and school (Williams, 2017). Though it may take longer to make a partnership work on the back of traditional snail mail, the benefits may sometimes outweigh the disadvantages.

The abundance of technology in use means that students are missing out on these more visceral and humanizing experiences.

CHAPTER 7

AVOIDING EQUITY PITFALLS

If you have come here to help me, you are wasting your time. If you have come because your liberation is bound up with mine, then let us work together.

—Lilla Watson

The best global partnerships are built on a foundation of equity and shared experience—a recognition of our common humanity. They are established on socially responsible and culturally responsive foundations that see every learner through an asset lens. As Lilla Watson (2016) suggests, we can only do this work together well if we recognize that our lives are interconnected. Despite good intentions, global educators encounter pitfalls when setting up an equitable relationship; they can address most of them by being more attuned to their partners.

Partnerships built on the assumption that one group has the capacity to help or even *save* the other rarely work, and they tend to ingrain the kind of inequitable thinking that global education should work to undo. The goal of an equitable partnership is to *walk together*, as the World Leadership School (n.d.) puts it, to recognize that the advantages of one group are often tied to the disadvantages of another, and to work together toward a more equitable world. Similarly, global health expert Paul Farmer (2011) describes *accompaniment* as the ideal model for global collaboration and development. It is only when we *accompany* others that we really understand their experiences.

Dana Mortenson, cofounder and executive director of World Savvy (www .worldsavvy.org), points out that global competency develops mostly through our encounters with others and our willingness to engage and be challenged by them, without assuming that we have all the answers on one side or the other (personal communication, October 28, 2016). This humility as learners, tied to the concept of learning *with* and *from* others, is vital to building an equitable and powerful global partnership. Try to approach your partnership with curiosity more than judgment, and with questions more than assumptions, so your students become humble global citizens who look for solutions in concert with a broader community.

As a historian, Tim Kubik sees how consistently humans repeat patterns of dominance and superiority all over the planet, and he challenges educators to work against those tides.

PERSPECTIVES ON REVERSING THE DIALECTIC: TIM KUBICK
Principal Consultant, Kubik Perspectives

I'm concerned that all too often, the developed side of the divide is setting the agenda in terms of what standards need to be accomplished, and is using the "global other" in a way that reduces them to exactly that, a global other. Like, "We need this perspective in order to meet this standard. I don't really care who I get, if they're Nigerian, Indian, Indonesian, Bolivian. It doesn't really matter, as long as I've got some other global perspective that I'm bringing in so I can 'recognize perspectives,' to use Center for Global Education at Asia Society's term." And that's great, to recognize perspectives. But when you're not recognizing that the other's perspective might be that they have standards that they're trying to accomplish, too, or that they have educational outcomes that their school system is demanding, you're not doing a damn bit of recognizing perspectives. Can we build a curriculum unit where Amazonian kids help North American kids figure out how to eat more healthfully? Could we reverse the dialectic, and say it's not about us helping others around the world but, What can we learn?

Source: T. Kubik, personal communication, May 21, 2016.

Not only do these pitfalls have the potential to keep your partnership from succeeding, but they can also reinforce inequitable paradigms that hurt global relationships and our collective future.

This chapter explores several of the most common global partnership pitfalls we need to address in order to "reverse the dialectic," as Kubik puts it, and make mutual benefit and true co-learning our central goals: exoticizing your partner; misperceiving your partner's academic capacity; focusing solely on helping; solving problems *for* your partner rather than *with* them; assuming your partner should have the same technology you have; and having conflicting priorities. Not only do these pitfalls have the potential to keep your partnership from succeeding, but they can also reinforce inequitable paradigms that hurt global relationships and our collective future. Combating the kind of postcolonial thinking that perpetuates such dynamics requires a different sort of global education and a more authentic sense of what it means to envision students collaborating globally. We need global citizens who build their sense of the world on real relationships and conversations, not on assumptions founded in supposed cultural deficits.

Avoid Exoticizing Partners

Even the best global educators can fall into the trap of *exoticism*, which means to view others as strictly different and alluring (Kelly, 1997). For example, years ago a well-meaning colleague complained to me after he'd been partnered with a teacher in Germany. He told me that Germany was too similar to the United States to lead to anything interesting, and that he was really hoping for a rural community in an African nation. While I could understand his interest in a more different partner, his assumption that Germany is just like the United States negated all of the differences that do exist between Germany and the United States, and suggested that German culture and history have nothing to teach U.S. students and teachers. His disappointment also underscored his belief that something more exotic would be more interesting for his students, a mindset that can easily turn potential partners into fascinating objects for students to examine as *other*, rather than as whole human beings. In truth, any two classrooms can learn from and with each other, even if they're blocks apart in the same city, and learning experiences are most powerful when students can explore both similarities and differences.

Exoticizing others, no matter how positively, diminishes their humanity; it can even suggest a sort of fetishism, which turns the "other" into a showpiece rather than a human. These complexities, no matter how unintended, can have the consequence of weaving exoticism into our students' worldviews, suggesting that one group explores while the other is explored or, in Kubik's (2012) words, is "included in global education primarily as an object of study, rather than as those with their own voices, and their own needs." As Kubik (2012) points out, this mindset is part of what has led humans to engage the world with an "explore and dominate" mentality that has done far more harm than good, historically speaking.

Be aware of the warning signs. Are you more interested in learning *about* your partner than in learning *with* and *from* your partner? Do you feel the urge to change partners every year or semester to mix it up, rather than dig deep with just one partner? Do you find yourself uninterested in cultures similar to your own in terms of race, socioeconomic status, and language? Ultimately, if the location is more exciting than your partner, this may be a sign that you're exoticizing your partner.

Avoid Misperceiving Academic Capacity

The often-unvoiced assumptions or biases we have about our potential partner's capacity can be incredibly destructive. In much of the developed world, we are raised to assume a sort of academic and intellectual superiority, which has created largely unconscious paradigms of educational dominance such as those explored in Carol Black's excellent film *Schooling the World* (Black, Grossan, Hurst, & Marlens, 2010). This is another form of *othering*. Cosima Rughiniș (2007) defines *oppressive othering* as when "a social group tries to obtain or to keep a privileged social position by defining another group as morally or intellectually inferior" (as cited in *About Discrimination and Exoticization*, n.d.). Whether it is clear in the consciousness of dominant nations or not, the most-developed nations have done exactly this to the rest of the world for centuries. According to Paulo Freire's (2000) work, education either functions as a tool for maintaining that social dominance or works to undo it.

Whether well-meaning educators intend this result or not, developing a global partnership often means overcoming unconscious biases. It can mean breaking down ideas about intellect and intelligence—largely Western concepts of what it means to be smart, educated, or learned—so that we can foster students' appreciation of other kinds of intelligence, knowledge, and skill, and learn to understand how a given educational system has grown out of a community's history without necessarily judging its quality based on an outsider's cultural lens. Some countries follow North American or European norms in terms of academic sequencing and age groupings, and some don't. Further, many children around the world are unable to consistently attend school, whether because of resources, location, or familial needs, so classrooms in many communities include a wide age range. It's not uncommon in many communities, for example, to see students graduating from high school at age twenty-one or older. Conflict and crisis can also impact the relative age of students at a given grade level. If you choose to partner with such communities, it's important to be flexible about the age and relative student preparation in your partner classroom—ideally without assuming the worst.

> *Whether well-meaning educators intend this result or not, developing a global partnership often means overcoming unconscious biases.*

In reality, lack of parity in age or academic preparation can be seen as opportunities for students to teach and coach each other, or to share local knowledge more than book knowledge. Many communities think differently about education, valuing oral traditions, fireside conversations, and ancestral knowledge more than written traditions or new technologies. Indigenous thought, for example, has long been devalued by Western systems of knowledge and education, yet indigenous peoples likely hold the keys to a more sustainable future on the planet. Rather than seeing these communities as less advanced, acknowledge that they offer ways of living and thinking that most developed nations could benefit from understanding. In the intersection between exoticizing and underestimating, there is valuing a partner simply for his or her humanity.

Watch for the warning signs for this pitfall, which are easy to notice. Do you find yourself worried about your partner classroom's ability to "keep up" or to match the rigor of your own classroom? Do you find yourself assuming your partner's students will be levels below yours in academic achievement? Let yourself be surprised, too, like the Canadian mathematics teacher I partnered, who assumed his partner classroom in rural Kenya would be at a lower academic level, only to discover that his partner's students were two years ahead of his own. These aren't moments in which to be embarrassed; they are moments for recognizing unconscious bias and improving how you engage with your partner.

Avoid Focusing Solely on Helping

The most dangerous pitfall that can significantly impede equitable relationships between classrooms is focusing too much on helping the partner classroom. *Helping* includes raising money or thinking you can improve its educational system, make them better teachers or students, or solve the partner's problems for it. While few global educators begin the work intending to take this route, and while some philanthropy can be a good thing, creating an inequitable relationship in which one community lifts up the other suggests that the latter doesn't already have the knowledge and skill to solve its own challenges.

The most dangerous pitfall that can significantly impede equitable relationships between classrooms is focusing too much on helping the partner classroom.

The warning signs are easy to see. Are you and your students focusing most of your time on what your partner *lacks*, rather than what it *offers*? Does your partnership feel like an opportunity for community service more than mutual collaboration and benefit? Do you find yourself assuming the final product will include a fund-raiser? Although this thinking usually comes from the best of intentions, it's a sign that you view your partner with a deficit mindset.

Avoiding all philanthropy isn't necessary, particularly if students see and want to respond to an authentic need, but ensure that you start your partnership with the assumption that your partner is capable of solving its own challenges with or without your support. Reframe the conversation for students and help them see themselves as *partners in change* rather than the *singular solution*. Teach students to begin by asking questions rather than assuming they have all the answers.

Freire (2000) emphasizes the importance of *true generosity* as compared to what he calls *false charity*, which just creates patterns and systems where those with less have to beg from those with more: "True generosity lies in striving so that these hands—whether of individuals or entire peoples—need be extended less and less in supplication, so that more and more they become human hands which work and, working, transform the world" (p. 27). This is a useful distinction for students to understand, and teaching them to choose true generosity over false charity can convert a pitfall into a learning opportunity. If philanthropy occurs within the context of what you're trying to accomplish with the partner classroom, or within the context of supporting a community that's addressing its own challenges, then it's not necessarily a bad thing. But it's important that students see themselves on equal footing with their partners, as walking alongside them rather than lifting them up.

In many cases, what an outsider sees as a problem, the community may not perceive as a challenge—or the community may already be working toward a culturally appropriate way of addressing it. This is why it's so important to teach young global citizens to ask questions rather than make assumptions. A powerful example of misguided philanthropy occurred in several small villages I visited in 1995, along the edges of Lake Atitlan in Guatemala. According to the locals I met there, a nongovernmental global development organization had decided that women in the region needed washing machines when they saw the women washing clothes in the lake, bent over and scrubbing on the rocks. The resulting project provided washing machines for every household, but it also plunged the women of these communities into severe depression because it completely removed the social element of their work, leaving them isolated inside their homes. The misperception that they even *needed* or *wanted* the machines began as an outsiders' assumption that what the developed world considers progress always makes life better, everywhere. When I returned to the region in 2015, I discovered that one of those villages now had very popular washing stations along the shoreline, simple wooden constructions that allowed the women to gather and wash under roofs and stand straight; according to the locals I spoke with, this was what happened when an NGO asked what the women *wanted*, rather than assuming that outside solutions were the best answer.

Avoid Solving *for* More Than *With*

Like other common pitfalls, this one stems from making negative assumptions about partners, however unintentionally, when it comes to problem solving. While solutions-oriented pedagogies are useful, be thoughtful when building solutions-oriented projects with schools in a different socioeconomic context. It is easy to fall into this trap, and the warning signs can be subtle, especially if action and solution building are key elements of your approach. Are your students trying to fix a problem they don't understand the same way their partners do? Are your students more interested in their own solutions than the opinions and ideas of their partners? It's not that students should never try to solve problems outside of their own neighborhoods, but that doing so without consistent partner input—and with no sense of local relevance—can easily lead to a savior mentality that's not the goal of global education.

Try to avoid projects where one side solves the other side's challenges—unless the design includes both sides offering solutions for the other's challenges. In other words, a mutual recognition of the need for more minds to solve a problem is great, but if students come away thinking they've saved their partners unilaterally or completely solved another community's challenges, you went in the wrong direction.

Try to avoid projects where one side solves the other side's challenges—unless the design includes both sides offering solutions for the other's challenges.

Instead, consider having teams solve their own problems using what they learn from their partners. Kubik offers the following advice for teachers:

> I think the really important question for students is, "How can I change my local situation with what I'm learning?" . . . That's my biggest frustration when I'm working with schools; they see global education as a kind of community service project. It makes us feel really good about ourselves as human beings, but it's really disempowering to the people who are the subjects of that learning experience. (T. Kubik, personal communication, May 21, 2016)

Some of the best solutions-oriented projects include students working simultaneously to solve a problem common to both communities. As in the example from Global Partners Junior in chapter 3 (page 49) and Arnetta Koger's partnership in chapter 4 (page 73), students collaborate around idea generation, critique, revision, and final products exhibition, but they work to understand and solve a challenge in their own communities, ideally a problem they have in common.

If you want to explore deeper social concerns and really want your students working on another community's challenges, just make sure that your students ground all of their work in the opinions of people inside that other community. The orientation should be toward collaborative change making, not one group solving for the other without its involvement.

Avoid Assuming Partners Can—or Should—Have the Same Technologies

While global education has advanced significantly as technology has become accessible in more parts of the world, it is dangerous to assume that your partners will have the same technology you do—or that they even *should* be set up to mirror your classroom. It's important to meet your partner where he or she is, technologically speaking. While Internet and computer access are increasing in much of the developing world, the truth is that the majority of schools in poorer nations are only barely equipped for the kinds of interactions teachers in other countries might consider common. As a result, it is important to understand the circumstances of your partner classroom, and to adjust the project accordingly.

Many of the technologies explored in chapter 6 (page 107) are low cost or free, and I've even seen teachers run videoconferences from their phones when poor broadband or firewalls got in the way of a fancier approach. Ultimately, global education and partnerships should be the domain of all schools, not just affluent ones; the more we can find inexpensive, creative ways to connect, the more accessible global learning will be for all students, regardless of whether they attend an affluent school.

> *Ultimately, global education and partnerships should be the domain of all schools, not just affluent ones; the more we can find inexpensive, creative ways to connect, the more accessible global learning will be for all students.*

To help developed world teachers understand the potential technological challenges in other parts of the world, and the creativity needed to address them, this anecdote from Sierra Leone can be helpful. I have worked with teachers and students in the rural village of Bumpe, in southeast Sierra Leone since 2010. There, leaders have relied for many years on the generosity of World Vision, a local charity about a mile walk from Bumpe High School. Limited groups of students and teachers can use the Internet connection during certain hours, as long as they pay for generator fuel. (There is only generator-based electricity in the region, and fuel is expensive.) The school's laptops, donated through a TakingITGlobal campaign on global giving, are carried to World Vision, which has the only Internet in the region, to upload and download asynchronous work, a technique referred to as *sneaker-net* across Africa, and for an occasional live Skype call. Laptops have traditionally charged in batches of six on a generator each night and in 2017 the computer lab integrated its first solar panels, donated by Sierra Leone Rising. While this might seem like a tenuous and unsustainable setup—and in many ways it is—Bumpe High School has run many successful videoconferences because of this network of nonprofit partnerships. Students are learning to code, and connectivity is changing the nature of their relationship with the world. Ultimately, it is the creativity of local leaders that has allowed for meaningful learning experiences between Bumpe

High School and schools in Canada, Costa Rica, Tanzania, and the United States, and leaders continue to work on more sustainable options for online engagement in the community.

Global educators from more affluent schools often take it on themselves to equip their partner classrooms to facilitate collaborative projects, and this approach has both pros and cons. On the positive end, equipping your partner classroom can mean engaging your students in purpose-driven fund-raising and can help establish modes of consistent, effective engagement. For example, the World Leadership Foundation project TabLab (http://tablabeducation.org) has opened up new partnership opportunities for several rural schools in Central America and East Africa by equipping them with teacher training, tablets, offline resources, and Internet solutions for blended learning. The resulting connectivity is good for students and teachers well beyond any global partnerships, as students and teachers are building technological literacy skills of benefit in many fields. One of the biggest advantages of creating access and equipment parity is that students from both schools can produce work of similar quality.

On the more negative end, equipping partners may rob students of the opportunity to understand what life is like in a less-connected environment, and to see their partners for who they are, as they actually live. Further, gifting technologies doesn't always help the partner classroom; in fact, many technology companies do regular *tech dumps*, in which out-of-date computers are given to underserved schools and end up becoming a recycling or electrical problem.

The bottom line is that not all partnerships need to be tech based, and students can learn a lot from understanding digital access disparities. I've seen amazing physical exchanges in which students hand-decorate letters about themselves and mail them to each other, and the impact of receiving a physical letter is the kind of formative, visceral experience that can ignite a lifetime of curiosity about the lives of others in the world. Communication takes much longer with traditional mail, but

Not all partnerships need to be tech based, and students can learn a lot from understanding digital access disparities.

building a partnership idea on the assumption of equipment and access parity is likely to waste far more time in the long run, particularly if you are interested in partnering with rural schools. Kubik (2012) puts the dangers in clear terms: "Where the [partnership] focus is solely on the technologies that allow us to interact with others, we risk solving the 'digital divide' only to broaden the cultural divides which separate us."

Watch for the warning signs of becoming too tech focused. Do you often find yourself thinking, "If only my partners had that essential device" or "If only my partners had faster Internet"? Do you feel overwhelmed by the time and effort involved in ensuring technologies work smoothly for both you and your partner? If so, try some problem solving with your students. Ask them how you might develop a robust partnership with your partner classroom *without* 21st century technologies.

Get students involved in navigating 20th century forms of communication in a 21st century context; doing so will help to nuance their sense of the world and how to meet people in the middle.

PERSPECTIVES ON THE TABLAB PROJECT: ROSS WEHNER
Founder, World Leadership Foundation and World Leadership School

TabLab partners with rural schools to transform teaching and learning. The nonprofit initiative grew out of World Leadership School, a U.S.-based organization that works mainly with private, North American K–12 schools to transform learning and create next-generation leaders. TabLab is a two-year program that allows under-resourced rural schools in Tanzania, Costa Rica, and the rural U.S. to leverage technology in order to create student-driven learning. The nonprofit is about dramatically improving education in rural schools and in the process, allowing schools of different social demographics to collaborate with one another.

TabLab's school-to-school partnerships are designed from the point of view of our rural schools, which increases the success rate of the global partnerships. We have found over the years that rural schools have particular curriculum demands (such as the Form IV exams in many African countries), and that the partnerships flourish if we engage the rural teachers to think about how our collaborative projects, enabled by technology, can help them deliver their curriculum in new and powerful ways. We then take the options explored with the rural school and see which are of interest to the North American school. In this way, we have the rural teachers driving the collaboration from the start, and also understanding its value.

A great example is a partnership that happened in 2016 between Appleby College, a private day and boarding school in Ontario, Canada, and rural schools in Costa Rica and Tanzania. Students at all three locations, using iPads and other technology, created some paper-based but also digital media products that really allowed students to explore their worlds, their myths, and their stories in very provocative ways. These partnerships were the result of a careful conversation between all schools about curriculum and common needs.

Source: Adapted from R. Wehner, personal communication, May 6, 2016.

Avoid Conflicting Priorities

Understandably, teachers can get so stuck in curriculum demands that they try to craft a global partnership to meet only their own needs, not the needs of the partner teacher and school. Inequalities of access and resources plague education from one country to another and even one school to another within a given city or region, so be mindful of creating an experience of equal value for both classrooms.

It's easy to get caught up in deadlines, standards, pacing guides, and time constraints, and to start asking a partner to bend to your needs. Doing so can lead to highly inequitable learning experiences for your partner classroom, and can squelch a partner teacher's enthusiasm—because after all, he or she has priorities too. Further, it can give students the message that people from other parts of the world exist to fill our needs, not as whole human beings with lives and needs of their own. Again, this can ingrain a worldview that mirrors historical patterns of dominance and perceived superiority found across the globe, rather than working to undo those patterns.

Sometimes, the best partnership topics are found in curricular elements that are flexible, not static, in terms of timing and approach. If you teach literature and have a book order because of district or building requirements, you may not want to base your partnership on a shared novel because it would require your partners to read it simultaneously. Many subject areas, such as mathematics and world languages, have a tight scope and sequence that can make partnerships challenging to time and align. Flexible elements of the curriculum, once you can identify them, often make the partnership easier and more enjoyable. Instead of focusing on reading a major work of literature together, for example, two literature teachers could partner on popular culture, poetry, or short stories, which they can weave in more flexibly. Similarly, designing a collaborative project that you can pass back and forth can allow partner teachers to address different curricula at different times and still build something together. For example, a physics teacher in one country and an engineering teacher in another might have students design one product they can pass back and forth between the two classes over several months, rather than having students build simultaneously.

Of course, you may find yourself working with a partner teacher who *does* want you to be an expert and take the lead, and being able to navigate such moments is also important. I know teachers who try to stay out of the expert role but find that some partners *want* them to take the lead, to shape the curriculum, and even to teach them new instructional practices. Working toward equitable partnerships and relationships requires being responsive to your partner's needs, whatever they are, even if that means taking an expert role sometimes. Just do everything you can to honor all the knowledge and experience that your partner brings to the table, constantly inviting him or her to share perspectives and make contributions.

Just do everything you can to honor all the knowledge and experience that your partner brings to the table, constantly inviting him or her to share perspectives and make contributions.

Watch for the warning signs of conflicting priorities. Do you find yourself crafting extensive curricular plans before you find a partner or communicate directly with him or her? Do you find yourself wanting to send all your curricular documents and plans to your partner once you find one? Do you have overly strict content pacing guides you need the partnership to cover? Do you find yourself so tied to the timing and content of your idea that it will be hard to compromise? If you answered *yes* to any of these questions, take a step back and think about your partner teacher. Think about his or her interests and curricular needs and consider this question: "Where do your individual priorities intersect, and how might you build a project on common ground, so that the needs of both communities are met?"

You may also find it helpful to use the Striving for Equity in Global Partnerships worksheet in figure 7.1 as you develop your plans. Exploring these questions can help lead you toward more equitable foundations in your partnership.

With colleagues or global partners, use these questions to guide you toward more equitable global relationships. You may also want to explore these questions with students before, during, and after global collaboration experiences.

- How do we ensure that we learn *with* our partners more than *about* them?

- What are the advantages of long-term partnerships over frequently changing partners?

- How do we ensure we aren't exoticizing our partners? How do we ensure we see them for who they are?

- Where do our priorities intersect with those of our partners?

- How might we build a project around the priorities we have in common?

- How might a project meet the needs on both sides of this collaboration?

- How might we build a project around simple technologies—or none at all?

- How might we ensure that all partners are able to create and share high-quality work?

- How might we make it comfortable for all students to engage, regardless of technological infrastructure differences?

- How might we de-emphasize service or helping, and emphasize learning and partnership?

Figure 7.1: Striving for equity in global partnerships worksheet.

- How might we build a project that focuses on actions other than fund-raising?

- What might we do to ensure that students see themselves as collaborative partners in change?

- If academic parity matters, can we be flexible about age parity?

- If age parity matters, can we be flexible about academic parity?

- What might we gain by approaching our partners with an asset mindset rather than a deficit mindset?

- What might we learn from our partners about how they see change in their community? What can we share about the challenges in our community?

- How might we create a project that solves a problem common to both communities?

Visit **go.SolutionTree.com/21stcenturyskills** *for a free reproducible version of this figure.*

A Few Concluding Thoughts

Certain pitfalls are common for global educators. Watch for the warning signs of potentially exoticizing or misperceiving your partner; focusing solely on helping or solving *for* your partner rather than *with*; assuming your partner should have the same technology; and putting your own priorities first. While building your partnership on equitable foundations can feel daunting, remember that the central point is to be open, real, and flexible with your partner. It's about developing your own collaborative skills and being transparent with your students about how you're trying to build equity. In fact, if you cue students to the fact that you need their help to learn *with* more than *about*, and to see your partners as whole human beings, you'll be surprised by how much students can contribute. They may be the first to recognize and point out inequities when they arise, and they may also be the first to recognize and point out moments of success. Don't hide this process from your students; bring them into the conversation and let them navigate what it means to maintain an asset mindset about others, no matter what their circumstances.

CHAPTER 8

EXPLORING SOCIAL JUSTICE CHALLENGES THROUGH PARTNERSHIPS

We have to create. It is the only thing
louder than destruction.

—Andrea Gibson

No matter the topic of your global partnership, differences of opinion will surface; in fact, it's a central *goal* of global partnerships, since only by engaging with people who think differently do we grow our own worldviews. The more controversial the topic, the more inevitable conflict and discord become—but that discord is a learning opportunity, not something to avoid. Even seemly innocuous topics, like girls' education and identity, can incite strong emotional responses from students, parents, and other community stakeholders. Understanding meatier social justice topics has to include understanding the inequities that cause combat, revolution, and discord, and I have found that students of all ages are deeply motivated by the opportunity to engage in social justice work. Rather than avoiding such topics, prepare for discord. If you have internal support and use the strategies in this chapter to help you avoid backlash, more controversial partnerships and social justice topics can be incredibly valuable for you, your students, and your partner classroom. This chapter offers strategies for knowing your community, getting administrative buy-in, gathering perspectives, addressing bias, using human rights frameworks, and being thoughtful about your choices, as well as providing examples to help you navigate and lean into the complexities of partnerships that focus on challenging topics. It also includes the voices of many educators who are eager to share what they have learned from their more controversial global partnerships.

Know Your Community

Obviously, knowing your community and how far you can—or should—explore controversial topics is key to doing this kind of work well. (Even the word *controversial* means very different things in different educational environments and parts of the world.) In each example in this chapter, educators had to gauge their community's readiness, pilot their ideas, and learn from any fallout or pushback. No one lost his or her job, and many (including me) learned a great deal about the importance of thoughtful messaging with and inclusion of parents and broader stakeholders. Interestingly, some of the most controversial work in education for social justice appears to be occurring in faith-based schools. Perhaps because many faiths emphasize social justice and action, teachers feel invited to explore such issues through a faith-based lens in their communities, a powerful contrast to the fear teachers described in the Ontario Institute for Studies in Education's research (Zoric et al., 2004), that we will explore later in this chapter.

PERSPECTIVES ON PARTNERING IN CONFLICT REGIONS: MARK THOMAS

Founder and Former Executive Director, Research Journalism Initiative

When we were working in Palestine, we had a whole group of young people we worked with on a regular basis, and we could legitimately call those young people our *partners.* They were dependable, they were available, they were accessible—linguistically accessible but also in terms of their youth and personality and global lens, their desire to reach out to young people abroad—and they were also predictable. I don't mean that the things they said were expected by our young people in the United States or Canada, or even that we knew what they were going to say, but they were predictable because they shared our vision of what we were trying to accomplish.

There have been lots of awkward exchanges, cringeworthy exchanges where what feels to a young person on one side as depth comes across to the group on the other side as the epitome of shallowness or lack of understanding—or just doesn't translate. So, our ability to rely on real partners, not just young people popping in for a session out of curiosity or novelty, was a really important part of our process. If we talk about partnerships as partnerships with human beings we love and care about and know their middle names, know their families, have dinner with them—those types of partners, that's infinitely better than partnership as the idea of a window that could be opened by one party when it's convenient. What I've just described can be summarized in the word *trust,* and a teacher who's subscribing to a service where he or she flips a switch and suddenly foreign faces appear in front of his or her students has no basis for trust. Why would the teacher?

Source: Adapted from M. Thomas, personal communication, May 8, 2016.

The tricky part is to develop an initial sense of what your community will support, while simultaneously trying to stretch your community to engage in harder dialogue. The Community Readiness and Preparation for Controversial Partnerships worksheet in figure 8.1 offers considerations as you plan your partnership and consider how you might communicate the goals most effectively within your particular community. When completing this worksheet, gather the teacher leaders, any key grade-level or disciplinary team members, and at least one administrator for this conversation.

Gather the lead teachers, any key grade-level or disciplinary team members, and at least one administrator for this conversation. Students can also offer insights as you assess the community's readiness and prepare to roll out potentially controversial partnerships.

Topic or region for partnership:

Grade levels and courses involved:

- What makes this partnership topic or region potentially controversial?

- Which specific stakeholders might resist the inclusion of this topic or partnership, and why?

- What do we know about the root causes of any potential resistance?

- What do we need to know about what might cause resistance, and how might we find out?

- What key messaging choices should we make when rolling out this partnership? How might we best present the project to students, parents, board members, and other stakeholders?

- Who are our key allies at this school for this topic or region? How might they help us with preparation, rollout, and any challenges that arise?

- Who are our potential opponents? How might we turn them into allies?

Figure 8.1: Community readiness and preparation for controversial partnerships worksheet.

continued →

- Does our partnership topic have any areas that will be challenging to effectively balance? Are there any ideological lines we need to stick close to in this partnership, given our school's demographics or mission?

- Which key resources do we need (speakers, films, books, and other educational materials) to ensure that we bridge ideological gaps and provide an appropriate level of perceived balance to the topic?

Visit *go.SolutionTree.com/21stcenturyskills* for a free reproducible version of this figure.

Get Administrative Buy-In

Mark Thomas notes that we never worry about how parents will respond to explorations of mathematics or science, yet the moment classroom conversations turn political, administrators, parents, and other stakeholders express concern (personal communication, May 8, 2016). The reality is that even our youngest students already see at least hints of conflict and controversy around them—and depending on where you live and teach, students may be experiencing social injustices daily. Teaching resilience can help increase healthy adaptation to unexpected events (American Psychological Association, n.d.). Resilience requires acknowledging the VUCA world, and globally competent teachers help students learn to navigate that volatility, uncertainty, complexity, and ambiguity. Thomas recommends that teachers avoid trying to "slip one past the censors," instead stressing that administrative support is paramount to any global partnership with or about a controversial region of the world:

> A teacher interested in doing this needs to have a principal standing by her side who is also convinced that this is a good idea. If a principal is standing behind the curtain ready to pull the plug, he or she probably will. If, on the other hand, a principal feels strongly that this is a good idea, that despite the risks—or even *because* of the risks—it is clearly a good idea, then he or she will be there to protect and support teachers who encounter resistance. I think most teachers feel perfectly comfortable confronting resistance from students and that's okay—but their parents can sometimes be a different issue. An administration willing to stand on the qualifications of educators and say, "Look, we trust them, and this is our curriculum, not an experiment," makes all the difference in how it is implemented, how challenges are overcome—even technical challenges. When a principal and an administration are willing to commit and support something, they throw that support behind the technical and the political resources necessary. (M. Thomas, personal communication, May 8, 2016)

Part of getting administrative buy-in may include finding ways to balance challenging conversations and topics. This can be hard to do, not only because conflict regions often produce a dominant narrative that leaves little room for marginalized voices, but also because many conflicts are in themselves so complex and power based that there is no such thing as true balance. Our schools are similarly complex and power based in many regards, whether we feel it directly as teachers or not, so it is important to consider the dominant narrative in your community before you decide how far to take your partnership. Most teachers who choose to tackle controversial topics do have a personal opinion about the region in question, and that makes it harder to separate self from politics. Just as Jeanne Boland demonstrated global competency by intentionally drawing in speakers and parents to help provide a broader array of narratives than she could offer personally (which she describes in Perspectives on Teaching Conflict Topics), any teacher can balance his or her own biases by providing diverse voices and resources.

Part of getting administrative buy-in may include finding ways to balance challenging conversations and topics.

The fact that very few resources exist to help teachers unearth the experiences of the disenfranchised isn't a problem in itself—it's exactly the reason global partnerships are so valuable. They can help students hear voices generally left out of the conversation.

PERSPECTIVES ON TEACHING CONFLICT TOPICS: JEANNE BOLAND

Former Middle-Years Social Studies Teacher, Odyssey Middle School in Denver, Colorado

A commitment to social justice and a commitment to a global perspective are evidenced throughout my curriculum. While studying the Israeli–Palestinian conflict through the lens of conflict resolution and peace building, students investigated multiple perspectives to hear varying narratives of historical events and present-day issues. Students utilized readings, watched films, and analyzed primary source documents to conduct research and engage in Socratic seminars. In addition, numerous experts came into our classroom: a Palestinian student and an Israeli student, a member of the American Israel Public Affairs Committee, the founder of Building Bridges (a Denver nonprofit that brings Middle East and U.S. youth together to address conflict through leadership skills), and several community members involved in peace organizations. I invited parents to be part of the dialogue by making my curriculum transparent and including them in activities, assignments, and discussions.

continued →

I believe the key for addressing parent concerns when investigating controversial issues in the classroom is honest, transparent communication. I made sure to fully hear parents and let them know that I found their concerns valid. I made the work my students and I engaged in fully available to them and involved parents as partners whenever possible—engaging them directly through student assignments, inviting them to visit my classroom, eliciting their support to connect with local experts (and sometimes being that expert), or having them serve as our audience for presentations of learning to the community.

Parents know that perspective-taking functions as an essential habit of mind in my classroom and that students are expected to read, consider, and respond to a variety of perspectives connected to any issue we investigate, whether historical or present day. While we examine concepts of bias and confirmation bias, we also come to understand the concept of differing narratives—the fact that different individuals or groups can hold vastly different interpretations of events, and that all can be valid and present the "truth" for that person or group.

I do my best to hear where parents are coming from and assure them that I have no agenda in terms of an intended outcome in having my students take sides (which is the concern voiced most frequently). Rather, I reiterate my goal: for students to recognize that events and issues affect individuals in different ways, that each is entitled to his or her perspective whether we agree or disagree, and to train students to be compassionate listeners who are willing to hear others speak their truth, engage in civil conversations on controversial topics, and come to their own conclusions based on doing so.

Source: Adapted from J. Boland, personal communication, May 9, 2016.

Gather Multiple Perspectives

It can be helpful for students to understand the potential tensions before they engage with their partners. No matter what the political lens, it's important for students to hear those perspectives, to try to understand where their partners are coming from, and to adjust their own worldview to make room for this different truth, regardless of whether they ever choose to agree. As a result, a focus on gathering perspectives can help keep controversial topics pluralistic without becoming contentious. As Jeanne Boland discovered when teaching about World War II and the Israeli–Palestinian conflict, if you frame your work as perspective taking, you can often address tensions in more constructive ways—and involve the stakeholders who might most resist your efforts (personal communication, May 9, 2016).

Lean Into Discomfort

Much of the challenge in addressing controversial topics in a partnership comes from the perceived sense that bias is a dangerous thing, and it certainly can be when hidden or disguised as an absolute truth. Most teachers work hard to *avoid* coming across as biased, but a person who denies his or her own bias, believing he or she is less biased than others, ultimately exhibits poor judgments and behavior (Scopelliti et al., 2015). Avoiding bias also means avoiding deep discussion of complex topics where bias can cause conflicts, and students are the first to notice when teachers are skirting their way around the mucky complexity of conflicting biases. One of the things we learned through the work in Palestine was that bias is a natural result of an individual's experiences, something to be understood and explored directly with students more than feared and avoided. Terry Godwaldt of the Centre for Global Education puts it this way:

> To say that bias is good or bad is the wrong question to ask because it just *is*. Everybody is biased, and it doesn't matter how informed, they're only able to have so many experiences. They can't have every experience. And every experience is unique, and comes with biases—that's intrinsic, that's how we encounter the world. And so our job as educators is not to ask, "Is bias good or bad?" but to recognize that bias intrinsically exists in the human experience. This makes it all the more important that we allow our students to encounter biases, which unfortunately isn't always possible when the prominent dialogue doesn't allow for other perspectives to be shared. (T. Godwaldt, personal communication, May 12, 2016)

Becoming comfortable asking real, hard questions lies at the heart of these more controversial global partnerships, particularly when those questions have no clear answer everyone can agree on. Instead of fearing or avoiding bias, the most courageous global educators explore it directly with their students, encouraging them to collect as many perspectives as possible before deciding what they consider their personal truth—if they ever need to choose at all. Seeing truth as fluid, as based on perspective and experience, is one of the best ways to equip our students for a changing world. This requires leaning into discomfort—both by teachers and students—but it's where deep transformation begins.

PERSPECTIVES ON STUDENT INSPIRATION: KATIE HORVATH
Activist and Nonprofit Cofounder, Symbiosis, Detroit, Michigan

When people ask me about my interest in Palestine or my connection to it, I often tell the story of skyping with someone in the West Bank who was just answering questions from curious teenage minds. Then somebody asked a question about suicide bombings, and the video went completely black and we were cut off, someone sent an explanation email, and our teacher read it to the class. It came out that there had been university officials in the room with our speaker, basically censoring him the whole time because they were afraid of retribution.

continued →

That was the first time I had any sort of direct experience with Palestine or anything to do with the Israeli–Palestinian conflict. I also took a class where we had a unit called Poetry of Witness, in which we got to actually interact with young people by reading poetry and looking at photographs by people living in the West Bank. They were regular young people living normal lives, but their normal lives were very different from ours.

I don't think there was one *aha* moment, but I remember being challenged by having to recognize my privilege in a way I hadn't previously. My parents had educated me about privilege of class and race, but that was in the United States. I vaguely knew that as an American, I had a lot of privileges that came at the expense of other people, but they were always just those faceless "others." I think that meeting people virtually, who were otherwise very similar to me in their interest in poetry, made me confront my own privilege as an American. I remember feeling discomfort in that, and the sense of "My life is so boring." I didn't have any illusions that living under occupation was exciting, but I did feel this sense of inadequacy. I was thinking, "What have I been through? How can I ever be a part of the struggle in a real way when I'm this fifteen-year-old white girl from a middle-class background, growing up in Colorado?"

I also remember the first time I was challenged by the now very familiar pro-Israeli discourse. It happened when a (high school) teacher showed some film clip . . . . It was this state-produced short film about how wonderful everything in Israel is. I don't remember the specifics; I just remember getting really mad, being very upset and not knowing if I should confront the teacher. It was my first sort of experience with trying to enter that fray, as far as Israel and Palestine go. The film touched me so personally because I had these personal relationships, and it wasn't just an impersonal debate anymore.

My desire to explore the world in a relationship-based way was encouraged by, or even sparked by, the kind of classroom relationships that these experiences initiated . . . . So when I joke about how my teens led me to radicalism, in all seriousness I think it taught me to question the mainstream narrative and to wonder what's behind the headlines. I want to learn the underdog's story, and I became skeptical of sound bites from the U.S. media—if what I'm being told about this through the media isn't true, what else am I being lied to about? That's a very valuable critical-thinking tool for students to gain at an early age because there are a lot of topics that will help with down the road. Learning to question the dominant narratives will not lead everybody to the same political perspective, but it will lead them to a more thoughtful and compassionate perspective on whatever they pursue.

Source: K. Horvath, personal communication, May 20, 2016.

Use Human Rights Frameworks

Educators from the University of Toronto's Ontario Institute for Studies in Education offer a comprehensive exploration of the challenges teachers face when teaching issues of inequity and social injustice (Zoric et al., 2004). They note that "many teachers remain hesitant to teach students how to challenge inequities because they lack either knowledge or confidence about what to do next" (Zoric et al., 2004, p. 40). Many teachers note a lack of support, as well as the pervasive sense that they might face repercussions from school and district administrators for lacking balance in their curriculum, particularly as students come to identify and act in response to injustices and inequities in their own communities:

> For a variety of reasons, beginning and newer teachers, in particular, often identify uncertainty about how to defend as responsible the posing of controversial issues from social justice perspectives. For example, adding to an already well-documented body of research on the fear and resistance of many teachers to equity education, Wane (2003) notes that student teachers often "perceive anti-racist approaches as risky, as something volatile, to be avoided all together [*sic*]." (Zoric et al., 2004, p. 40)

In their exploration of solutions to these challenges, Zoric et al. (2004) note that "the thoughtful combination of human rights–focused teaching with an explicit emphasis on the development of critical inquiry skills" (p. 40) can go a long way to helping teachers successfully integrate controversial topics into the classroom, helping students, parents, and other stakeholders see their value beyond any discomfort they may have with the specific inequities being explored. Whether you use an existing framework (for example, the United Nations' Universal Declaration of Human Rights or sustainable development goals) or one developed by the school, having a road map for the work, as well as a clear sense of why it is relevant to the curriculum, will help you navigate the challenges and develop the best messaging possible.

Enrich work around human rights and social justice with intentional use of inclusivity strategies and restorative justice practices that help students become comfortable with often divisive topics and develop their conflict-resolution skills, an important global (and local) competency. The use of a collaborative process formally called *Tribes*, for example, can help establish democratic group processes and a safe, positive environment for growth and learning. According to researchers at the Ontario Institute for Studies in Education (Ballagh & Sheppard, 2004), using Tribes allows students to practice the collaboration skills needed to work together in small and large communities, including attentive listening, encouraging others, expressing ideas, making decisions, and resolving conflict. By making sure "All interactions are based on a set of community agreements that include attentive

Enrich work around human rights and social justice with intentional use of inclusivity strategies and restorative justice practices that help students become comfortable with often divisive topics and develop their conflict-resolution skills.

listening, mutual respect, appreciation/no putdowns, and the right to participate/pass," Tribes can help create a sense of community inquiry and inclusion inside each classroom in a global partnership, and in the work students do together (Ballagh & Sheppard, 2004, p. 31). Such comprehensive strategies often help hesitant teachers take new risks by providing methods and approaches, a sort of toolkit that makes teachers feel more equipped to take on topics of race, identity, religion, and conflict.

PERSPECTIVES ON UNDERSTANDING AND TEACHING CONFLICT: JENNIFER D. KLEIN

Author and Former Educational Director, Research Journalism Initiative

The Research Journalism Initiative (RJI), a nonprofit founded by U.S. activist Mark Thomas, was dedicated to bringing Palestinian voices into North American classrooms. RJI's vision was based on the belief that certain voices were missing from international dialogue about the Israeli–Palestinian conflict, particularly in media and schools, and that bringing authentic perspectives into the classroom required direct contact with people living the conflict. As it turned out, much of the work focused on the needs of teachers as they took on this often volatile topic inside their communities. The more hostile the reaction to RJI's goals, the more important it felt to be working in that school—but we also had to find reasonable ways to navigate those tensions so that opponents became advocates. We didn't want innovative teachers to live in fear of losing their jobs or to create political turmoil within these communities; we just wanted students to hear a more varied set of narratives.

But it was hard, emotional work, and while my colleague Mark was living alongside Palestinians in the West Bank, facilitating videoconferences through An-Najah National University, I was coaching U.S. teachers through their emotional turmoil before, during, and after those life-changing videoconferences. In one memorable case, I got an unexpected call from a crying teacher, a Lebanese American herself, who didn't know how to continue her school day after a particularly powerful videoconference with a young Palestinian poet.

In the case of RJI, partnership meant not just connecting two classrooms but connecting two very different worlds, and the kinds of emotional ground we covered changed the lives of students, teachers, and our young partners in the West Bank as well. We built trust on deep levels, and we relied on that trust to help us manage the political and emotional complexities of the region we'd chosen to focus on. And we discovered, among other things, that using photography, visual arts, and poetry to connect students was far more powerful—and more effective—than setting up political dialogue. By humanizing the topic so deeply, the arts became a vehicle for avoiding a classroom debate mindset and shifting the focus to human beings and their very real expressions of experience. Using the arts as our medium helped students connect with each other even when their worldviews diverged. This helped my students see conflict not as a cut-and-dry topic with one right side and one that was definitively wrong, but rather as a complex dance of needs and rights in which all parties had their own truth to share.

Choose Social Justice Partnerships Thoughtfully

None of what you are exploring in this chapter is meant to suggest that conflict and controversy belong in all classrooms. It's important to make thoughtful choices, considering the age and developmental readiness of your students, as well as the readiness of your broader community. Avoid assuming that students are too young to understand war and conflict when, in reality, they may already be experiencing conflicts in their own lives and need help navigating the challenges of bias and perspective. Many elementary teachers push these boundaries, exploring conflict, discord, and difficulty with students in an open, transparent, and still developmentally appropriate way. These approaches build students' navigational skills when it comes to conflict in their own lives, and avoiding such topics in elementary school means that students will encounter middle school bullying and highly charged social dynamics without the skills to handle them.

Even topics that seem less controversial can cause challenges for the teachers. Take the case of Heidi Hutchison, whose partnership caused challenges both inside and outside the classroom.

PERSPECTIVES ON CONTROVERSIAL GLOBAL PARTNERSHIPS: HEIDI HUTCHISON

Fifth-Grade Teacher, Global Classroom Project Leader, Friends School of Baltimore, Maryland

I didn't want the project just to be about Malala Yousafzai specifically; I wanted students to go in their own direction and boy, did they ever. I had to give them enough background information; that's the hard thing about doing these projects—you want to give them appropriate information for their age. But that ignites them to want to go deeper to understand the driving question.

I did run into some controversy; the boys in my class were like, "Why are we just talking about girls? Why aren't we talking about boys?" That was really interesting, and that led to such great conversations about gender inequity. You get to go in areas you never would be able to explore by just teaching. I shared the book about Malala, but they were making meaning themselves. And they got very interested. *Girl Rising* came out at the same time, then the next year *Blackfish* came out at the time as the program. I had no idea these things were going to happen. We did a community showing of *Girl Rising*. I had to get special permission for the kids to be able to see it and decide where the proceeds were going to go. The kids learned about girls having to walk miles and miles for water.

Other kids learned about other areas of interest to raise money for. They made pamphlets, and they stood on little soap boxes in the courtyard where the students were at lunchtime. They handed out pamphlets about the barriers that girls faced and gave speeches. It was really successful. Some of the struggles that came out of that for me personally was that I started receiving emails in Arabic. I received an email from the Syrian National

continued →

Army requesting that I help it because it saw the work I did around Malala. My IT department regularly reached out to me asking what I was doing, since it was getting an influx of Arabic traffic. My father was getting very nervous, and what I got to learn was how nervous people are about the misinformation they are receiving.

Because I have a digital footprint and I am who I say I am online, I ended up getting contacted a lot, from others asking for help. From a teacher's perspective, doing these types of projects opens you up. I was contacted by an ex-headmaster from a school in India, sending his resume and this long letter asking if he could work for the Malala project and if I would consider hiring him. As a teacher, as an adult, as a citizen of this world, to see my little Baltimore classroom putting something out there in the world and then being contacted—I just see such great need. People are searching to get connected.

Source: Adapted from H. Hutchison, personal communication, May 20, 2016.

A Few Concluding Thoughts

Many parts of and issues in the world stimulate controversy, yet the more controversial a region's challenges, the more likely there are multiple truths hidden in the layers of complexity any given injustice contains—and many educators and students are anxious to dig into those layers. I experienced deep dialogue in my own classroom when students explored heavily charged topics, like whether dictatorships were better than democracies at curbing humans' worst tendencies. I remember thinking I'd be seen as a communist for even bringing such a question to the table. Instead, these conversations built students' curiosity to know more; exploring controversy actually made students *less* certain about their worldviews, not *more* sure. And that uncertainty is exactly what leads to a lifetime of critical inquiry and constructive engagement of the kind Katie Horvath describes.

One of my favorite global learning moments occurred when my creative writing students asked a young Palestinian author, Falastine Dwikat, why she participated in videoconferences with students in the United States. Her reply, which was poetry in itself, was that she wanted her poetry to be a bridge. She told my students that peace has to be built "from word to word, from heart to heart, and from line to line" (F. Dwikat, personal communication, October 23, 2008). The point of social justice work in global partnerships isn't to solve problems in a black-and-white way, to choose a side, or to decide on one definitive truth. Instead, it's about building bridges that allow us to understand each other's experiences; it's about exposing students to very real complexities around truth, identity, and human rights; and it's about empowering students to really grapple with the grey areas they encounter. And ultimately, it's about students becoming critical media consumers who always look beyond the headlines to understand the lives and experiences that lie behind them.

CHAPTER 9

ASSESSING GLOBAL COMPETENCIES, PARTNERSHIPS, AND PROGRAMS

Masters are not experts because they take a subject to its conceptual end. They are masters because they realize that there isn't one.

—Sarah Lewis

We are educating in a data-driven era, so our ability to assess the quality of educational experiences—and student growth—is paramount. In growth-oriented school communities, gathering data improves project planning and implementation; and formative assessment allows students multiple opportunities to give and receive growth-producing feedback on their path to mastery.

Additionally, there is an important distinction between grading and assessing. The educational culture in many countries focuses on what standardized tests identify as valuable, and in some cases what isn't on the test isn't taught because there simply is no time to devote to it (Smith, 2016; Turner, 2014). Ken Robinson and Lou Aronica (2016) point out China's *gaokao* system as an example of this problem, noting that Shanghai's top rankings on PISA come "as a result of relentless drilling and nearly exclusive focus on test-taking performance" (p. 240). But competency is not a moment in time. Far more interesting—and important—is growth. High-quality assessment is about that growth—about helping students recognize the opportunity for improvement in their own work and their peers' work; and creating space for multiple attempts at demonstrating knowledge and skill. In the words of author and researcher Sarah Lewis (2015), "Mastery is also not the same as success—an event-based victory based on a peak point, a punctuated moment in time. Mastery is not merely a commitment to a goal, but to a curved-line, constant pursuit" (p. 5). In truth, we can reduce very few elements of education to "event-based victories," and global competencies aren't among them. In fact, most people in globally oriented fields consider themselves and their efforts a work in progress. As World Savvy Executive Director Dana Mortenson puts it, "Building global competence is a journey; it is by definition aspirational, we never fully arrive there" (personal communication, October 28, 2016).

> *The goals of assessment in global partnerships are twofold:*
> *(1) assessing students' global competencies and (2) adapting and retaining global partnerships.*

The goals of assessment in global partnerships are twofold, and this chapter explores both: (1) assessing students' global competencies in a partnership and (2) adapting and retaining global partnerships. Thoughtful assessment will help improve your work and retain your partner over the coming years. This chapter also explores how to assess opportunities for growth in your broader global programming, as global partnerships should become just a portion of what makes your school global, one of many global experiences students are having across grade levels, disciplines, and teachers.

Assess Students' Global Competencies in a Partnership

Keeping in mind that assessment's goal is growth measurement, teachers should assess students' global competencies—and have students reflect on their own growth—at least twice during a global partnership (most teachers do a pre- and post-assessment), and at several points during students' academic career. It's important that your assessment criteria, both academic and global, do not rely on your partner classroom's behavior or follow through, however. For example, assess your students' communication skills, but don't assess based on whether their partners replied. Even if the goal is co-creation, keep assessment focused on your *own* students' contributions. Build for your students' success regardless of what their partners contribute, so that partners' contributions enrich the experience but are irrelevant to formulating a complete sense of your students' academic growth.

One of the challenges of assessing global competency is the unquantifiable nature of so many of global education's goals. In *Why School?*, education reform advocate Will Richardson (2012) points out that assessment systems are based on a time when knowledge was scarce and hard to access, not on paradigms in which "if we have an Internet connection, we have fingertip, on-demand access to an amazing library that holds close to the sum of human knowledge and, equally important, to more than two billion people with whom we can potentially learn" (Kindle location 91). This new paradigm means giving value to more than just content knowledge; it means valuing what we can *do* with what we learn from and with the world.

While global competencies such as research, world language, and geography skills are fairly easy to assess in quantifiable terms, some of the most important goals are not. How do you measure unquantifiable skills such as empathy or humility, and how do you know that a student has acquired such values beyond a superficial demonstration? How do you measure the growth of curiosity, resilience, and open-mindedness? How do you quantify the ability to connect in a humanizing way across cultural and geographic borders? How do you measure the balance between critical thinking and acceptance when students encounter particularly challenging cultural practices? And if the answer is that you can't (at least not as easily as you can quantify the correct tense of a verb), then how do you ensure these *immeasurables* are given importance alongside more easily measured outcomes?

> *How do you measure unquantifiable skills such as empathy or humility, and how do you know that a student has acquired such values beyond a superficial demonstration? How do you measure the growth of curiosity, resilience, and open-mindedness?*

At the very least, ask students to reflect on their growth in these more amorphous competencies. Often, key challenges emerge more clearly from student reflections than from more traditional assessments, and they tell us more than exams can about how students are doing, about the kinds of people they are becoming. In one example, a project in which seventh graders built prosthetic hands for a specific sport, the teacher I was coaching discovered only at the very end through student reflections that students had developed deep sympathy for the differently abled, but it was bordering on pity, not empathy. From that, he and I developed remediations for the following year, to ensure we humanized the differently abled more fully for students. In another example, a project I helped facilitate on the world water crisis turned out to be exacerbating the trope of poor Africans walking miles for water, not because the single story hadn't been addressed and broken down along the way, but because the project launched with videos on water scarcity that demonstrated a stereotype the students held onto.

Student reflections can often tell us more about the immeasurables than any other form of assessment, and making time for journal writing and quick exit-ticket reflections can go a long way to making growth and abstract learning more concrete for you and your students. If you want to know how students see a given immeasurable, ask them, "How would you define humility, and how do you know when you are seeing it? What are the key distinctions between empathy and sympathy, and how might we measure the growth of empathy in this partnership?" A class discussion or journal entry can reveal more about students' thinking and growth than a more formalized, teacher-created task, and can even offer student-generated criteria for rubric development later. For example, ask your students how they *feel* about what they're learning from their partnership. When have they experienced discord, and when have their previous opinions been upheld? What has been easy to learn, and what has been hard to hear? How has their thinking grown or been impacted by the perspectives they've heard? Reflective questions can tell us a lot more about the social-emotional learning our students are experiencing, and they have the double benefit of helping students deepen their learning by reflecting on it (Dewey, 2012).

Develop specific competency *look-fors* and *listen-fors*—indicators you might see and hear when students demonstrate the competencies, such as students asking questions more than making assertions, handling setbacks without blaming peers, and the like. Work with collaborative teams during department or grade-level meetings to identify the kinds of language and behaviors you want to catalog during class. Refer back to tables 1.1, 1.2, and 1.3 (pages 19, 21, and 22) for global competencies and choose those most relevant to your partnership. Then, develop capture tools like the one in figure 9.1 so that assessment indicators are as concrete as possible for these largely subjective goals. Ensure that each group ends up with a well-defined list of look-fors and listen-fors connected to the competencies most relevant to its partnerships (such as empathy, resilience, respect, curiosity, initiative, passion, entrepreneurial thinking, inquiry, creativity, collaboration, and intercultural communication). If a team records *hear respectfulness* or *see a sense of safety* when a student is demonstrating *empathy*, ask the group to be as specific as possible about what respectfulness sounds like or what safety looks like.

---

1. Agree on the competencies your team will assess in the partnership.

2. Split into small or large groups, depending on how many immeasurables you plan to assess.

3. Draw one T-chart on a piece of paper for each global competency, writing the competency across the top of the T.

   - On one side of the T, have teachers brainstorm what they will *see* when a student is competent in this area.

   - On the other side of the T, have teachers brainstorm what they will *hear* when a student is competent in this area.

4. Gather all relevant look-fors and listen-fors onto a note catcher teachers can easily use to record evidence when students are working or having a discussion during class.

Figure 9.1: Capture global competency evidence.

*Visit **go.SolutionTree.com/21stcenturyskills** for a free reproducible version of this figure.*

Figure 9.2 shows T-chart examples for competencies including empathy, humility, and resilience.

Competency to Assess: Empathy	
Look-Fors	**Listen-Fors**
• Understanding actions such as verbally comforting a peer, giving pats on the back, hugging a student who is upset • Helpful actions such as helping a peer with a task • Supportive body language such as smiles and nods	• Understanding words such as "I know how you feel" or "I'm sorry you're feeling bad." • Encouraging language such as "You can do it!" • Supportive language such as "I can tell you worked hard."
Competency to Assess: Humility	
Look-Fors	**Listen-Fors**
• Draws peers in for their perspectives • Is receptive when new learning negates existing opinions or knowledge • Plays well as a team member; encourages and focuses on having all views considered	• Questions rather than makes assertions • Uses language that suggests flexibility with knowledge, such as "I think I know" and "I wonder" • Compliments about others' ideas, even when they conflict with their own
Competency to Assess: Resilience	
Look-Fors	**Listen-Fors**
• Takes setbacks well; bounces back quickly • Hears feedback well; can adapt as a result • Demonstrates a growth mindset; keeps working at something until successful • Looks for alternative routes or solutions	• Uses flexible language such as "How might I approach this differently?" when encountering setbacks • Uses receptive language such as "That's really helpful" in response to feedback • Shows improvement and problem-solving language, such as "I wonder if I might try . . ."

Figure 9.2: T-charts for making global competencies more concrete.

A few organizations effectively define global competencies in less abstract terms, even establishing what they look like in different disciplines. In partnership with EdSteps and the Council of Chief State School Officers, the Center for Global Education at Asia Society developed discipline-specific rubrics for global competency assessment within the core subject areas and across grade bands, always through the four domains: (1) investigating the world, (2) recognizing perspectives, (3) communicating ideas, and (4) taking action (Mansilla & Jackson, 2011). Several discipline-specific global competency rubrics are available in the free 2011 publicatione *Educating for Global Competence: Preparing Our Youth to Engage the World* (Mansilla & Jackson, 2011).

Regardless of whether you develop your own or use existing rubrics, or even use district-mandated proficiency scales for your academic standards, weaving in assessment points for global competencies helps legitimize 21st century skills alongside academic knowledge. Figure 9.3 is a Center for Global Education at Asia Society rubric example for fifth-grade social studies. Based on benchmarks from the four domains of global competency, specifically Investigate the World, this rubric gives teachers and students a sense of what a learner might be able to do, from the beginning level (emerging) through the most advanced. (The full rubric provides a full page of criteria for each of the four domains.)

Figure 9.4 (page 163) is another example of a Center for Global Education at Asia Society rubric, this time for fifth-grade mathematics. Again, the rubric aligns with the specific elements of the Investigate the World domain that apply to mathematics, and it defines a spectrum of achievement levels for students with a specific focus on mathematical skills.

The Center for Global Education at Asia Society (2015) has also developed an extraordinary set of free public materials for fostering and assessing students' global leadership skills, including rationales, *I can* statements, performance outcomes, and rubrics for grades 3, 5, 8, 10, and 12, again framed around the four domains and 2017 assessment materials for grades K–2. Figure 9.5 (page 165) is the Investigate the World page of the global leadership rubric for fifth grade. This rubric has many similarities to the fifth-grade social studies rubric in figure 9.3, given that investigation in both fields takes a similar form. You may find it useful to explore the other pages of the global leadership rubric online (http://bit .ly/2pEQ4h3) as well, to envision how you might assess recognizing perspectives, communicating ideas, and taking action.

Teachers can weave these criteria in with academic standards and 21st century competencies on rubrics and other assessments, as they deal with students' ability to turn knowledge into action and participation. The Center for Global Education at Asia Society (2015) notes that these materials are meant for use across all disciplines to encourage active participation and direct engagement in the topics students are studying.

Investigate the World: What is the evidence that students can situate and analyze social questions beyond their immediate environment and time?

	Emerging	Developing	Proficient	Advanced
Pose significant researchable questions.	Identifies a local, regional, or global issue and poses a question to investigate that is disconnected from the social sciences	Identifies a local, regional, or global issue and poses a question that is loosely connected to the social sciences	Identifies a local, regional, or global issue and poses a social science-related question relevant to the issue	Explains a local, regional, or global issue and poses a social science-related question that matters to the local, regional, or global community
Select varied sources.	Uses a provided source to address a question	Selects one secondary source relevant to the question	Selects multiple secondary sources relevant to a social science-related question	Selects relevant primary or secondary sources that vary in format
Analyze source origins.	States information as fact and uses direct quotes without citation	Uses direct quotes or specific information without citation	Provides accurate source information when using direct quotes and facts	Introduces sources by referring to their origins, and provides accurate source information when using direct quotes and facts
Analyze source credibility.	Understands or represents information from sources as fact	Questions the credibility or bias of a source without presenting a clear reason	Questions the credibility or bias of a source and includes a logical reason	Questions the credibility or identifies the bias of a source using specific details

continued →

Figure 9.3: Graduation performance system—social studies rubric for grade 5.

	Emerging	Developing	Proficient	Advanced
Compare sources.	Relies primarily on one source	Uses more than one source but does not compare or group information from the documents	Uses information from multiple sources to support a claim	Makes connections between documents by comparing information or types of sources
Draw evidence-based conclusions and raise logical implications.	Restates a conclusion from a source in response to a global question. Identifies a question or proposes an action that is not supported by the source	Adopts and accurately restates a conclusion from a source in response to a global question. Identifies a question related to the topic or proposes an action related to the findings	Draws simple conclusions based on evidence from a source in response to a global question, and raises an unanswered question related to the source or issue	Draws conclusions based on evidence from sources in response to a global question, and raises unanswered questions for further investigation

Source: Center for Global Education at Asia Society, n.d.a.

Investigate the World: How well does the student use mathematics to model and investigate a given issue, situation, or event?

	Emerging	Developing	Proficient	Advanced
Develop models.	Recognizes the need to simplify a globally significant issue using mathematical modeling; may need assistance to list types of mathematical models, and to select an appropriate one	Understands what a mathematical model is; identifies parts of a globally significant issue that may be included in a mathematical model, but needs some assistance to develop an appropriate one	Builds a simple mathematical model using concrete referents (objects, drawings, diagrams, and actions) to describe a globally significant issue; attends to some but not all given constraints	Builds a mathematical model using both concrete referents and abstractions (symbols and equations) to describe a globally significant issue, or applies a model that has been successful previously in similar situations; attends to most given restraints
Revise models.	Recognizes that a model can be used to represent a particular situation, but may need assistance to connect an appropriate model with the situation	Understands the purpose of a mathematical model, and can relate parts of a problem or situation to a model, but may omit data or information	Describes how elements in a model relate to elements in a situation; uses models that rely primarily on concrete referents (objects, drawings, diagrams, and actions)	Describes how elements in a model relate to elements in a situation; uses models that have both concrete referents (objects, drawings, diagrams, and actions) and abstractions (symbols and equations)

continued →

Figure 9.4: Graduation performance system—mathematics rubric for grade 5.

	Emerging	Developing	Proficient	Advanced
Use appropriate tools strategically.	Recognizes that mathematical tools, procedures, and representations can be used to explore a global issue, situation, or event, but may need some assistance in selecting the appropriate tools, procedures, or representations	Selects and uses mathematical tools, procedures, and representations to explore a global issue, situation, or event, but may not select the most efficient tool or procedure to explore the given issue, situation, or event	Employs appropriate mathematical tools, procedures, or representations to explore a global issue, situation, or event	Distinguishes between appropriate mathematical tools, procedures, and representations to explore a global issue, situation, or event; articulates why a particular tool or procedure was selected

Source: Center for Global Education at Asia Society, n.d.d.

Investigate the World: What is the evidence that a student can initiate investigations of the world by framing questions, analyzing and synthesizing relevant evidence, and drawing reasonable conclusions about global issues?

	Emerging	Developing	Proficient	Advanced
Pose significant researchable questions.	Identifies a local or regional topic or issue for study; relevance to the global community must be inferred	Poses a broad question on a local or regional issue, and identifies relevance to the global community	Poses a question on a local or regional issue, and identifies significance to the global community	Poses a researchable question on a local, regional, or global issue, and provides a general reason for its significance to the global community
Select varied, relevant evidence.	Uses evidence from a provided source to address a local or regional question	Relies on a single source relevant to a local or regional question	Selects and uses a few sources to identify evidence that addresses a global question	Selects and uses a variety of sources to identify relevant evidence that addresses a global question
Analyze, integrate, and evaluate sources.	Restates accurate information that is relevant to a local, regional, or global question	Provides a partial summary of evidence from sources that are relevant to a local, regional, or global question	Provides an accurate summary of evidence from sources that are relevant to a global question	Analyzes and integrates evidence from sources to develop a response to a global question; demonstrates understanding of the issue
Develop an evidence-based position and draw conclusions.	Restates an opinion from a source in response to a global question	Adopts and accurately restates an opinion, and at least one piece of supporting evidence from a source, in response to a global question	Develops an opinion based on evidence from a source in response to a global question; draws simple conclusions	Develops a position, based on evidence from sources, that reflects a particular perspective in response to a global question; draws conclusions that reflect a partial understanding of the issue

Source: Center for Global Education at Asia Society, n.d.c.

Figure 9.5: Graduation performance system—global leadership rubric for grade 5.

Imagine, for example, that you are partnering a fifth-grade classroom in Canada with a fifth-grade classroom in Greece. Both classes are studying human geography, specifically the refugee crises around the world. Both communities are also receiving a high number of refugees, but for different reasons and at different points along the journey. The classes could strive to achieve benchmarks from the International Studies Schools Network *I can* statements for fifth-grade social studies, mathematics, and leadership. Students could investigate the current and historical treatment of refugees together; use mathematics to understand the related statistics; explore varied perspectives on the best solution for the refugee crises (including exploring the controversy and hateful rhetoric in some parts of the world, and trying to understand and articulate their own perspectives); communicate their ideas about solutions to their partners and real stakeholders; and take action in their local communities to support the needs of new refugees.

Weave these criteria in with academic standards and 21st century competencies on rubrics and other assessments.

The teachers could weave the most relevant criterion from the fifth-grade global leadership rubric in figure 9.5 (page 165) with criteria from the discipline-specific rubrics for social studies and mathematics in figure 9.3 (page 161) and figure 9.4 (pages 163), as well as any key content or skill goals for social studies (from the Common Core State Standards, for example), to make one partnership-specific rubric with concrete criteria for fostering and measuring growth in relevant global competencies and academic content. This is a good way to simplify the assessment work, and you can make the rubric development even richer by asking students to weigh in about what they're learning. The sample rubric in figure 9.6 can work as a starting point.

If your students are using technology in new or unusual ways as a part of their partnership experience, it's worth being intentional about their digital literacy growth as well. If your school doesn't already have rubrics and other tools for guiding and assessing technological student growth and achievement, visit **go.SolutionTree .com/21stcenturyskills** for live links to EdTechTeacher assessment resources, including media-specific resources, tools, and rubrics for formative and summative assessment. You'll also find live links to ISTE rubrics you can weave into technology-enabled global partnerships, many of which are particularly appropriate to assessing those types of partnerships. (The ISTE standards for being a creative communicator and a global collaborator are particularly appropriate for use in global partnerships.) The goal is not to sit down with five different rubrics for each authentic performance task your students complete, but rather to pull together the most salient criteria from multiple sources, building one rubric that includes one or two global competencies or 21st century skills, between two and four academic competencies, and one or two technological competencies (if relevant).

Project: Refugee Partnership	Emerging	Developing	Proficient	Advanced
Collaborate				
Empathize				
Analyze and evaluate sources (social studies).				
Use mathematical statistics and graphing tools to understand a problem (mathematics).				
Draw evidence-based conclusions and raise logical implications (social studies and leadership).				
Act creatively and responsibly to improve the conditions of refugees locally (leadership).				

Figure 9.6: Rubric sample.

Sometimes growth in student thinking and behavior comes in the form of slow changes over time, which is almost impossible to measure within the project, course, or school year. While you may not be able to capture such growth quantitatively, it is important for global partnerships to include opportunities for students to reflect on shifts in their thinking. Mark Thomas notes that global partnerships wear away prejudices over time, but their effects are rarely seen immediately:

> One of the most important things for educators to understand or establish is a reasonable level of expectation. A forty-five–minute exchange with young people across the world is not going to change very much, actually. It's probably not going to change anything for either group, other than maybe to plant some seeds for the future. The best thing we can accomplish here is to plant some seeds, and those seeds are probably destructive as opposed to constructive. It does happen that a young person will have that tiny seed of possibility implanted in her, and she fosters it over the next three years of high school, transitions to university, and then goes off to try to change the world. But I think more important are the seeds of destruction that can be planted, and what I'm talking about is the ability for an exchange to put a crack in the foundation of prejudice, a prejudice that hasn't fully materialized yet.
>
> The vast majority of the prejudices in play in these exchanges are latent: they are subliminal, they are subcontextual, they are unrealized. Students are learning how political discourse works; slowly, they're building vocabularies for exchanging ideas. They're learning what type of language is accessible, and they're learning about the value of empathy or the lack of value for empathy, and subconsciously they're accumulating an understanding of what's acceptable. We won't know the true benefit of these seeds of discord until these young people are no longer our students but are teachers themselves. (M. Thomas, personal communication, May 8, 2016)

Many global schools use journaling, capstone projects, and graduation portfolios to try to map students' growth over time. Many globally oriented high schools are implementing global certification programs, such as Appleby College's Global Leadership Diploma (www.appleby.on.ca/page.cfm?p=2697), Fountain Valley School of Colorado's (2017) Global Scholar Diploma (http://bit.ly/2rzihGG), and Parish Episcopal School's Academy of Global Studies (www.parishepiscopal.org). In such programs, students are asked to chart their learning through a variety of global courses and experiences, culminating in final portfolios that they present to a panel their senior year. Each program has different requirements, including experiences like global travel, service, speakers, classroom projects, and capstone experiences.

Another way to capture competency growth over time is through more overarching and often fee-based global competency measurements, including the Global Competence Aptitude Assessment for Education (www.globallycompetent.com/home.html). The University of Michigan's Center for Research on Learning and Teaching "Tools for Assessing Intercultural and Global Competence" (www.crlt.umich.edu/interculturalcompetence) maintains a list of broader global competency assessments. Such assessments may not be useful for assessing growth before and after a specific project, as several require a trained facilitator and all require a financial investment, but you could use them with students at entry and exit points, such as fifth and eighth grades, or ninth and twelfth grades. Such assessments can be very helpful in furthering systemic growth, especially if they lead to deeper consideration of current programming and a willingness to remediate challenges.

It is worth noting that the international business field is doing some excellent work around assessing global competency as well. As business leaders move their companies in increasingly global directions, the need to define, foster, and assess the global competencies of employees and business leaders becomes paramount to a company's success. Two of the most popular measures include the Global Competence Aptitude Assessment for Business (www.globallycompetent.com/aboutGCAA), and the Thunderbird School of Global Management's (n.d.) Global Mindset Inventory (http://bit.ly/2rlWtSB). Educators can gain an even more nuanced understanding of what global competency looks like—and strong arguments for its importance in the business world—by exploring such business models and even using them to assess more advanced students.

Adapt and Retain Global Partnerships

Most teachers struggle to see their successes because their failures—or perceived failures—weigh so heavily on these well-intentioned and passionate educators. Frankly, even one Skype session is a success worth celebrating, and even one pen pal exchange can begin shifting student perspectives. As you consider the challenges you've encountered in the course of your partnership, don't forget to pat yourself on the back for your successes, too, however small they may seem.

As you consider the challenges you've encountered in the course of your partnership, don't forget to pat yourself on the back for your successes, too, however small they may seem.

The goal of partnership assessment should be, above all, to identify remediations to improve the project the following year. Don't spend too much time bemoaning your challenges and regrets; stay focused on why they happened and on planning constructive adaptations. Whenever possible, partnership assessments should be done with your partner teacher, as reworking the project together to ensure deeper success is the only way to effectively retain a partner over many years. If you work closely with your partner teacher to develop a strong curriculum and adapt it regularly together, your partnership can outlive any changes in building, grade level, or discipline taught, even if one or both of you are constantly being moved to teach in different schools, as is the case for public school teachers in many parts of the world. Your capacity to work together and adapt the curriculum as a team will allow you to adjust.

Remember, too, that your perspectives on success and failure may be quite different than your partner's, so having an open conversation that allows you to understand your partner's impressions will lead to better choices for both of you in the long run. An experience that felt unexciting on your end may well have been the highlight of your partner's experience, and it's important for both partners to know what succeeded and fell flat on both sides. If you rework the exchange *without* your partner, you are likely to create remediations that suggest your priorities matter more than his or hers, or that lead you away from his or her needs—or even what produced success. All of this makes it less likely that your partner will want to keep working with you.

Your perspectives on success and failure may be quite different than your partner's.

Evaluating partnership successes and identifying remediation areas should include students' perspectives on both sides of the partnership as well. Students often notice before educators when a given task is irrelevant or feels like busywork, and they will be the first to report when a project or strategy isn't working as long as teachers give them the opportunity to voice those opinions and really hear the feedback. Students can also help you notice areas of success and resonance where you might see none. For example, student journals from a partnership experience can show you where deep insights and connections occurred, and reflective writing or discussion can help you see the nuances of students' experiences.

Don't give up if you have a rocky start. Ask the students what worked for them, what they need next, and build from there. Remember, too, that changing partners frequently means starting from scratch repeatedly. Most of the time, the initial hiccups go away as you get to know your partner teacher and can understand the rhythms of his or her work and school year, his or her limitations and strengths—and as your partner learns the same about you. Giving up too soon turns your search for the right partner into a dating game; if you think of your partnership as a marriage, that means digging as deep as you can for the sake of the children.

Don't give up if you have a rocky start.

Once in a while, of course, it *is* appropriate to start from scratch with a new partner. If the challenges or differences between you and your partner feel insurmountable, then it makes sense to try someone new. For example, over the course of two years, a Spanish teacher I coached in the United States really tried to make a language partnership work with a computer science teacher in Spain. But there were several essential problems in their dynamic, and time and effort didn't fix the teachers' incompatibilities. The teacher in Spain didn't trust her students to post appropriately on their Edmodo page, so she posted everything for them. Meanwhile, the U.S. teacher wanted her students to *learn* to post appropriately through practice. Students couldn't learn anything about each other directly, as the Spanish partner didn't want her students to have their own accounts or profiles. Even more challenging, the teachers' educational goals were different. The U.S. teacher wanted her students to develop a passion for communication that would increase their motivation to learn Spanish, while the teacher in Spain wanted her students to edit the Spanish that the U.S. students wrote, and to learn to use English correctly by having the U.S. students identify their mistakes. But the U.S. students were deflated by getting their Spanish introductions back with extensive edits, and were uncomfortable correcting the work of counterparts they couldn't even get to know directly first. Both teachers did all they could to communicate and find common ground, but the decision to move on was best for both of them.

As you reflect on your experiences, consider using a form such as the one in figure 9.7 for measuring students' and teachers' opinions of the partnership.

Both partner teachers and their students should complete this worksheet. The partner teachers should then discuss the responses together.

Partnership or project title: _____

Grade level and discipline: _____

Circle one: Student   Teacher   Other (specify): _____

How many times did you have live contact with your partner classroom?

How regularly did you communicate with your partner classroom asynchronously?

What form did your partnership take? Circle one:
  Exchange   Collaboration   Co-Creation   Other (specify): _____

What were some of the highlights of this partnership? Describe a few of your favorite experiences.

What were some of the challenges you encountered during this partnership?

Figure 9.7: Partnership evaluation and reflection worksheet.

continued →

Which global competencies or other new skills do you think you developed through this partnership?

What was your biggest takeaway from this partnership?

How might we improve this partnership next year?

Please share any ideas you have for new global projects, either with this partner or another:

Visit *go.SolutionTree.com/21stcenturyskills* for a free reproducible version of this figure.

Assess and Improve Broader Global Programming

It can be useful to take a deep look at your current programming and school culture as you discuss expanding and deepening global partnerships and other global work across your community. (For information on this topic, see chapter 10, page 177.) There are many ways to approach global programming self-assessment. As educators continue defining best practices in this relatively new educational movement, all assessments likely have something to offer depending on your community, how deeply you want to dig, and the nature of your goals.

One of the oldest free global programming assessments is Fred Czarra's (2002) *Issues in Global Education: Global Education Checklist for Teachers, Schools, School Systems and State Education Agencies*, published online by the American Forum for Global Education. While a few of Czarra's (2002) delineations assume that teachers can accurately judge what students do and do not know, and ask teachers questions that might be better answered by students, this checklist does focus on excellent ideas about what strong global programming should include—and could easily be adapted for students to complete as well. It addresses enough aspects of global education to be a useful resource throughout several months of re-envisioning and planning if key leaders, teachers, students, and parents complete the portion relevant to their domain. At the very least, collaborative teams can use the checklist to provoke conversation and deeper reflection, identifying areas of strength and opportunities for growth in your community.

For schools that can afford them, most fee-based evaluation programs offer deep asset analysis and ongoing support. The broader the cross section of stakeholders evaluating your community's global strengths and challenges, the more complete your results will be.

The following sections describe a few such programs: Future Friendly Schools, the Global Education Benchmark Group, the Center for Global Education at

Asia Society's International Studies Schools Network, and World Savvy's School Partnership Program.

Future Friendly Schools

Future Friendly Schools (FFS; www.futurefriendlyschools.org) was established in 2013 by TakingITGlobal for Educators in Toronto, to "nurture student voice, global citizenship, and environmental stewardship through technology-rich and project-based learning" (Future Friendly Schools, n.d.). The FFS program includes showcasing work across a network of schools, professional development, and a certification process that includes deep surveys geared toward a variety of stakeholder groups (teachers, students, parents, administrators) to help schools identify challenges and perform ongoing growth assessments. The survey questions focus on the three FFS pillars: (1) global citizenship, (2) student voice, and (3) environmental stewardship. TakingITGlobal provides deep analysis of assessment results, helping schools in their network identify strategies that will allow for growth in challenge areas.

PERSPECTIVES ON BUILDING AND ASSESSING GLOBAL PROGRAMS: MICHAEL FURDYK

Cofounder, Future Friendly Schools at
TakingITGlobal for Educators, Toronto

We created Future Friendly Schools to respond to the growing interest in the three values: global citizenship, student voice, and environmental stewardship. . . . But beyond that, student learning that responds to these values is relevant, authentic, and deep, and can help our classrooms and schools play a role in shaping a better world. Here in Canada, data from June 2016 highlight that 88 percent of grade 12 students worry about the state of the planet, and 85 percent agree that people will have to make lifestyle choices to solve climate change (Anderssen, 2016). What better way to help students see that their actions matter than to guide their learning in a way that makes a difference? Future Friendly Schools is committed to being at the forefront of that work, and to reflecting on how it can continually improve.

Creating the indicators and benchmarks for the program was a very creative process. It was part of my master of design in inclusive design research project, and we developed a portal that allowed anyone interested (students, educators, administrators, parents, nonprofit partners) to post ideas, vote on others, and leave comments to dig into the ideas of other participants. We had over four thousand participants in this process from over one hundred countries, so we're proud of how global this process was. The best part? Of the fifteen program principles we settled on (five in each value area), eleven came exclusively from ideas and insights shared by people outside of our own internal research and experience.

continued →

Across each of the FFS value areas, we offer an accredited graduate course to help educators build classroom projects that deepen their practice, and that work has been measured by the Toronto District School Board's research department. After the FFS course cycle, 95 percent of educators said the content was relevant to their school's improvement plan and goals, and 86 percent gained new knowledge and skills that had direct and practical value for doing their job.

What about the students? That question will take longer to answer, but in an analysis of the provincewide Office of Education Quality and Accountability assessments of the two families of schools participating, there was an increase of 5 percent to 6 percent of students achieving the provincial standard in the family that joined our first year of courses, and 4 percent in the family of schools that joined in the second year. It's not possible to conclude that all this improved achievement has been the direct result of the engagement with us across the FFS values, but the Toronto District School Board's (2015) reporting concludes, "We are certain that the professional learning has provided participating educators an opportunity to collaborate within their learning communities, share best practices, and actively engage their students in their daily learning."

Source: Adapted from M. Furdyk, personal communication, June 25, 2016.

The Global Education Benchmark Group

The Global Education Benchmark Group (http://gebg.org) was founded to help connect communities working to globalize their schools. The group's low membership fee offers several benefits, including a listserv, a wiki for resource sharing, and an annual conference that brings together innovative global educators for sharing and learning.

Most important to its work is the actual *benchmarking* that gave the group its name, and one of the most valuable benefits of membership. Member schools gather data yearly, and then receive an analysis of their results, calibrated alongside the aggregated data from other network schools. This combination of individual and group data offers schools insights into their own work and into the efforts of schools they can learn from and partner with. The Global Education Benchmark Group also runs accreditation visits to schools looking for deeper analysis of their programming and insights into how to improve their work. The group strives to promote community and growth among its member schools and is a worthwhile investment for schools looking to deepen their self-assessments and global networks.

Center for Global Education at Asia Society's International Studies Schools Network

The Center for Global Education at Asia Society's International Studies Schools Network (http://asiasociety.org/education) offers conferences, professional development workshops and coaching, and site visits that provide a deep global programming analysis based on a qualities matrix reflective of high-level global programs. While International Studies Schools Network membership requires a fee, it also includes a more robust opportunity for professional development, growth, and achievement than most global education initiatives can offer.

The meat of the framework lies in the curriculum, assessment, and instruction sections, which provide methods for assessing the alignment of curriculum with mission and standards; access to authentic, performance-based assessments (including a capstone project and graduate portfolio); and an emphasis on using varied instructional strategies that develop literacy, numeracy, action, and career readiness.

World Savvy's School Partnership Program

World Savvy's School Partnership Program (www.worldsavvy.org/school-partnership) includes opportunities for comprehensive assessment of schoolwide global programming. World Savvy works directly with schools to provide a formative assessment and feedback process that analyzes school climate, classroom practices, and schoolwide programs, with a particular focus on global competency development. (See table 1.2, page 21, for details.) The goal is to help schools determine where they are in relation to their global competence goals in teaching, learning, and school culture. World Savvy cofounder and executive director Dana Mortenson believes that such evaluation programs are essential in an era in which schools often add initiatives without fully understanding what their strengths might be already: "[Schools] dive in aggressively and expand programming without fully understanding what assets may already exist, and how to leverage them. So [our assessment] mitigates that and attempts to set schools up for better, more efficient, long-term planning" (D. Mortenson, personal communication, October 28, 2016). The assessment reviews curriculum and instruction, evaluation, community partnerships, teacher capacity, and leadership capacity using a participatory approach that engages stakeholders across all those same groups.

A Few Concluding Thoughts

While knowing how to assess global competency is certainly important to educators, being able to foster its growth is the more important goal. Use assessments to help enrich and develop best practices, and collect anecdotal evidence as students graduate and head into the world. Some of the most useful assessments come from the ways former students shape their lives around the experiences they've had with us. Learning that former students are planning to teach in the developing world, to start a meaningful global project, or to work locally for social change matters more than anything that

Use assessments to help enrich and develop best practices, and collect anecdotal evidence as students graduate and head into the world.

can be measured inside a classroom. It's those "enduring understandings" (McTighe & Wiggins, 2012) that matter most, and those are rarely elements that you can measure easily while students are still inside the schoolhouse.

CHAPTER 10

BUILDING A CULTURE OF GLOBAL ENGAGEMENT ACROSS THE COMMUNITY

Revolutionary change does not come as one cataclysmic moment . . . .
We don't have to engage in grand, heroic actions to participate in the
process of change. Small acts, when multiplied by millions of people,
can transform the world.

—Howard Zinn

It is isolating when innovative teachers feel they are the only ones in their communities who value global engagement. If change requires "small acts . . . multiplied by millions of people," as historian and activist Howard Zinn (2004) suggests, then there is a need to include as many colleagues as possible in these efforts. Town School for Boys in San Francisco, California, is an example of a school that is intentional about bringing global experiences to all stakeholders schoolwide, and about making community a concept that includes both local and global connections for students (F. Mugambi-Mutunga & K. Goggins, personal communication, October 28, 2016).

At schools like this one, global engagement goes well beyond a buzzword or just another initiative; instead, global thinking and engagement become a central part of school culture and expand the way the whole school thinks about community. While a private school like Town School for Boys has fewer restrictions on how it can use money, its success is not about funding; it stems from the school's intentionality, creativity, internal capacity building, and space for teacher choice in professional development. This kind of deep global learning can happen anywhere if educators are motivated toward growth and innovation.

This chapter explores ways teachers can build a global education revolution by developing enthusiasm and buy-in, teaching your community about global education, initiating district and policy changes, inspiring global fluency through student travel, understanding the impact of global partnerships on partners and their communities, and fostering a constructive worldview across your own community.

Build a Global Education Revolution

Key to developing a successful schoolwide global citizenship program is having a team of globally minded faculty and administrators develop a well-defined plan, according to researchers at the University of Toronto's Ontario Institute for Studies in Education (De Caria, Garthson, Lettieri, O'Sullivan, & Sicilia, 2004). They note that despite many educators addressing international issues in their courses, those educators do not necessarily "see these experiences in a broader context or framework of international issues, trends or challenges" (De Caria et al., 2004, p. 160). As a result, researchers find that bringing together stakeholders to develop a comprehensive plan for global learning helps build more cohesive, effective programming (De Caria et al., 2004).

Several publications offer ideas about how a school might build a road map for such comprehensive growth, including the scope and sequence of global educational programming across grade levels. Given the commonalities between global education and diversity or inclusivity work in many schools, it can be useful to develop such a road map in collaboration with your inclusivity leaders. Alignment will help both movements gain strength and community buy-in.

Oxfam's (2015) free online publication, *Education for Global Citizenship: A Guide for Schools*, provides a comprehensive overview of what a robust global citizenship program might look like. In this publication, Oxfam identifies how teachers might integrate global thinking into each disciplinary area, and extensive charts clarify the grade levels at which particular Oxfam's global citizenship framework goals are most appropriately addressed in terms of alignment to educational standards and developmental appropriateness. Breaking down each benchmark under the categories explored in table 1.1 (page 19) as definitions of global competency, Oxfam offers rich definitions of what developing each competency might look like for students ages 3 through 18, offering a starting place for building a global education scope and sequence across the preK–12 spectrum. While schools need to develop their own definitions of global competency and citizenship, their own frameworks, and their own scope and sequence (since doing so can help build the alignment and understanding crucial to success), the Oxfam guidelines offer collaborative teams a clear starting place for integrating global thinking across the curriculum.

Before you start expanding global programming at your school, take a close look at your school's culture and the culture of its surrounding community. Beyond that, you can create schoolwide events and plan strategies for the community; introduce and pursue professional development and growth strategies for teachers and curricular leaders; and initiate district and building policy changes. The following sections help you with these steps.

Your Community's Culture

If you have teachers and other community stakeholders who don't understand the importance of global learning, or who continue to believe it's an episodic topic for specific classes rather than a lens through which to teach across disciplines and grade levels, it can be useful to start by investigating *why* the broader community is less than invested. Is there history to investigate and understand before colleagues can move forward? Are there political tensions around what *global* means—or who should have access? Are your colleagues exposed to global learning experiences? Does your school have a culture of innovation or does a *culture of no* prevail when it comes to new ideas?

Particularly if you live in a largely homogenous region, helping your community become more global will require meeting community stakeholders where they are and helping them see this work's value and urgency—first and foremost to prepare students for our VUCA world. Foster global competencies across the school community, including deep, ongoing professional development for teachers, in order to shift school culture toward compassionate and constructive global engagement. Wiley (2014) adds that a globally oriented community has "a school climate in which sharing, risk taking, and curiosity are norms," and stresses that such schools support and encourage "faculty travel, language learning, and other experiences that will further develop their own global competence" (pp. 155–156). While few schools have the luxury of making global competencies a central part of their hiring profiles, any school can find ways to build teachers' and leaders' global competencies and student-centered instructional practices through workshops, conferences, and travel programs. Wiley (2014) also emphasizes the importance of increasing student voice in global schools, noting that "Schools that want their students to be globally competent should provide them with a role in the development of course content and the direction of their learning" (p. 141).

Particularly if you live in a largely homogenous region, helping your community become more global will require meeting community stakeholders where they are and helping them see this work's value and urgency.

Dan Lutz, founder of the original Denver Center for International Studies at Montbello magnet program inside West High School in Colorado, discovered that many teachers and community members were initially suspicious of the word *global* in the 1980s (D. Lutz, personal communication, May 22, 2016). Perhaps even more challenging for Lutz and other progressive education pioneers was the pervasive perception, which lingers, that an international studies program is the domain of middle- and upper-class white students, not cultural and socioeconomic minorities (D. Lutz, personal communication, May 22, 2016). Lutz ultimately created a school culture that counteracted that perception. His story helps educators think about the challenges they might encounter as they develop global programming:

> In the first month after I was hired to develop and direct the program, it became clear to me that a key reason for locating the program at [my school] was to have a program that would attract middle- and upper-class white students from around the city to a minority school with low achievement. The assumption was that an international studies program would appeal to middle- and upper-class white families whose children could improve the school's test scores and its image throughout the school district.
>
> After becoming aware of this view, my first reaction was disgust at this insidious discriminatory attitude. But I soon chose to take on the challenge of equity for the students that enrolled in [the Center for International Studies], knowing that learning connected directly to significant meaning would lead to higher achievement. After several years, we started to disaggregate DCISM students' standardized test scores (Iowa Test of Basic Skills) from the rest of the student body, and found them on average to be 21 percentile points above the rest of the school. (D. Lutz, personal communication, May 22, 2016)

Both Lutz and progressive education pioneer Arnie Langberg (personal communication, March 16, 2017), founder of the Jefferson County Open School in Colorado, note that the collaboration of motivated, creative teachers was paramount to their success. Lutz describes his use of an "intentional distributive leadership approach that meant each teacher was an essential actor" in the program's development (personal communication, May 22, 2016). Similarly, Langberg had a core of creative, motivated teachers who had felt constrained in their previous teaching positions; their enthusiasm, creativity, and life experiences naturally drove the school's direction. As Langberg puts it, "It all grew out of teachers wanting to get the same value out of the [Jefferson County] Open School that the kids were getting" by having the opportunity to build programming and craft curriculum from their own sense of passion and purpose (personal communication, March 16, 2017).

While these globally oriented goals were unique among schools in the 1970s and 1980s, the Open School and other frontrunners in globally connected, personalized, democratic schooling have consistently maintained huge waiting lists, achieved high-level learning, and sent their graduates on to make significant contributions in a wide array of fields (Langberg, 1993; Posner, 2009; Zhao, 2012). Communities just beginning their global journeys can learn a great deal from schools like the DCISM and the Jefferson County Open School, which built exemplary programs through the motivations of their teachers and students. Langberg insists that this kind of empowered, student-centered education can work with any demographic; some schools just "have more unlearning to do" (personal communication, March 16, 2017). Langberg gives an example of that unlearning in a Denver school he founded in gang territory in the 1980s: "It took three years to change the culture. The first year, if there was a fight [between students], everyone came around and put fuel on the fire. The second year, if there was a fight, [other students would] leave and let the two of them work it out. The third year, if there was a fight, the others would break it up. Three years" (personal communication, March 16, 2017). I can think of no better story for demonstrating how globally connected programs can build empathy and a broader sense of community, if given time to shift community culture.

Schoolwide Events and Strategies for Engaging the Community

Ensuring that school leaders and teachers engage in global learning themselves is key, as only through intentional work can school leaders develop the skills needed to take their communities global. Many schools build global education teams, usually made up of administrators and teachers who are sold on the power of global learning, while others hire a global studies director to support teachers. Australian educator and author Julie Lindsay (2016) notes that global education leaders need to develop a specific set of *global awarenesses* that allow them to work with teachers and students in a meaningful way. Lindsay (2016) quotes from a list of awarenesses originally established by Robert G. Hanvey in his 1982 landmark piece, *An Attainable Global Perspective* (2016). Hanvey's awarenesses include perspective consciousness (understanding that individual views are not shared across the world); state of the planet consciousness (understanding global conditions and trends); cross-cultural awareness (understanding the diversity of ideas and societies, and how one's own might be viewed); knowledge of global dynamics (understanding mechanisms and systems for change); and awareness of human choices (understanding the challenges created by individual and collective choice). Lindsay (2016) also stresses the importance of embracing teachers who are "self-directed to create an innovative pedagogy," and what she calls *teacherpreneurs*,

> *Ensuring that school leaders and teachers engage in global learning themselves is key, as only through intentional work can school leaders develop the skills needed to take their communities global.*

those teachers who use new technologies and educational best practices to create new programs (pp. 77, 79). Such teachers can feel isolated, since they are often what Lindsay (2016) calls "outlier teachers," but a good, innovative leader can draw these teachers into the heart of global educational growth (p. 79).

Showcasing global projects, particularly students sharing their own work and ideas, can help the community buy into global learning in general and partnerships in particular. Seeing those projects helps the community internalize the value such experiences have for students. Invite parents and board members to a student work exhibition, and you will hear far fewer concerns about the place of global learning in your community because they will be so impressed with what students are producing. Find ways to showcase students' global work in public spaces in your building, too. At the DCISM, for example, globally oriented student artwork and photos from student travel are visible in every hall, as are powerful quotations from Paulo Freire, Mahatma Gandhi, Martin Luther King, Jr., and other global thought leaders. Increasing the global nature of your building's aesthetics can go a long way to creating a culture of global engagement. Make sure that maps and cultural imagery are given as much visual importance as athletic trophies. While such visuals can lead us back toward flags, folks, and festivals, as long as they are student created and serve as an entry point into deeper levels of cultural learning, they can go a long way to creating a global culture.

In their book *The Global Education Toolkit for Elementary Learners*, Homa Sabet Tavangar and Becky Mladic-Morales (2014) share many examples of global celebrations, events, and activities a school might host to ensure that global experiences become part of the school culture. With examples that engage all age groups and disciplines, Tavangar and Mladic-Morales (2014) insist that it's never too early for students to start exploring the world. In fact, starting early is key: "The sooner [students] start thinking about the wider world, the better they'll do—not because they are motivated by panic or competition but because they enjoy interacting with new friends around the world, discovering new interests, and imagining doing big things in it" (p. xx). While an international night or festival can promote the superficial Fs of global education (see chapter 2, page 36), such events can still go a long way to building inspiration and enthusiasm among community members who need a lighter entry point than global poverty, conflict, or human rights. If you think of the Fs as an entry point, there is a lot of rich learning beneath each of them (for example, *why* we see the clothing design we do in certain places, *why* festivals in two different countries might have similarities, and so on). While it may not happen *constantly*, global learning should happen *consistently* and in a variety of meaningful ways across all facets of the school. As long as the experiences and cultural representations are authentic and personal, exploring lighter celebrations can help open the door to deeper, more meaningful global engagement.

To develop deeper global events that dig into solving global issues through collaboration and multiple perspectives, consider getting your school involved in the Global Issues Network (http://globalissuesnetwork.org). With a focus on J. F. Rischard's (2012) book on global development priorities, *High Noon: Twenty Global Problems and Twenty Years to Solve Them*, the Global Issues Network brings together students, both regionally and internationally, for robust conferences with a focus on empowering young people to collaborate, innovate, and solve the world's biggest challenges. Their free online resources can also help students identify passions and begin projects of their own, either with or without a teacher's support. Having students attend Global Issues Network events or hosting a conference at your school can do a great deal to connect you to a network of globally oriented partners, as well as increase the focus on global issues and student-led learning in your community.

It's also important to do outreach to the broader community when students have meaningful global experiences. Have students present on their global learning projects at faculty meetings, back-to-school nights, PTA meetings, and school board meetings. Appoint student ambassadors to run school tours with a focus on how the program is developing their global competencies and citizenship. Have students share learning beyond your school walls, and get the press involved when something particularly exciting is happening, such as an international videoconference or a local action project. This kind of outreach helps shift the community culture by creating space for students

> *Have students share learning beyond your school walls, and get the press involved when something particularly exciting is happening.*

to articulate their passion for being change makers rather than spectators. Involve internationally connected parents and other community members, especially interpreters and content or product experts, to participate as experts during students' collaborations and as panelists for final presentations. Invite the broader community to student exhibitions and film showings. Anything you can do to communicate the *why* behind global initiatives will help, particularly if your students can articulate that *why* for themselves.

Much like writing across the curriculum, an interest in making connections to global issues or perspectives should permeate the way a community functions. Be intentional about running schoolwide events with a global focus. For example, when students are putting on plays and concerts, include international works. Singing in a world language can ignite an interest in deeper language study, and understanding cultural traditions and views through the arts can be a powerful entry point for inspiring global learning across the community. Early in my career, an excellent student production of Federico García Lorca's *The House of Bernarda Alba* (*La Casa de Bernarda Alba*) created incredible waves of intercultural dialogue across the community at St. Mary's Academy in Denver, mostly about gender norms and associated rules of sexuality in different parts of the world, and my ninth graders investigated questions the play brought up for weeks.

Professional Development and Growth Strategies for Teachers and Curricular Leaders

It's important to encourage global thinking across all grade levels and disciplines in age-appropriate and relevant ways. Doing so helps avoid an episodic mentality about global engagement and instead makes it as much a part of what schools do as fostering students' literacy skills.

Vivien Stewart (2007) expresses much the same, asserting, "Teaching students about the world is not a subject in itself, separate from other content areas, but should be an integral part of all subjects taught." Our daily lives are increasingly globalized in myriad ways, and allowing global thinking to become siloed or episodic in schools is inauthentic to the way students actually engage the world already. But integrating global thinking more consistently means ensuring that all teachers find ways to create global connections in their courses at least some of the time, whether those are connections to global issues, perspectives, or both. Preparing teachers for this shift requires significant professional development.

The interdisciplinary approach can actually make both global learning in general and partnerships in particular more manageable for teachers. While interdisciplinary projects require more collaborative planning time and better communication skills to work well, effective interdisciplinary teachers tend to share the load. They work to bring their disciplines together, often lightening the load for teachers who would otherwise have to teach outside their disciplines when running global projects alone. Interdisciplinary teams can also provide students with a much more authentic, layered, and nuanced look into the causes of and possible solutions to global challenges. For example, Hillary Rubenstein and Jason Dorn, sixth-grade science teachers I coached at The Berkeley Carroll School in Brooklyn, New York, have students explore the world water crisis through the driving question, How might we use our science knowledge to help solve the world water crisis? Students Skype with Hindogbae Kposowa in Sierra Leone and connect with researchers and scientists in the New York area as well. In their first year, the science teachers drew in the humanities team, so students studying the science of water quality and access could read, write about, and reflect on Linda Sue Park's *A Long Walk to Water* in the context of their humanities course, while also questioning the single story of walking for water and trying to understand girls' experiences in a nuanced way. Their next step is to draw in the mathematics team to help analyze global water access and quality

The interdisciplinary approach can actually make both global learning in general and partnerships in particular more manageable for teachers.

statistics. To create this kind of rich interdisciplinary project, the entire grade-level team must be convinced of the power of global learning.

One of the best ways to ensure that your colleagues grow in global directions is to ensure that they have humanizing global experiences themselves. Help your colleagues see the importance of this work by involving them in deep intercultural immersion programs that shift their worldview and classroom approaches. Chapter 5 (page 93) explores several teacher travel programs with a professional development focus, and most require no previous global experience. Several grant programs support teacher travel, while others are fee-based programs usually paid for through the school's professional development funding. For beginners, the best programs are those with built-in professional development experiences, homestays, and other immersive elements that draw teachers out of their comfort zones and into another community's life. (See the World Leadership School [www.worldleadershipschool .com] and Global Exploration for Educators Organization [https://geeo.org].) For the more advanced, programs like Fund for Teachers (www.fundforteachers.org) and the Fulbright Distinguished Awards in Teaching Program (http://bit.ly/2qfyAdM) allow teachers to design their own course of study around a destination of their choice. The bottom line? Get yourself and your colleagues out into the world as much as you can; doing so strengthens your global partnerships and your ability to lead students toward global competency.

There are a growing number of online and in-person conferences with a global focus that can provide significant professional development exposure for teachers eager to bring global issues and perspectives into their classrooms. In-person conferences such as the Global Education Benchmark Group's annual conference (http:// gebg.org/conference-materials/general-information) or the International Society for Technology in Education conference (https://conference.iste.org) are valuable, but are more costly to attend because they require physical travel. Particularly for teachers outside the United States, online conferences provide much easier and more equitable access to professional growth. As a result, many organizations are developing online conferences, webinars, and massive open online courses (MOOCs) to make professional learning opportunities more accessible to more of the world's teachers. Because MOOCs can enroll thousands of participants and usually require no real-time coursework (they are made up almost entirely by videos, readings, assignments, and peer review activities), they have revolutionized access to higher education for much of the world. Visit http://mooc.org to browse through a plethora of open courses; read more about how MOOCs have impacted education around the world in *MOOCs and Open Education Around the World* (Bonk, Lee, Reeves, & Reynolds, 2015).

One of the most significant global spaces for conversation and connection among educators is the Global Education Conference network (www.globaleducation

conference.com), which runs the free annual online event GlobalEdCon (see chapter 5, page 93) in addition to myriad other global education events throughout the year. With over twenty-four thousand members from more than 170 countries, this professional learning community is a rich space for international dialogue and learning (GEC, 2016). Participants have also created smaller communities inside the global platform, to allow for more focused dialogue and sharing.

On a more local level, Wisconsin's Global Education listserv (www.global wisconsin.org), one of the oldest global education networks in the United States, provides information on globally oriented events and opportunities in its region, as well as running an annual Global Youth Summit. Colorado's World Denver (www. worlddenver.org) community hosts significant events to connect local communities to global visitors, helps find local homes where visiting educators or students might stay, and generally connects globally minded people in the region to learn more about global issues and topics. Similar organizations exist in many cities around the world, many connected to local universities or international education programs. Curricular organizations with a global element, such as Facing History and Ourselves (www.facinghistory.org), also have regional offices where they offer free workshops for local teachers, usually in partnership with local and international experts and nongovernmental organizations. They also offer webinars you can attend from anywhere.

Some of the best conferences for intercultural conversations focus on diversity and inclusivity, such as the National Association of Independent Schools' People of Color Conference (http://pocc.nais.org). The challenges and goals of global and inclusive education are similar, as both seek to honor all identities and to equip students with the ability to engage in meaningful intercultural dialogue and collaborative action. Encourage your colleagues to seek out new learning about culture, identity, and intercultural competencies to learn more about culturally responsive pedagogies and restorative justice practices. Doing so can inspire them to create increasingly inclusive, globally connected classrooms and learning experiences.

> *Encourage your colleagues to seek out new learning about culture, identity, and intercultural competencies.*

In Lindsay's (2016) view, professional development for global educators should happen inside a school building, but should also occur within online global personal learning networks that engender a sense of purpose and trust across schools and communities. As Lindsay (2016) notes, "A global educator knows that connected learning is about not working in isolation, but learning with and from others" (p. 11). Helping your colleagues build such networks inside your building and beyond will help them feel more connected and see the value of global learning, providing a wealth of innovative ideas and best practices as well as new opportunities for professional feedback on their ideas and plans.

Often, all teachers need is an opportunity to reflect on the value of a given initiative before joining. Consider posing the essential and practical questions for global educators in figure 10.1 before, during, and after global experiences to help teachers process their learning and turn it into actionable classroom change. By digging into their own childhood family culture, and those moments when they saw beyond the boundaries of their own experiences and increased their *global pluralism* (navigating multiple ways of thinking and being), teachers can tap into much deeper, more intrinsic reasons for doing this work and teach it better as a result.

Bring faculty and administrators together in small or large groups for conversations about their global experiences. Be sure that participants are able to choose which questions they wish to answer, and establish community norms around respecting confidentiality so that the conversation is safe for participants. No one should ever be forced to answer a question, though all participants should be encouraged to lean into discomfort. (Note: You can adapt this activity to become a weekly journal assignment, a ten-minute talk at the beginning of every faculty meeting, or another long-term approach, as long as the participants choose which questions to explore and when.)

Essential Questions

What makes me want to bring global issues and perspectives into my classroom or administrative role? What experiences or beliefs lie behind that motivation?

Who were the teachers or other mentors who helped me connect with the world during my education? How do I model my work after them?

What are the key elements of my personal worldview, and where did they come from in my childhood, family history, and life experience? How do they inform my teaching or administrative work?

What memorable experiences included a deep connection with the experiences of people outside my own cultural family?

When have I failed to see someone else's perspective? How might I have handled that situation differently?

Figure 10.1: Essential and practical questions for global educators.

continued →

Which students, backgrounds, and perspectives am I best at honoring in my classroom or administrative role? Why?

Which students, backgrounds, and perspectives am I less receptive to in my classroom or administrative role? How might that affect my work?

How do my own ethnicity and cultural or religious upbringing inform the choices I make as a teacher or administrator?

How might I use my own perspectives and experiences to enrich my classroom or administrative work?

How might I honor a wider, more diverse range of students and perspectives?

How might I become more globally pluralistic for the benefit of my students?

Which global issues do I tend to avoid in my classroom? Why? How might I navigate and overcome those challenges?

What have been some of my best global education moments? How did my choices facilitate that success?

What have been some of my worst global education moments? What have I learned from conflict, discord, or avoidance?

How do I define global citizenship? When I imagine a graduate of my school or classroom, what are the skills, knowledge, behaviors, and values I want him or her to embody?

Practical Questions

When we try to imagine the ideal global education program for our school, what does it include? What are the obstacles?

What are some small, easy ways we could immediately globalize the curriculum or other elements of our programming?

How fully does the current curriculum reflect our ideas about global learning? Where have we held back? Where do we most want to increase the global components?

What global projects, ideas, and organizations have caught our interest? Why? How might we adapt them to work in our context?

What global strengths do our school's academic departments, grade levels, or divisions have? How might we better take advantage of those strengths?

How might we use global and cultural stories to enrich and enhance work within our department or grade-level team?

How might we work with colleagues to develop authentic global projects as departments or across grade levels?

What are some of the challenges at our school when it comes to shifting school culture and prioritizing global thinking? How might we help foster change?

What are our school community's greatest strengths when it comes to global education and a shift in school culture? How might we build on those strengths to further develop programming?

*Visit **go.SolutionTree.com/21stcenturyskills** for a free reproducible version of this figure.*

District and Policy Changes

In places like the province of Alberta in Canada and the District of Columbia in the United States, educational policy is turning toward global education as a 21st century imperative on a broader scale. In Alberta, the revised benchmarks for K–12 education emphasize 21st century skills and global competencies more overtly (Government of Alberta, 2010). In District of Columbia Public Schools, an office of key support people helps develop and grow global programming districtwide (K. Ireland, personal communication, June 8, 2016). These programs and initiatives signal a significant shift in global education; rather than remaining the work of a few motivated educators in a handful of affluent schools, these initiatives are putting global learning front and center for every student in every school.

PERSPECTIVES ON BUILDING DISTRICT INITIATIVES:
KATE IRELAND

Director, Global Education, District of Columbia Public Schools,
Washington, DC

There was a decision in 2014 for District of Columbia Public Schools (DCPS) to invest in a global education team at the central level. That was really decided on as a response to and in recognition of work that is happening nationally around K–12 global competence building, and a realization that we are in arguably the most global city in the United States, with a wealth of resources at our fingertips. We need to be sure we are using those resources to the best of our abilities and ensuring that they are reaching our children in an equitable way, really making sure that global education is accessible to every student. Global competence is not just a nice skill or a recognition of what our community is all about, but really is a *critical* skill that is extremely urgent to build with our students. If we are going to ensure that they are going to be successful in both career and college, they need this skill.

We start multilingual instruction in preschool (PK3) and prekindergarten (PK4). Students in elementary school have a minimum of forty-five minutes of instruction a week in one of the seven target languages we offer. . . . Diplomats from the embassies come up throughout the course of the year to meet with students and teach them about their countries and their cultures. That is augmented by visits from teaching artists from the Washington Performing Arts Society, who teach about the different cultural visual arts and performing arts of their particular regions.

Then, we have a lot of global voices that we are able to bring in through virtual learning spaces. Virtual exchange used to be a one-time experience that wasn't necessarily connected to what's happening in the classroom, but that is shifting. Virtual partnerships would be very powerful ways to prepare students for their travel, to add that humanizing aspect and that personal connection. When we are thinking about the home for these connections, certainly we imagine embedding them into classroom curriculum. For us, this is an opportunity to leverage the unique character and design of our city. We are this global city, but not all of our students feel that.

Global education is incredibly urgent and necessary for all K–12 students moving forward, and we are making that a part of the DCPS expectation. We are working very hard to ensure that global is not reserved for a few but becomes the expectation for all students in Washington, DC. We are a high-profile district, a majority African-American district, and our second largest demographic is Latino students. These are students who traditionally have not had access to these opportunities, so we're changing that narrative. If we have every graduate excited about the world and excited to learn about it, and seeking out new ideas and people, I think that's going to be a tremendous thing—not only for our students, but for our city and our schools.

Source: Adapted from K. Ireland, personal communication, June 8, 2016.

One important way to globalize your broader district is to bring international teachers into your community. This strategy can sometimes have broader impact than sending teachers out. The organization Participate (www.participate.com) partners with schools and districts to support these kinds of teacher exchanges. These cultural exchange teachers bring new global ideas, lessons, and firsthand knowledge to not only their students, but to the schools and communities in which they work and live, and the impact on broader school culture lasts beyond their presence. Participate leverages its continuous learning platform to increase opportunities for its international teachers in districts like Edgecombe and Onslow Counties in North Carolina, so that visiting and local teachers can network and maintain public and private learning communities where educators share resources, ideas, and interactive courses. According to Dave Potter, director of Participate's Global Schools Network, equity of access to global learning lies at the core of its philosophy:

> The challenge has always been to make the collaboration among teachers and students inclusive and equitable. If we seek to build empathy and mutual respect, we have to be very careful not to design programs where only some students have the global learning opportunities that all students need to thrive. Participate meets this challenge by leveraging its cultural exchange teachers and continuous learning platform to prepare all educators at a school to be global learners. Since all teachers at Participate schools are building awareness, empathy, and knowledge about global issues, so are all of their students. No one has to ask, "What about the other students?" (personal communication, March 28, 2017)

Inspire Global Fluency Through Student Travel

Travel remains one of the most powerful ways to develop global fluency and citizenship, and in-class experiences often spark a desire to travel. This is true for both students and teachers, and it is equally important to create opportunities for both, as well as for key administrators who are in a position to make or break a community's global efforts. As is the case for teachers, immersive experiences are key to more deeply transforming students' worldviews as well. Many educators and global leaders cite physical travel as a key element of any global programming, impossible to re-create in all its nuances from inside the classroom.

Travel remains one of the most powerful ways to develop global fluency and citizenship, and in-class experiences often spark a desire to travel.

The best student travel is immersive and humanizing, taking students off the tour bus both literally and figuratively. As much as possible, students should have the opportunity to involve themselves in a community's day-to-day workings, through homestays and a focus on local life more than tourist sites. Service learning components should include consistent collaboration with the community itself, to avoid the savior mentality addressed in chapter 7 (page 129). The landscape of international student travel is rife with programs that give students the impression that a little sightseeing and a little volunteering mean they've saved the world, and the voluntourism debate rages on (Garlick, 2011). Organizations intentionally developing more immersive, less voluntourist approaches to student travel include Atlas Workshops (www.atlasworkshops.com), Envoys (https://envoys.com), Experiment in International Living (www.experiment.org), Where There Be Dragons (www.wheretherebedragons.com), and World Leadership School (www.worldleadershipschool.com), among others.

Making such immersive travel accessible to all students can be very challenging; I've seen schools work around this through student-driven fund-raising events, social networking, and student- or teacher-led grant writing. In cases like Washington, DC Public Schools, district buy-in to global learning includes funding student travel each year, so that all students have one opportunity to travel internationally at some point in their academic careers (K. Ireland, personal communication, June 8, 2016). In many inner-city schools, administrators develop partnerships with airlines and travel providers to lower costs. Even in private schools, I've seen administrators build scholarship programs and work travel expenses into tuition, so that financial aid for travel mirrors aid for enrollment and all students have access to international experiences.

Holly Emert, who manages K–12 educational exchanges at the Institute of International Education, makes the distinction between virtual and in-person experiences this way:

> If we can make person-to-person connections happen, that is preferable because there's nothing like human-to-human contact to get people to dive into conversation. Virtual is two-dimensional, whereas I see the human component as three-dimensional.
>
> There are advantages to connecting in person. For example, many countries in South America are relationship-based cultures. They know you're coming, and they're excited you're coming. But you're not real until they see you face-to-face, so there's a cultural element as well. Any experience where you lived in a different culture changes your whole world perspective—for

the better. It makes you look outward instead of inward. It's not about you *or* us, it's about *all* of us, and we really need that right now. (H. Emert, personal communication, May 20, 2016)

Princeton graduate Katie Horvath (read her testimony on page 149 in chapter 8) agrees that in-person experiences alongside virtual connections are essential:

I don't think the virtual is a substitute for the real thing. There is certainly a deep value to actually interacting with people as opposed to Skyping or reading. But I think that these virtual experiences actually push people toward travel and then can be linked to a trip, to flesh out the experience in a more three-dimensional way, with person-to-person and virtual together. I think there's a value to an embodied experience that you can't capture with any technology.

A lot of what I learned about my host families and the places I lived was in the times between things that were happening. In a classroom, you're skyping to talk about the poem or the conflict, and you're not just hanging out. Anthropology, which was my major, is all about the deep hanging out. A lot of it was just forming relationships with people, and those relationships are always going to be limited if they remain virtual because so much of the deeper experience has to do with that filler time, with just having experiences with people instead of talking about something specific. (K. Horvath, personal communication, May 20, 2016)

Susan Lambert, founder and director of Away 2 Be (http://away2be.com), also makes the distinction between in-person and virtual experiences. Though she's always seen the two as deeply interconnected, with relationship building at the core of both, she notes that something unique occurs when students travel outside their home countries or cultures:

I think that something happens when you leave your comfort zone and engage with others. It's just as much about that engagement as it is being able to peel back layers of self that much quicker in person. Traveling abroad, not only are you placed in a personal challenge but then you're adding seeing others in their personal lives. You're much more able to notice similarities and differences than you could through a screen. I think one of the really poignant things is what you learn about yourself when you're stretched. Then you're able to engage in a more authentic way. (S. Lambert, personal communication, May 22, 2016)

A huge part of the impact comes from small, everyday experiences in between the planned experiences— moments when students see life through a different lens.

In many cases, global travel can ignite curiosity and lead to lifelong pursuits that focus on global collaboration and progress. As both Lambert and Horvath note, a huge part of the impact comes from small, everyday experiences in between the planned experiences—moments when students see life through a different lens. This was the case for Kennedy Leavens, who traveled internationally almost by accident as a teenager, and whose life was reshaped by her learning during and after her travels to Peru (personal communication, May 24, 2016).

PERSPECTIVES ON STUDENT TRAVEL: KENNEDY LEAVENS
Founder and Executive Director, Awamaki, Peru

I signed up for the Peru trip because my friend was signing up, and I thought it would give me something to write about in my college essays. My clearest and happiest memories of the trip, and the times where most of the cultural connection happened for me, were at the hostel where we were staying. It was run by a family, and I remember sitting in the grass, shelling beans for lunch. I remember not knowing that peas came from bean shells. We were shelling these beans and having a fabulous time, and then we got to eat them. That was a moment I still remember really vividly.

Part of the experience was the group coming together to do something hard. But a huge part of it was just realizing how things happened in the rest of the world. I remember coming back from the trip and telling one of my friends that we could only take a shower every three days and it could only be five minutes because we were at this little hostel and it didn't have very much hot water. She thought that sounded awful; to me, it was a highlight. I thought this was so cool, that we never took showers. I didn't even know you could take a shower every three days.

Walking around one evening in Peru by ourselves, we just stumbled across these kids playing soccer in the street, so we played soccer with them. We would sit in front of a store and drink a Fanta out of a glass bottle, then we would have to return the bottle to the store. We were just learning how life was there, and starting to participate in it. I think being a part of the community and participating in life in that way, the authenticity of it, was part of what stuck with me. Like shelling beans—we don't shell beans here, we buy them in a package at the store. I wouldn't go to the street in front of my house and hang out with a bunch of kids coloring with sidewalk chalk. But that's basically what we did there. While we were there, I was not at all interested in making this my life. It didn't even cross my mind.

When I started college, I signed up for Latin history. I had real experiences to connect to the class, and it was really exciting. So I took another Latin America class. It began building, and I ended up majoring in Latin American studies.

I just moved to Ollantaytambo in Peru. I started volunteering for this organization that we had visited while I was in high school. The organization didn't have very strong leadership. So as a twenty-two year old with no experience, I was able to take on a lot of responsibility. I stayed for two years, and then the organization ended up folding. So, with my connections in Peru, I started another organization, Awamaki, so that we could keep doing what we were doing. I was twenty-four years old when I founded my nonprofit. We eventually settled on what we think we are best at, which is helping women's artisanal cooperatives connect to skills training and gain direct access to markets, helping them learn to represent their own businesses so that they can be successful entrepreneurs.

I think that creating classroom connections is the best way to create a generation of smart, intentional global citizens—people who care about the world beyond their doorstep. There are really big problems in the world, and we all need to care in order to solve them . . . . We might be investing in it so that students know what's really important; so they live their lives in a way that allows these things to happen. They travel responsibly when they travel, they buy fair trade, they take a job working with an organization doing good in the world rather than bad, or whatever it is. They don't have to grow up and start a big nonprofit that directly solves the problems . . . . At the most basic level, it's important to understand how our actions connect to the people, the rivers, and the hospitals in other countries, because they do.

Source: Adapted from K. Leavens, personal communication, May 24, 2016.

The little moments Leavens describes, like shelling beans or playing soccer with local children, can change a person's worldview and trajectory completely. Sometimes just one story makes the difference. For example, a Canadian teacher with me on a professional development program in Peru remarked, after meeting Leavens, that her story made him want to be the kind of educator who helps inspire his students toward the kind of life she has chosen to lead. Just as most teachers feel a sense of passion and purpose in connection to their grade level or disciplinary focus, global experiences for students and professional development programs for teachers should hook into a sense of passion and purpose, which helps shift participants' lives and practice in tangible ways.

Global partnerships can help sow seeds of curiosity and connection before travel. They can also be an excellent way to ensure that personal and curricular connections aren't lost—and can be taken deeper—when travel is over. If international travel is the only way a school engages globally, it becomes too easy for students to see global learning as something they engage in only briefly during school breaks, and only

> *If international travel is the only way a school engages globally, it becomes too easy for students to see global learning as something they engage in only briefly during school breaks, and only when they're outside their home country. Global citizenship is—or should be—a year-round pursuit.*

when they're outside their home country. Global citizenship is—or should be—a year-round pursuit.

Some of the best global partnerships include an intentional combination of both in-person and virtual experiences, as is the case for middle schoolers at Ensworth School in Nashville, Tennessee, a school I worked with for several years. Ensworth's seventh graders travel to Belize each June, but only after studying the coral reefs in science class. During the classroom explorations, students skype with marine biologists working on the Cayes to prevent environmental destruction from bleaching, ocean acidification, climate change, and invasive species. Students explore these issues in class, making virtual connections with people doing the work. When the students arrive in Belize, they come with a different, more authentic curiosity about seeing all of this in person, and they get to meet and work with some of the biologists they've met via Skype sessions. This is an ideal and more humanizing balance, as students get the benefit of both forms of connection.

Australian student Sophia Fuller participated in online partnership experiences through TakingITGlobal's DeforestACTION (http://dfa.tigweb.org) project, and her high school science teacher, Christopher Gauthier (read his testimony on page 77 in chapter 4), has taken Fuller on two physical trips to Borneo since she graduated from high school in 2012. Asked about the impact of these experiences, Fuller shared how travel helped her find her passion and focus for higher education:

> My two trips to Borneo have had a great impact on my life; I am now studying tourism management in the hopes to enter into the ecotourism industry and show others what it's like in places like Tembak [Borneo]. To finalize my university degree, I am also looking into studying the Indonesian language in order to end with a bachelor of business, majoring in tourism management and languages (Indonesian). With this, I can one day further my study and complete a teaching degree as well. (S. Fuller, personal communication, March 11, 2016)

It is important to make connections between travel experiences and classroom learning, as Gauthier tries to do during his students' explorations of deforestation, because doing so helps students like Sophia see potential academic pursuits and career paths connected to the places and topics they're most passionate about.

Understand the Impact of Global Partnerships on Partners and Their Communities

Some impacts of global partnerships are less easily recognized in our own classrooms—those are the effects on our partner teachers and schools. I've referenced Hindogbae Kposowa of Bumpe, Sierra Leone, for his partnerships with several schools in North and Central America. These partnerships have explored health, water, sanitation, renewable energy, and digital literacy programs. Kposowa says his community is committed to connecting students in Bumpe with young people in other parts of the world and is experiencing the power of being connected for the first time in the community's history.

PERSPECTIVES ON THE IMPACT OF COMMUNITY PARTNERSHIPS: HINDOGBAE KPOSOWA

Law Student, Teacher, and Global Education Leader, Bumpe Ngao Chiefdom

Virtual connections have created awareness among our students that collaborative global learning is feasible and enriching. Many students are now proud of having email and Facebook accounts to connect with their peers, which was never the case until we started partnering with classrooms and schools. Our students have made new peer connections and are understanding what life or school is like with other students in different parts of the world. These virtual connections have provided room for our students to learn how to code, and many have become computer literate. Bumpe High School is the only school in Sierra Leone teaching students how to code since the establishment of our computer lab (in 2015)—an effort initiated by me after understanding the crucial need for virtual connections. I learned leadership skills virtually, and I brought back support for empowering others in my community through those virtual connections.

Many parents have come to understand what is possible through virtual connections. They have come to understand cultures of other people from the connections their children are making through the use of technology. Teachers in Bumpe High School have stepped into 21st century teaching; they are learning computer skills slowly to meet the speed at which their students are discovering the usefulness of technology. Personally, I've learnt the skills necessary for collaboration programs, and leaving students to explore is one of them. Most importantly, more kids are yearning to learn from their peers, and youth are aware that they can create an impact in the world by making their voice heard through technology.

Source: H. Kposowa, personal communication, May 17, 2016.

Samuel Ochieng Phabian, a computer science teacher at St. Theresa's Girls Secondary School in Kisumu, Kenya, has also partnered his students with many schools through World Leadership School, TakingITGlobal, and Adobe Youth Voices (http://adobeyouthvoices.tigweb.org), another excellent global project that allows students to produce and share unique media projects with their global counterparts (S.O. Phabian, personal communication, May 14, 2016). Phabian's students have most enjoyed partnerships connected to topics like peace and education, multimedia production, drug abuse prevention, and comparison of government election systems. As a motivated global educator, Phabian commits to connecting students to the world in authentic ways:

> Global partnerships have enabled me to create awareness in learners and teachers locally and globally. Partnering has helped the students and teachers to learn together, to share issues affecting us across the globe, and to explore how to solve them together. My students have learnt how to share their ideas and who can solve issues in the society. They learnt that people behave as they do because they have chosen to do so. (S.O. Phabian, personal communication, May 14, 2016)

Foster a Constructive Worldview

Whether all students are aware of it, the global experiences they have as early as preschool become part of their worldviews, and their classroom experiences over the years determine in large part whether those views expand or contract.

Whether all students are aware of it, the global experiences they have as early as preschool become part of their worldviews, and their classroom experiences over the years determine in large part whether those views expand or contract. Global experiences can be transformative, changing the lives of teachers and administrators, but the most important impact is on students. These young people, like Kennedy Leavens, Katie Horvath, and Sophia Fuller, are the new generation of leaders who will decide how the future looks for all of us. As their consciousness of our most serious global challenges grows, their urge to respond will increase as well. Each of them has the capacity to shape change, and their early global experiences have a lot to do with whether they choose to take a constructive and innovative role.

Every one of our classrooms has the capacity to help create constructive global graduates, young people who know that learning from the real experiences of others leads to better choices and solutions in our own lives as well, and who recognize that they have as much to learn from the rest of the world as they might have to impart. In reflecting on his experiences in ninth-grade global studies at Parish Episcopal School in Dallas, Texas, one student put the impact of making global connections this way:

> The ultimate way in which I will be different is my perspective on the world. We are simply not able to support ourselves forever living on the earth. From now on, I will

> do my best to be more conscientious about the envi-
> ronment, and to take pride in my education so that I
> can be a leader in solving these issues when I grow up.
> (A. Jennings, personal communication, May 12, 2016)

When asked how he might support the rights of children everywhere, a kindergarten student at Town School for Boys (with some help from a fourth-grade
buddy) wrote, "I hope that everybody gets fresh water. I want to keep learning
about access to fresh water so that I can make a solution when I'm older" (A. Miller,
personal communication, May 17, 2014). If global connections can help create
this awareness in a five-year-old as much as in a fifteen-year-old, teachers have the
potential to change the world through their classrooms with any age group, one
student at a time.

A Few Concluding Thoughts

Building a culture of global engagement across a community starts in the classroom. Making authentic connections will help students
cultivate an open, thoughtful worldview that honors all perspectives. And even small acts, as Zinn (2004) notes, become
significant contributions when multiplied by millions.

Borderless problems require borderless teams of constructive change makers who know how to listen to and learn from each other so that action is grounded in socially responsible and culturally equitable foundations.

I am encouraged and motivated by the image of millions of
young people working together in collaboration across borders, languages, and politics to improve their communities,
cities, states, countries, and shared planet. I imagine them
as passionate, purposeful young global citizens who have
engaged the world authentically in their youth and know
how to problem solve with their global counterparts. They
are young leaders who embody what poet Andrea Gibson
(2011) calls a "captivated audience refusing to be held captive
in the thought that they can only listen and watch" (p. 87),
and who recognize that borderless problems require borderless teams of constructive
change makers who know how to listen to and learn from each other so that action
is grounded in socially responsible and culturally equitable foundations.

Every classroom can prepare students to thrive in our world of volatility, uncertainty, complexity, and ambiguity. Creating classrooms that help foster change
makers is an essential first step toward better schools, more equitable societies, and
a more peaceful, sustainable future for all of us.

References and Resources

About discrimination and exoticization. (n.d.). Accessed at http://antiracist-toolkit
.users.ecobytes.net/pdfs/04_en_About_discrimination_and_exoticization.pdf on
December 30, 2016.

Adichie, C. N. (2009, July). *Chimamanda Ngozi Adichie: The danger of a single story*
[Video file]. Accessed at www.ted.com/talks/chimamanda_adichie_the_danger
_of_a_single_story on December 13, 2016.

American Psychological Association. (n.d.). *Building resilience to manage indirect exposure to
terror.* Accessed at www.apa.org/helpcenter/terror-exposure.aspx on December 30, 2016.

Anderssen, E. (2016, June 28). Through the eyes of Generation Z. *The Globe and Mail.*
Accessed at www.theglobeandmail.com/news/national/through-the-eyes-of
-generation-z/article30571914 on March 22, 2017.

AZEdNews. (2014, August 7). *Google's Jaime Casap on classroom innovation.* Accessed at
http://azednews.com/googles-jaime-casap-on-classroom-innovation on May 15, 2017.

Ballagh, P., & Sheppard, K. (2004). Creating inclusive classrooms for global perspectives.
In M. Evans & C. Reynolds (Eds.), *Educating for global citizenship in a changing
world: A teacher's resource handbook* (pp. 30–39). Toronto: Ontario Institute for
Studies in Education. Accessed at www.oise.utoronto.ca/cidec/UserFiles/File
/Research/Global_Citizenship_Education/chap2.pdf on December 12, 2016.

Black, C. (Director), Grossan, M. (Producer), Hurst, J. (Producer), & Marlens, N.
(Producer). (2010). *Schooling the world: The white man's last burden* [Motion
picture]. United States: Lost People Films.

Bonk, C. J., Lee, M. M., Reeves, T. C., & Reynolds, T. H. (Eds.). (2015). *MOOCs and
open education around the world.* New York: Routledge.

Boss, S. (2012). *Bringing innovation to school: Empowering students to thrive in a changing
world.* Bloomington, IN: Solution Tree Press.

Boss, S. (2013a, April 29). *Stove project sparks global youth action* [Blog post]. Accessed at www.edutopia.org/blog/stove-project-global-youth-action-suzie-boss on March 11, 2017.

Boss, S. (2013b, July 11). *Want to amplify student voice? Write a book together* [Blog post]. Accessed at www.edutopia.org/blog/amplify-student-voice-write-book-together-suze-boss on November 10, 2016.

Boss, S. (2016, October 26). *How are you helping your students become global citizens?* [Blog post]. Accessed at www.edutopia.org/blog/how-are-you-helping-your-students-become-global-citizens-suzie-boss on December 12, 2016.

boyd, d. (2014). *It's complicated: The social lives of networked teens.* New Haven, CT: Yale University Press. Accessed at www.danah.org/books/ItsComplicated.pdf on March 18, 2017.

Center for Global Education at Asia Society. (n.d.a). *History and social studies are global competencies.* New York: Author.

Center for Global Education at Asia Society. (n.d.b). *Leadership is a global competence.* Accessed at http://asiasociety.org/education/leadership-global-competence on December 13, 2016.

Center for Global Education at Asia Society. (n.d.c). *Leadership is a global competence: Global leadership rubric—grade 5.* Accessed at http://asiasociety.org/files/uploads/522files/globalleadership_5_rubric.pdf on November 10, 2016.

Center for Global Education at Asia Society. (n.d.d). *Mathematics are global competencies.* New York: Author.

Center for Global Education at Asia Society. (2005). *The four domains of global competence.* New York: Author.

Center for Global Education at Asia Society. (2015). *Graduation performance system: Grade 5—Global leadership I can statements.* New York: Asia Society. Accessed at http://asiasociety.org/files/uploads/522files/globalleadership_5_ican.pdf on December 12, 2016.

Conference of the Parties 21. (2015). *Decarbonize: Teacher's guide.* Accessed at https://docs.google.com/document/d/1JnvdsFDJB-Lztyqf1YObPdkZvuRtzRwW2w85dif1JJc/edit on November 10, 2016.

Cooper, E. (2013, May 22). *Student's rant speaks volumes for what ails our classrooms* [Blog post]. Accessed at www.huffingtonpost.com/eric-cooper/students-rant-speaks-volu_b_3314806.html on May 8, 2017.

Critical Thinking Community. (2015). *Defining critical thinking.* Accessed at www.criticalthinking.org/pages/defining-critical-thinking/766 on March 25, 2017.

Czarra, F. (2002). *Issues in global education: Global education checklist for teachers, schools, school systems and state education agencies.* New York: American Forum for Global Education. Accessed at www.nccap.net/media/pages/Global%20Education%20 Checklist1.pdf on December 12, 2016.

Damon, W. (2009). *The path to purpose: How young people find their calling in life.* New York: Free Press.

Darling-Hammond, L. (2010). *The flat world and education: How America's commitment to equity will determine our future.* New York: Teachers College Press.

Davies, I., Hatch, G., Martin, G., & Thorpe, T. (2002). What is good citizenship education in history classrooms? *Teaching History, 106,* 37–43.

Davis, M. (2016, May 6). *8 travel grants and fellowships for educators* [Blog post]. Accessed at www.edutopia.org/blog/teacher-travel-grants-resources-matt-davis on June 20, 2016.

De Caria, P., Garthson, W., Lettieri, J., O'Sullivan, B., & Sicilia, V. (2004). Infusing perspectives of global citizenship through school-wide initiatives. In M. Evans & C. Reynolds (Eds.), *Educating for global citizenship in a changing world: A teacher's resource handbook* (pp. 158–169). Toronto: Ontario Institute for Studies in Education. Accessed at www.oise.utoronto.ca/cidec/UserFiles/File/Research/Global _Citizenship_Education/chap8.pdf on December 12, 2016.

#Decarbonize. (n.d.). *A global mobilization of youth perspectives on climate change.* Accessed at http://decarbonize.me on March 25, 2017.

DeforestACTION. (2012). *History of DeforestACTION.* Accessed at http://dfa.tigweb .org/about on December 12, 2016.

Dewey, J. (2012). *Democracy and education.* Hollywood, FL: Simon & Brown. (Original work published 1916)

E2 Education & Environment. (n.d.). *This is ours.* Accessed at www.e2education.org /this-is-ours-1 on March 17, 2017.

Evans, R., Hawes, R., Levere, R., Monette, L., & Mouftah, N. (2004). Building collaborative partnerships for inquiry and engagement in global citizenship. In M. Evans & C. Reynolds (Eds.), *Educating for global citizenship in a changing world: A teacher's resource handbook* (pp. 115–137). Toronto: Ontario Institute for Studies in Education. Accessed at www.oise.utoronto.ca/cidec/UserFiles/File/Research/Global _Citizenship_Education/chap6.pdf on December 12, 2016.

Farmer, P. (2011, May 25). Transcripts: 'Accompaniment' as policy. *Office of the Secretary-General's Special Advisor.* Accessed at www.lessonsfromhaiti.org /press-and-media/transcripts/accompaniment-as-policy on March 23, 2017.

Fountain Valley School of Colorado. (2017). Global education: Global Scholar Diploma. Accessed at www.fvs.edu/page/academics/global-education/global-scholar-diploma on May 19, 2017.

Freire, P. (1970). *Pedagogy of the oppressed* (M. B. Ramos, Trans.). New York: Continuum.

Freire, P. (1998). *Pedagogy of freedom: Ethics, democracy, and civic courage* (P. Clarke, Trans.). Lanham, MD: Rowman & Littlefield.

Freire, P. (2000). *Pedagogy of the oppressed* (30th anniv. ed.; M. B. Ramos, Trans). New York: Continuum.

Fund for Teachers. (n.d.). *About us.* Accessed at www.fundforteachers.org/about-us.php on March 18, 2017.

Future Friendly Schools. (n.d.). *Background.* Accessed at www.futurefriendlyschools.org /about/background on January 11, 2017.

Galloway, H. (2016, Fall). Opening doors—and minds. *Independent School.* Accessed at http://assets.levelupvillage.com/wp-content/uploads/2016/10/NAIS-Website.pdf on March 22, 2017.

Garlick, S. (2011). *The voluntourism debate.* Accessed at http://archive.skoll.org /2011/01/03/the-voluntourism-debate on December 12, 2016.

Gerras, S. J. (Ed.) (2010). *Strategic leadership primer* (3rd ed.). Carlisle, PA: United States Army War College, Department of Command, Leadership and Management. Accessed at http://docplayer.net/9940589-Strategic-leadership-primer-3rd-edition.html on May 8, 2017.

Gibson, A. (2011). Yellow bird. In *The madness vase* (pp. 85–87). Long Beach, CA: Write Bloody.

Global Education Conference. (n.d.). GlobalEdCon welcome & information. Accessed at www.globaleducationconference.com/forum/topics/2016-global-education -conference-starts-sunday-important-informat on May 26, 2017.

Global Nomads Group. (n.d.). *Our impact.* Accessed at http://gng.org/our-impact on January 6, 2017.

Global Partners Junior. (n.d.). *Home.* Accessed at http://gpjunior.tiged.org on January 17, 2017.

Government of Alberta. (2010). *Inspiring action on education.* Accessed at www.oecd.org /site/eduilebanff/48763522.pdf on January 2, 2016.

Hall, E. T. (1976). *Beyond culture.* Garden City, NY: Anchor Press.

Hanvey, R. G. (1982). *An attainable global perspective.* New York: Global Perspectives in Education.

Harth, C. (2010, Fall). Going glocal: Adaptive education for local and global citizenship. *Independent School.* Accessed at www.nais.org/Magazines-Newsletters/ISMagazine /Pages/Going-Glocal.aspx on December 12, 2016.

Hill, K. G. (2013, March 7). *Global youth summit: What students want in their schools, communities* [Blog post]. Accessed at http://international.wisc.edu/global-youth -summit-what-students-want-in-their-schools-communities on November 10, 2016.

Institute of Design at Stanford. (n.d.). *Use our methods.* Accessed at http://dschool.stanford .edu/wp-content/themes/dschool/method-cards/interview-for-empathy.pdf on December 16, 2016.

Institute of International Education. (n.d.). *About us.* Accessed at http://iie.org/en /Who-We-Are/Mission-and-Values on December 12, 2016.

International Education and Resource Network. (n.d.). *About.* Accessed at https://iearn.org/about on June 20, 2016.

Jackson, A. (2015, June). *Opening remarks.* Presentation at the Summer Institute of the International Studies Schools Network, the Center for Global Education at Asia Society, Los Angeles, CA.

Jacobs, H. H. (2014). Interdisciplinary global issues: A curriculum for the 21st century learner. In H. H. Jacobs (Ed.), *Mastering global literacy* (pp. 87–110). Bloomington, IN: Solution Tree Press.

Jacobs, T. O. (2002). *Strategic leadership: The competitive edge.* Washington, DC: National Defense University, Industrial College of the Armed Forces.

Jefferson County Open School. (n.d.). *About JCOS: Goals.* Accessed at https://sites.google .com/a/jeffcoschools.us/jcos/philosophy on December 14, 2016.

Jenkins, K., & Meyers, J. (2010, May–June). U.S. policy diplomacy depends on citizens learning other languages. *International Educator.* Accessed at www.nafsa.org/_/File /_/mayjun10_frontlines.pdf on March 9, 2017.

Kelly, U. A. (1997). *Schooling desire: Literacy, cultural politics, and pedagogy.* New York: Routledge.

Kist, W. (2014). Taking the global and making it local: A qualitative study. In H. H. Jacobs (Ed.), *Mastering global literacy* (pp. 53–66). Bloomington, IN: Solution Tree Press.

Klein, J. D. (2017, February 2). *Culture in the classroom: Replacing misrepresentation with authenticity* [Blog post]. Accessed at http://principledlearning.org/1/post/2017/02 /culture-in-the-classroom-replacing-misrepresentation-with-authenticity.html on March 25, 2017.

Global Education Conference. (n.d.). GlobalEdCon welcome & information. Accessed at www.globaleducationconference.com/forum/topics/2016-global-education -conference-starts-sunday-important-informat on May 26, 2017.

Kubik, T. (2012, November 26). *Perspectives on the state of global education: Global education as THE dialogue among civilizations* [Blog post]. Accessed at http://kubik perspectives.com/1/perspectives-on-the-state-of-global-education on November 10, 2016.

Kubik, T. (2016, April 28). *The world . . . immediately: Three tweets that won't change the world, but might help you make a world in which you can live* [Blog post]. Accessed at http://kubikperspectives.com/1/the-world-immediately-three-tweets-that-wont -change-the-world-but-might-help-you-make-a-world-in-which-you-can-live on November 10, 2016.

Kucey, S., & Parsons, J. (2012). Linking past and present: John Dewey and assessment for learning. *Journal of Teaching and Learning, 8*(1), 107–116.

Langberg, A. (1993). Empowering students to shape their own learning. In G. A. Smith (Ed.), *Public schools that work: Creating community* (pp. 129–154). New York: Routledge.

Larmer, J., Mergendoller, J., & Boss, S. (2015). *Setting the standard for project-based learning: A proven approach to rigorous classroom instruction.* Alexandria, VA: Association for Supervision and Curriculum Development.

Lewis, S. (2015). *The rise: Creativity, the gift of failure, and the search for mastery.* New York: Simon & Schuster.

Lilla Watson. (n.d.). In *Wikipedia.* Accessed at https://en.wikipedia.org/wiki/Lilla_ Watson on November 10, 2016.

Lindsay, J. (2016). *The global educator: Leveraging technology for collaborative learning & teaching.* Eugene, OR: International Society for Technology in Education.

Lindsay, J., & Davis, V. A. (2013). *Flattening classrooms, engaging minds: Move to global collaboration one step at a time.* Boston: Pearson.

Mansilla, V. B., & Jackson, A. (2011). *Educating for global competence: Preparing our youth to engage the world.* New York: Asia Society. Accessed at https://asiasociety.org /files/book-globalcompetence.pdf on November 10, 2016.

Maxwell, J. C. (2000). *Failing forward: Turning mistakes into stepping stones for success.* Nashville, TN: Nelson.

McTighe, J., & Wiggins, G. (2012). *Understanding by design framework.* Alexandria, VA: Association for Supervision and Curriculum Development. Accessed at www.ascd .org/ASCD/pdf/siteASCD/publications/UbD_WhitePaper0312.pdf on November 10, 2016.

Meyer, E. (2015, December). Getting to si, ja, oui, hai, and da. *Harvard Business Review.* Accessed at https://hbr.org/2015/12/getting-to-si-ja-oui-hai-and-da?utm _campaign=harvardbiz&utm_source=twitter&utm_medium=social on March 21, 2017.

Michaelsen, A. S. (2013). *Connected learners: A step-by-step guide to creating a global classroom.* Virginia Beach, VA: PLP Press.

Murdoch, K. (2014, February 21). *How do inquiry teachers . . . teach?* [Blog post]. Accessed at https://justwonderingblog.com/2014/02/21/how-do-inquiry-teachers-teach on November 10, 2016.

Nabokov, V. (1980). *Lectures on literature*. F. Bowers (Ed.). New York: Harcourt Brace Jovanovich.

Narrative 4. (2015). *What we do*. Accessed at www.narrative4.com/mission-vision on November 10, 2016.

National Geographic Society. (n.d.). *Grosvenor Teacher Fellow program: Honoring excellence in K–12 geographic education*. Accessed at http://nationalgeographic.org /education/programs/grosvenor-teacher-fellows on December 13, 2016.

New York City Global Partners. (2015). *Colorful communities* [Handout]. Accessed at www1.nyc.gov/assets/globalpartners/downloads/pdf/2015–16-curriculum-overview.pdf on December 23, 2016.

No Child Left Behind (NCLB) Act of 2001, Pub. L. No. 107–110, § 115, Stat. 1425 (2002).

Nye, N. S. (2008). Gate A-4. In *Honeybee: Poems & short prose*. New York: HarperCollins.

Organisation for Economic Co-operation and Development. (2016). *Global competency for an inclusive world*. Paris: Author. Accessed at www.oecd.org/education/Global -competency-for-an-inclusive-world.pdf on March 9, 2017.

Oxfam. (2015). *Education for global citizenship: A guide for schools*. Oxford, England: Author. Accessed at www.oxfam.org.uk/education/global-citizenship/global -citizenship-guides on November 10, 2016.

Posner, R. (2009). *Lives of passion, school of hope: How one public school ignites a lifelong love of learning*. Boulder, CO: Sentient.

Reimers, F. (2009). *Educating for global competency: Excerpts from chapter 14 of* International Perspectives on the Goals of Universal Basic and Secondary Education. Accessed at www.neafoundation.org/content/assets/2012/11/Educating%20for%20Global%20 Competence%20by%20Fernando%20Reimers.pdf on November 10, 2016.

Reimers, F., Chopra, V., Chung, C. K., Higdon, J. & O'Donnell, E. B. (2016). *Empowering global citizens: A world course*. North Charleston, SC: CreateSpace.

Reis, H. T., & Shaver, P. (1988). Intimacy as an interpersonal process. In S. Duck (Ed.), *Handbook of personal relationships: Theory, research, and interventions* (pp. 367–389). Hoboken, NJ: Wiley.

Rich, A. (2013). *The dream of a common language: Poems 1974–1977*. New York: Norton. (Original work published 1978)

Richardson, W. (2012). *Why school? How education must change when learning and information are everywhere* [Kindle version]. Accessed at Amazon.com.

Ripp, P. (2017). *Reimagining literacy through global collaboration*. Bloomington, IN: Solution Tree Press.

Rischard, J. F. (2002). *High noon: Twenty global problems, twenty years to solve them*. New York: Basic Books.

Robinson, K., & Aronica, L. (2015). *Creative schools: The grassroots revolution that's transforming education*. New York: Viking.

Roth, M. S. (2012, September 5). Learning as freedom [Editorial]. *The New York Times*. Accessed at www.nytimes.com/2012/09/06/opinion/john-deweys-vision-of-learning -as-freedom.html?_r=0 on November 10, 2016.

Rughiniş, C. (2007). *Explicaţia sociologică*. Iaşi, Romania: Polirom.

Sachs, J. D. (2005, March 14). The end of poverty: In a world of plenty, 1 billon people are so poor, their lives are in danger—How to change that for good. *Time, 165*, 42–54. Accessed at www.unmillenniumproject.org/documents/TimeMagazine Mar142005-TheEndofPovertysmall1.pdf on November 10, 2016.

Scopelliti, I., Morewedge, C. K., McCormick, E., Min, H. L., Lebrecht, S., & Kassam, K. S. (2015). Bias blind spot: Structure, measurement, and consequences. *Management Science, 61*(10), 2468–2486. Accessed at http://pubsonline .informs.org/doi/abs/10.1287/mnsc.2014.2096 on December 31, 2016.

Smith, W. C. (Ed.). (2016). *The global testing culture: Shaping education policy, perceptions, and practice*. Oxford, England: Symposium Books.

Sobel, D. (2005). *Place-based education: Connecting classrooms and communities* (2nd ed.). Great Barrington, MA: Orion Society.

Stanford University, Center for Teaching and Learning. (2001). Problem-based learning. *Speaking of Teaching, 11*(1), 1–7.

Stewart, V. (2007). Becoming citizens of the world. *Educational Leadership, 64*(7), 8–14. Accessed at www.ascd.org/publications/educational-leadership/apr07/vol64/num07 /Becoming-Citizens-of-the-World.aspx on November 10, 2016.

TakingITGlobal. (2016). *About TakingITGlobal*. Accessed at www.tigweb.org/about on November 10, 2016.

TakingITGlobal for Educators. (2015). *TIGed helps educators foster deep learning competencies through real-world problem solving*. Accessed at www.tigweb.org/tiged/?npc on November 10, 2016.

Tavangar, H. S., & Mladic-Morales, B. (2014). *The global education toolkit for elementary learners*. Thousand Oaks, CA: Corwin Press.

Thomas, P. (2016, April 9). *What's the difference between design thinking and making?* [Blog post]. Accessed at https://medium.com/@parkerthomas/what-s-the-difference -between-design-thinking-and-making-614cb089bc5e#.2hojfey8n on November 10, 2016.

Thomson, G., & Godwaldt, T. (2016, March 12). Thomson and Godwaldt: Showing climate leadership in Alberta schools. *Calgary Herald*. Accessed at http://calgary herald.com/opinion/columnists/thomson-and-godwaldt-showing-climate-leadership -in-alberta-schools on November 10, 2016.

Thunderbird School of Management. (n.d.). *Global mindset inventory*. Accessed at https://thunderbird.asu.edu/faculty-and-research/najafi-global-mindset-institute /global-mindset-inventory on May 19, 2017.

Toffler, A. (1980). *The third wave*. New York: Morrow.

Tolisano, S. R. (2014). The globally connected educator: Talking to the world—not just about the world. In H. H. Jacobs (Ed.), *Mastering global literacy* (pp. 31–52). Bloomington, IN: Solution Tree Press.

Toronto District School Board. (2015). *Internal report of the TDSB research department on TakingITGlobal social innovation professional learning supported by the Ontario Council of Directors (CODE)*. Toronto, Canada: Author.

Turner, C. (2014, April 30). *U.S. tests teens a lot, but worldwide, exam stakes are higher*. National Public Radio. Accessed at www.npr.org/2014/04/30/308057862 /u-s-tests-teens-a-lot-but-worldwide-exam-stakes-are-higher on March 24, 2017.

United Nations. (n.d.). *Sustainable development goals*. Accessed at https://sustainable development.un.org/sdgs on April 3, 2017.

Wagner, T. (2012). *Creating innovators: The making of young people who will change the world*. New York: Scribner.

Wiley, B. L. (2014). Leading for global competence: A schoolwide approach. In H. H. Jacobs (Ed.), *Leading the new literacies* (pp. 123–160). Bloomington, IN: Solution Tree Press.

Williams, A. (2017, March 21). A call for fewer screens in the classroom. *Education Week Teacher*. Accessed at www.edweek.org/tm/articles/2017/03/21/a-call-for-fewer -screens-in-the.html?cmp=SOC-SHR-FB on March 23, 2017.

Wonderment. (n.d.). *Educators*. Accessed at http://thewonderment.com/educators on November 10, 2016.

World Leadership School. (n.d.). *Student travel*. Accessed at www.worldleadershipschool .com/student-travel on March 19, 2017.

World Savvy. (2014). *Global competence matrix*. Accessed at https://static1.squarespace.com /static/541b08ace4b03814779bda86/t/5425b0ade4b0a13786495f02/141175620 5854/World+Savvy+Global+Competence+Matrix+2014.pdf on November 10, 2016.

Wright, R. (1998). *Black boy (American hunger): A record of childhood and youth*. New York: Perennial Classics.

Zhao, Y. (2012). *World class learners: Educating creative and entrepreneurial students*. Thousand Oaks, CA: Corwin Press.

Zinn, H. (2004, September). The optimism of uncertainty. *The Nation*. Accessed at www.thenation.com/article/optimism-uncertainty on November 10, 2016.

Zoric, T., Ast, D., Lang, H., Vamvalis, M., Weber, M., & Wong, M. (2004). Examining social justice and our human rights: Developing the skills of critical inquiry. In M. Evans & C. Reynolds (Eds.), *Educating for global citizenship in a changing world: A teacher's resource handbook* (pp. 40–69). Toronto: Ontario Institute for Studies in Education. Accessed at www.oise.utoronto.ca/cidec/UserFiles/File/Research/Global _Citizenship_Education/chap3.pdf on November 10, 2016.

Index

21st Century Skills
Edited by James A. Bellanca and Ron Brandt
Examine the Framework for 21st Century Learning from the Partnership for 21st Century Skills as a way to re-envision learning in a rapidly evolving global and technological world. Learn why these skills are necessary, which are most important, and how to best help schools include them.
BKF389

Creating the Anywhere, Anytime Classroom
Casey Reason, Lisa Reason, Crystal Guiler
Discover the steps K–12 educators must take to facilitate online learning and maximize student growth using digital tools. Each chapter includes suggestions and examples tied to pedagogical practices associated with learning online, so you can confidently engage in the best practices with your students.
BKF772

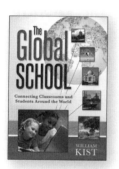

The Global School
William Kist
Prepare students for an increasingly flat world where diverse people from divergent cultures learn and work together rather than in isolation. Learn specific steps to globalize your classroom and encourage higher-order thinking, all wrapped in a 21st century skills framework.
BKF570

Mastering Global Literacy
Edited by Heidi Hayes Jacobs
Discover how educators can cultivate globally literate learners while becoming globally connected themselves. The authors explore ways to bring global issues into the classroom and personalize them using new digital tools. Find strategies for implementing global-awareness studies into the traditional school curriculum.
BKF415

Wait! **Your professional development journey doesn't have to end with the last pages of this book.**

We realize improving student learning doesn't happen overnight. And your school or district shouldn't be left to puzzle out all the details of this process alone.

No matter where you are on the journey, we're committed to helping you get to the next stage.

Take advantage of everything from **custom workshops** to **keynote presentations** and **interactive web and video conferencing**. We can even help you develop an action plan tailored to fit your specific needs.

Let's get the conversation started.

Call 888.763.9045 today.

SolutionTree.com